P9-BVC-718

POLITICAL ECONOMY

A BEGINNERS' COURSE

By

A. LEONTIEV

Proletarian Publishers
P. O. Box 40273
San Francisco, Ca. 94140

CONTENTS

CHAPTER I—WHAT IS POLITICAL ECONOMY AND WHAT DOES IT TEACH?

CHAPTER II—HOW DID SOCIETY DEVELOP TO CAPITALISM?

CHAPTER III—COMMODITY PRODUCTION

CHAPTER IV—THE ESSENCE OF CAPITALIST EXPLOITATION

Page

CHAPTER V—WAGES AND THE IMPOVERISHMENT OF THE WORKING CLASS UNDER CAPITALISM

CHAPTER VI—DIVISION OF SURPLUS VALUE AMONG THE CAPITALISTS

CHAPTER VII—CAPITALISM IN AGRICULTURE

CHAPTER VIII—REPRODUCTION AND CRISES UNDER CAPITALISM

CHAPTER IX—IMPERIALISM—THE EVE OF THE SOCIALIST REVOLUTION OF THE PROLETARIAT

CHAPTER X—THE WAR AND THE GENERAL CRISIS OF CAPITALISM

CHAPTER XI—THE CONTEMPORARY WORLD CRISIS OF CAPITALISM

CHAPTER I

What Is Political Economy and What Does It Teach?

In its struggle the proletariat is guided by the teachings of Marx, Engels, Lenin and Stalin. These great teachers and leaders of the proletariat have forged a powerful weapon. They have created and developed the revolutionary theory of the proletariat.

Marxism-Leninism—the doctrine of the proletariat

The Marxist-Leninist teaching is a guide for the working class in its struggle under capitalism. Marxism-Leninism is a powerful weapon in the hands of the class conscious workers of all countries who enter the struggle against capital, and after the triumph of the proletarian revolution it shows the working class the way to conduct successfully the further struggle against all enemies of socialism, it enables them to carry out a correct policy ensuring the building of a complete socialist society.

In his explanation of the first draft program of the Bolshevik Party, Lenin wrote more than thirty years ago that Marxian theory

> ". . . for the first time transformed socialism from a utopia into a science, established a firm basis for this science and indicated the road along which to proceed in developing and elaborating this science further in all its details. It uncovered the essence of modern capitalist economy, explaining how the hiring of labour, the purchase of labour power, masks the enslavement of millions of propertyless people by a small group of capitalists, the owners of the land, factories, mines, etc. It showed how the entire development of modern capitalism tends towards the crushing of small enterprises by large ones, creating conditions which make possible and necessary the establishment of a socialist order of society. It taught one to distinguish—under the veil of established customs, political intrigue, tricky laws and tangled teachings—the *class struggle,* the struggle of propertied classes of all sorts with the propertyless masses, with the *proletariat,* which leads all the propertyless masses.

It made the real task of the revolutionary, socialist party clear: not the concoction of plans for the reorganization of society, not sermons to the capitalists and their henchmen about improving the conditions of the workers, not the organization of conspiracies, but the *organization of the class struggle of the proletariat and the leadership of this struggle, the final aim of which is—the capture of political power by the proletariat and the organization of socialist society.*" *

Marxism was the first to give a scientific approach to the study of the history of mankind. Bourgeois scientists are powerless to explain the laws of development of society. They represent the history of society as a continuous chain of pure accidents in which it is impossible to find any definite law connecting them. Marx was the first to show that social development like natural development follows definite internal laws. However, unlike the laws of nature, the laws of development of human society are realized, not independently of the will and acts of man, but, on the contrary, through the action of the broad human masses. Marxism discovered that the capitalist system, by virtue of the contradictions inherent in it, is unswervingly advancing towards its own destruction. Marxism teaches, however, that the destruction of capitalism will not come of itself, but only as the result of a bitter class struggle of the proletariat against the bourgeoisie. The social-democratic theory that, since society presumably develops according to definite laws, the working class can sit down with folded hands and wait for these laws to bring about socialism in place of capitalism is a crass distortion of Marxism. The laws of social development do not realize themselves automatically. They forge their way through the class struggle taking place in society.

The proletariat, armed with the Marxist-Leninist teaching, carries on the struggle for socialism with certainty. It knows the laws of social development; with its struggle, its work, its activity, it follows these laws, which lead to the inevitable destruction of capitalism and the victory of socialism.

Marxism-Leninism teaches one to lay bare the class struggle of the disinherited against their oppressors. Marxism-Leninism

* Lenin, *Collected Works*, Vol. II, "Our Program," p. 491, Russian ed.

teaches that the only road to socialism leads through the determined class struggle of the proletariat for the overthrow of the rule of the bourgeoisie and the establishment of its own dictatorship.

Class differences under capitalism

Let us take any capitalist country. Whether it is an advanced or a backward country, the first thing that strikes one is class differences. In splendid mansions on streets lined with lawns and trees—a few rich people live. In dirty, smoky houses, squalid tenements or rickety shacks on joyless streets—live the workers, the creators of the tremendous incomes of the rich.

Under capitalism society is divided into *two* great enemy *camps*, into *two* opposed *classes*—the bourgeoisie and the proletariat. The bourgeoisie has all the wealth and all the power in its hands; it has all the plants, factories, mines, the land, the banks, the railroads; the bourgeoisie is the *ruling class*. The proletariat has all the oppression and poverty. *The contrast between the bourgeoisie and the proletariat*—that is the most important distinction in any capitalist country. The *struggle* between the working class and the bourgeoisie—that is what takes precedence over everything else. The *gulf* between these two classes grows ever deeper, ever wider. With the growth of class contradictions the indignation of the masses of the working class grows, their will to struggle grows, as do their revolutionary consciousness, their faith in their own strength and in their final victory over capitalism.

The crisis brought untold suffering to the proletariat. Mass unemployment, lower wages, thousands of suicides of people brought to desperation, death from starvation, increased mortality of children—these are the joys of capitalism for the workers. At the same time the bourgeoisie gets its tremendous incomes as usual.

Thus, for instance, according to German newspapers, 43 directors of the dye trust get 145,000 marks a year each; 4 directors of the Schubert and Saltzer Firm—145,000 each; 2 directors of the Ilse Corporation—130,000 each; 7 directors of the Mannesmann Corporation—135,000 each; 22 directors of the Alliance Insurance Co.—80,000 each.

Millions of people go hungry so that a handful of parasites may live in luxury and idleness. This is the picture which capitalism presents, this is the picture of the class contradictions, sharpened to the extreme by the unprecedented crisis.

The interests of the bourgeoisie and the proletariat are opposed to each other. The bourgeoisie tries to hold on to its rule by all the devices of violence and deceit. The proletariat tries, in proportion to the growth of its class consciousness, to do away with capitalist slavery and to substitute the socialist order for it.

The bourgeoisie and the proletariat are the *basic classes* in capitalist countries. Their interrelations, their struggle—these are what determine the fate of capitalist society. However, in capitalist countries, together with the bourgeoisie and the proletariat, there are other, intermediate, strata. In many countries these intermediate strata are fairly numerous.

The intermediate strata consist of the small and middle peasants (farmers), artisans, and handicraftsmen. These strata we call the petty bourgeoisie. What makes them kin to the bourgeoisie is that they own land, instruments and tools. But at the same time they are toilers, and this makes them kin to the proletariat. Capitalism inevitably leads to the impoverishment of the intermediate strata. They are being squeezed out under capitalism. Insignificant numbers break through into the ranks of the exploiters, great masses are impoverished and sink into the ranks of the proletariat. Hence, in its struggle against capitalism, the proletariat finds allies in the broad masses of the toiling peasants.

What are classes?

The bourgeoisie and the proletariat—these are the two main classes in every capitalist country. The bourgeoisie rules. But the bourgeoisie cannot exist without the working class. The capitalist cannot prosper if hundreds and thousands of workers will not bend their backs and be drenched in sweat at his plants and factories. The blood and sweat of the workers are converted into jingling coin to fill the pockets of the rich. The growth and strengthening of bourgeois rule inevitably call forth the growth of the working class, an increase in its numbers and in its solidarity. Thus the bourgeoisie prepares its own grave-digger. As the capitalist system develops, the forces of the new, socialist society ripen at its core. Classes, their struggle, the contradictions of class interests—this is what constitutes the life of capitalist society.

But what are classes? Lenin answered this question as follows:

> "What is meant by classes in general? It is what permits one part of society to appropriate the labour of another. If one part of society appropriates all the land, we have the classes of landlords and peasants. If one part of society owns the plants and factories, shares and capital, while the other part works in these factories, we have the classes of capitalists and proletarians." *

What is the secret, however, which renders it possible for one part of society to appropriate the labour of another part of that society? And what are the reasons for the appearance of whole groups of people who "sow not, but reap"?

In order to understand this it is necessary to examine *how production is organized* in society. Every worker, every toiling farmer knows very well what production means. People must have food, clothing and shelter in order to exist. Every toiler knows very well the labour it requires to build houses, cultivate land, produce bread, perform the necessary work in plants and factories to produce the things man needs—because every worker, every toiling farmer, himself takes part in this work.

By means of labour, people change objects found in nature, adapt them for their use and for the satisfaction of their wants. In the bowels of the earth people find coal, iron ore, oil. By their labour they extract these useful objects and bring them to the surface of the earth. Here the iron ore is smelted and made into iron. The iron is in turn converted into the most diverse things—from a locomotive to a pocket knife or needle.

Everyone knows that people do not work singly but *together*. What could one man, by himself, do with a coal mine, an iron mine, a plant or a factory? And first of all, could there be such undertakings altogether without the united effort of thousands and tens of thousands of people? However, it is not only on large undertakings that individual effort is unthinkable. Even the indivi-

* *Ibid.*, Vol. XXV, "Speech at the Third Congress of the Russian Young Communist League," p. 391, Russian ed.

dual peasant working a small plot of land with the help of his old mare could not do so if other people would not furnish him with a whole number of necessary things. The handicraftsman and artisan who works by himself could not get very far either without the instruments and materials which are the product of the labour of others.

We thus see that production proceeds in society. Production is *social,* but it is organized *in various ways.*

In order to produce, land, factory buildings, machinery and raw material are needed. All these are called *the means of production.* But the means of production are dead without *human labour,* without live *labour power.* Only when labour power is applied to the means of production does the process of production begin. The *place and significance in human society of different classes are determined by the relation of each of these classes to the means of production.* For instance, under the feudal system the principal means of production—the land—is owned by the landlord. By means of his ownership of the land, the landlord exploits the peasants. Under the capitalist system all enterprises, all the means of production, are in the hands of the bourgeoisie. The working class has no means of production. This is the basis for the exploitation of the proletariat by the bourgeoisie.

Capitalism was not the creator of classes and class differences. Classes existed before capitalism, under the feudal system and even earlier. But capitalism substituted new classes for the old. Capitalism created new methods of class oppression and class struggle.

> "Classes are large groups of persons, differing according to their places in the historically established system of social production, according to their relations (mostly fixed and formulated in laws) to the means of production, according to their roles in the social organization of labour and consequently according to their methods of obtaining and the size of the share of social wealth over which they dispose. Classes are groups of persons, of which one group is able to appropriate the labour of another, owing to a difference in their respective positions in a definite order of social economy." *

* *Ibid.,* Vol. XXIV, "The Great Initiative," p. 337, Russian ed.

Marxism was the first to disclose the laws of development of human society. Marx showed that economics lies at the basis of social development and that the mainspring of social development is the class struggle. The struggle of the oppressed classes against their oppressors—this is the fundamental motive force of history.

Productive forces and production relations

We have already seen that classes differ according to the places they occupy in a given system of social production. We have also seen that the place occupied by any class is determined by the relation of this class to the means of production. In the process of production definite relations are established between people.

We already know that social production is variously organized. In capitalist countries there is one social system, in the *Soviet Union* there is a totally different one. In capitalist countries the proletariat is compelled to work for the capitalist, is subjected to submission and arbitrary rule. There the plants, the factories, the railroads, the land, the banks—all belong to the bourgeoisie. The bourgeoisie has all the means of production in its hands. This makes it possible for the bourgeoisie to drain the life sap out of the workers, to oppress and enslave the working class. The relations between the bourgeoisie and the proletariat, between the capitalist oppressors and the exploited workers, put a decisive stamp on the entire order of any capitalist country. In the Soviet Union, on the contrary, the proletariat occupies the ruling position in the plants, the factories and in the entire state.

In the course of production, definite relations are established between people, between entire classes. These relations we call *production relations.* The relations between workers and capitalists can serve as an example of production relations. Every social system, every system of social production, is characterized by the production relations dominant in it. In the Soviet Union production relations are entirely different from those in capitalist countries.

What determines production relations in society, on what do they depend? Marx showed that production relations depend upon the stage of development of the *material productive forces of society.* At different stages of its development a society commands different levels of productive forces. At present, production takes place principally in large plants and factories, by means of complex machinery. Even in agriculture, where for ages the ancient wooden plough held sway, complex machinery is being used to an ever greater extent. In the past, however, human labour was totally different. Modern complex machinery was not even dreamt of then. In very ancient times a stone and a stick were the only instruments known to man. Many thousands of years have elapsed since then. Gradually man discovered newer and newer methods of work, learned to make new instruments. Instruments and machinery are the servants and helpers of man. With their aid human labour power produces enormous quantities of things which were undreamt of before. Of course, with the change of the means of production, with the introduction of new machinery, the very labour of man changes. During the last century to century and a half, technical progress has been particularly rapid.

About a hundred and fifty years ago people did not yet know anything about the steam engine; electricity came into use only about fifty years ago. Railroads have been developed only during the last hundred years. Automobiles became common only during the last few decades, tractors—even more recently. People still remember very well the first appearance of aeroplanes—it was only a short time before the war. The radio was developed only since the war.

However, it is not only man's tools—his inanimate assistants—that grow and develop. At the same time the living productive forces of society develop. *The greatest productive force* consists of the toiling classes themselves, man himself. The ability, the skill and the knowledge of man increase with the development of machines and the advances in technique. There could be no aviators while there were no aeroplanes, there could be no chauffeurs before the appearance of automobiles. Man learns not only to work with the assistance of complicated machines, first of all he also learns to create them, to construct them.

Together with the development of the productive forces, production relations change. Marx says that social production relations change simultaneously with the change and development of the material means of production, with the change in productive forces.

Further, the transition from one form of class dominance to another is inseparably linked up with the development of the productive forces of society. Thus, for example, the development of capitalism is linked up with the spread of large-scale production and with the appearance of machines.

We have already seen, for instance, that in primitive times the state of development of productive forces was very low. The instruments of labour were not yet developed. Man could only inadequately struggle with nature. Primitive tribes could only just manage to feed themselves on the products of the hunt. There were no reserves whatever. Therefore there could not be a system of classes wherein one lives at the expense of the other. The division of society into classes appears at a higher stage of development of the productive forces.

Up to a certain point production relations stimulate the development of the material productive forces. Thus, for instance, capitalism radically changed the old methods of labour, evoked and developed large-scale machine production. But at a certain point in their development, the productive forces begin to clash with the production relations within which they developed.

> "From forms of development of productive forces these relations turn into their fetters. Then comes the period of social revolution." *

At the present time we are living in such a *period of social revolution.* The production relations of capitalist society have turned into chains hampering the further development of the productive forces. Overthrowing the power of capital, the proletariat breaks these chains. The proletarian revolution frees the productive forces from the chains of capitalism and opens up an unlimited scope for their development.

The scope of study of political economy

The capitalist system, resting as it does on the brutal exploitation of the toiling masses, will not get off the stage of its own accord. Only the heroic *revolutionary struggle* of the working class, relying upon its alliance with the basic mass of peasants and toilers in the colonies, will bring about *the overthrow of capitalism* and *victory of socialism* the world over.

* Marx, *Critique of Political Economy,* Preface, p. 12, Charles H. Kerr & Co., Chicago, 1908.

How is capitalism organized, how is the apparatus organized by means of which a handful of capitalists enslave the working masses? It is important to know this in order to take a conscious and active part in the great struggle which is now going on all over the world between capitalism and socialism.

The development of capitalism leads to the victory of the proletarian revolution, the triumph of the new, socialist system. This was established by Marx many years ago. Marx came to this conclusion through a thorough study of the capitalist system of production, through discovering the laws of its development and decline.

From this it is clear what *tremendous significance* there is in political economy, which, in the words of Lenin, is "the science dealing with the developing historical systems of social production." This science occupies a very important place in all the teachings of Marx and Lenin.

In his introduction to *Capital,* Marx says:

> ". . . it is the ultimate aim of this work to lay bare the economic law of motion of modern society," *i.e.,* capitalist society.

Marx set himself the task of discovering the law of development of capitalist society in order to guide the proletariat in its struggle for freedom.

> "The study of the production relationships in a given, historically determined society, in their genesis, their development, and their decay—such is the content of Marx's economic teaching," * says Lenin.

The servants of the bourgeoisie try to "prove" that the capitalist system, capitalist relations, are eternal and immutable. Their purpose is perfectly evident. They would like to convince the workers that there can be no question of the overthrow of capitalism. The fall of capitalism, they say, is the fall of humanity. Humanity, according to them, can exist only on the basis of the capitalist system. Hence they try to represent all the basic laws of capitalism, all the most important social relations of the capitalist system, as

* Lenin, *Marx-Engels-Marxism,* p. 15, International Publishers, 1935.

eternal laws, as immutable relations. Thus it has been—thus it will be, say the hirelings of the bourgeoisie.

The political economy of Marx and Lenin does not leave a single stone of this dream edifice of the reactionaries standing. The Marxist-Leninist theory shows how capitalist relations arise from the ruins of the previous system, how they develop, and how the development of the ever sharpening internal contradictions of capitalism inevitably leads to its destruction, leads to the victory of the socialist revolution of the proletariat—the grave-digger of the bourgeoisie.

The history of mankind tells us that man lived on this earth for thousands of years knowing nothing of capitalism. This means that the laws which political economy discloses in capitalist production are neither eternal nor immutable. On the contrary, these laws appear only together with capitalism and disappear with the destruction of the capitalist system which gave rise to them.

It means, in addition, that political economy cannot confine itself to the study of only the capitalist order of society, but must also study the *previous epochs* in the development of society.

Marxist-Leninist political economy penetrates deeply into all the innermost recesses of the capitalist system of coercion and exploitation. It uncovers the true nature of class relations which the learned hirelings of the bourgeoisie try to befog.

Marxism-Leninism studies the production relations of people in capitalist society in their development, in motion. The productive forces of human society develop, as we have already shown, within the framework of definite production relations. The development of capitalist society, however, reaches the point where the productive forces outgrow the limits imposed upon them by the production relations within the framework of which they grew and developed for a time. The contradictions between the productive forces of capitalist society and its production relations then grow sharper and deeper. These contradictions find their expression in the class struggle between the bourgeoisie, which defends the system of exploitation, and the proletariat, which fights for the abolition of all exploitation of man by man.

Marxist-Leninist political economy centres its attention on the developing contradictions of capitalism, which lead to its destruction and to the victory of the socialist revolution of the proletariat.

The social revolution is conditioned by the contradictions between the productive forces and the production relations under capitalism, which find their expression in the class struggle. These contradictions inevitably grow keener as capitalist society develops.

Political economy and the building of socialism

Socialism comes to replace capitalism. Under socialism, production relations in society are entirely different in structure from those under capitalism. Must political economy study these new relations? Of course it must. Lenin has shown that political economy is "the science dealing with the developing historical systems of social production."

Engels—who was Marx's closest companion-in-arms—has pointed out that:

> "Political economy, in the widest sense, is the science of the laws governing the production and exchange of the material means of subsistence in human society." *

Consequently, political economy must study not only capitalism, but also the epochs which preceded it and the order of society which is coming *to replace it.*

Does this mean that for all systems of social production the same laws prevail? Not at all. On the contrary, every system of social production has its own peculiar laws. The laws which prevail in the capitalist order lose their force and their significance under socialism.

At present, when socialism is being victoriously built on a sixth of the globe, the great practical importance of also studying the economic structure of socialism and the transition period from capitalism to socialism is clear.

To us theory is not a dogma (*i.e.*, a dead, religious doctrine), but *a guide to action.* Theory is of great significance to the revolutionary struggle. The greatest liberation movement in the world of an oppressed class, the most revolutionary class in history, is impossible without revolutionary theory, Lenin has stressed numerous times.

* Engels, *Herr Eugen Dühring's Revolution in Science (Anti-Dühring).* p. 167, International Publishers, 1935.

"You know that a theory, when it is a genuine theory, gives practical workers the power of orientation, clarity of perspective, faith in their work, confidence in the victory of our cause. All this is, and must be, of enormous importance for the cause of our socialist construction," * says Comrade Stalin.

Political economy must give a clear and precise understanding not only of the laws governing the development and decline of capitalism, but also of the laws governing the new socialist order that arises from the ruins of capitalism. Marxist-Leninist political economy throws a bright light on the picture of the decaying capitalist world and also on the picture of the socialist world under construction in the U.S.S.R.

It is clear that attempts artificially to confine political economy within the narrow walls of studying only the capitalist system play into the hands of the enemies of socialist construction. Such attempts prevent the theoretical comprehension of the vast experience of the Soviet Union in economic construction, experience of the utmost importance for the working class of the entire world. Such attempts lead to theory lagging behind practice, to the separation of theory from practice, which plays into the hands of our enemies. Such a conception of political economy, as a science dealing exclusively with the capitalist system, is held by many economists, on the initiative of one of the theoreticians of social-democracy, Hilferding, who attempts an idealist revision of Marxism. Lenin came out sharply against such a conception.

Two worlds—the world of capitalism and the world of socialism—this is what at present constitutes the centre of attention in political economy.

Two worlds, two systems

Unprecedented destruction and disintegration are taking place in capitalist countries. Beginning with the autumn of 1929 a crisis of unwonted depth and power has been devastating these countries. This crisis has exceeded any crisis previously experienced by the capitalist world in its severity, in its protracted nature and in the distress it has caused to the toiling masses.

* Stalin, *Leninism,* Vol. II, "Questions of Agrarian Policy in the Soviet Union," p. 253-54, International Publishers, 1933.

The crisis brought tremendous ruin both to industry and to agriculture. Because of the lack of markets, production has been curtailed to an ever increasing extent, shutting down plants and factories and throwing millions of workers out of employment. In the countryside the areas under cultivation were reduced, and millions of farmers ruined. Great quantities of goods were simply destroyed: in Brazil coffee was dumped into the ocean, in the United States wheat was used to fire locomotives, milk was spilled into rivers, fish thrown back into the sea, cattle destroyed, harvests ruined—all in order thus to reduce the quantity of foodstuffs thrown on the market. At the present time when the lowest depths of the crisis have already been passed, capitalism has succeeded in somewhat easing the position of industry by means of the utmost intensification of the exploitation of the workers, by increased robbery of the farmers, by still further pillaging the colonies. Nevertheless, there can be no talk of any serious economic recovery in capitalist countries, since capitalism is living through the period of its decline, its disintegration. The bourgeoisie seeks a way out of the crisis by increasing the exploitation of the masses of workers, by paving the way for a new imperialist war and intervention against the U.S.S.R. The bourgeoisie is passing to fascist methods of rule to an ever greater extent, in an attempt to keep the workers in subjection by means of bloody terror.

During the years of this profound crisis in the capitalist world, the U.S.S.R. has successfully fulfilled its First Five-Year Plan of socialist construction in four years. At the present time, the U.S.S.R. is victoriously carrying out the even greater task of the Second Five-Year Plan—the building of classless, socialist society.

The U.S.S.R. has laid the foundation of socialist economy during the years of the First Five-Year Plan period. Socialist large-scale industry—the fundamental base of socialism—has grown enormously. Dozens of new industries have been created that had never before existed in Russia. In particular, heavy industry, which is the backbone of the entire national economy, has made great strides forward.

During the period of the First Five-Year Plan, the U.S.S.R. has also accomplished the tremendous task of reorganizing agriculture on socialist principles. The new system of collective farms (*kolkhozes*), that opened the door to a well-to-do and cultured life for the millions of peasants, has triumphed in the village. The basic masses of the peasantry, the collective farmers, have become solid supports of the Soviet power, and the last bulwark of capitalism---the kulak (the rich, exploiting peasant)—has been routed.

The working class has grown enormously. The living conditions of the broad masses of workers have improved. The Soviet Union has been transformed into a land of advanced culture. Universal education has been introduced and the illiteracy of tens of millions of people has been done away with. Millions of children and adults are studying at various schools. Tremendous success has been achieved in the inculcation of socialist labour discipline. The energy and activity, the enthusiasm of the millions of builders of socialism, have grown tremendously.

> "As a result of the First Five-Year Plan, the possibility of building socialism in one country was for the first time in the history of mankind demonstrated before hundreds of millions of toilers of the whole world." In the Soviet Union "the worker and collective farmer have become fully confident of the morrow, and the constantly rising level of the material and cultural living standards depend solely upon the quality and quantity of the labour expended by them. Gone is the menace of unemployment, poverty and starvation for the toiler of the U.S.S.R. Confidently and joyfully each worker and collective farmer looks into his future, and presents constantly rising demands for knowledge and culture." *

At the same time, in the lands of capital the masses of toilers suffer untold and unprecedented privations. The army of unemployed grew with each year of the crisis until it reached the stupendous figure of fifty million. This means that the present crisis doomed to all the tortures of unemployment and hunger a number of workers who, together with their families, exceed the population of the biggest capitalist country—the United States of America. Now that the lowest point of the crisis has been passed not only is there no improvement in the conditions of the masses of workers,

* *Resolutions and Decisions of the Seventeenth Congress of the C.P.S.U.*, p. 9, Moscow, 1934.

but, on the contrary, their conditions are continually growing worse. The slight increase in production in capitalist industry is taking place primarily at the expense of the increased exploitation of the employed workers and the greater intensity of their labour.

> "Amidst the surging waves of economic shocks and military-political catastrophes the U.S.S.R. stands out alone, like a rock, continuing its work of socialist construction and its fight to preserve peace. While in capitalist countries the economic crisis is still raging, in the U.S.S.R. progress is continuing both in the sphere of industry and in the sphere of agriculture. While in capitalist countries feverish preparations are in progress for a new war, for a new redistribution of the world and spheres of influence, the U.S.S.R. is continuing its systematic and stubborn struggle against the menace of war and for peace; and it cannot be said that the efforts of the U.S.S.R. in this sphere have been quite unsuccessful." *

After the end of the civil war in Russia, after the transition to economic construction, Lenin said: "Now we exert our main influence upon the international revolution by our economic policy." Hence the tremendous *international* significance of the victory of socialism in the U.S.S.R. is evident. The workers of capitalist countries, groaning under the pressure of the crisis, under the yoke of fascism, regard the U.S.S.R. as the fatherland of the world proletariat. The success of the U.S.S.R. encourages the workers of capitalist countries to struggle. The world-historical triumphs of socialism in the U.S.S.R. are a tremendous factor in the *world socialist revolution.*

The capitalists and their lackeys are beginning to think with anxiety *about the fate of the capitalist system.* The radical difference, the gulf between the turbulent socialist construction in the Soviet Union and the decay of capitalism, is all too striking. *To whom does the future belong*—to communism or to capitalism—this is the question which the foes of socialism now put before themselves ever more frequently.

The struggle of two systems (*i.e.,* social orders)—capitalism and

* Stalin, *Report on the Work of the Central Committee of the C.P.S.U. to the Seventeenth Congress of the C.P.S.U.*, p. 8, Moscow, 1934.

socialism—that is the central issue of our times. Two diametrically opposite worlds are facing each other: the world of labour, the world of the workers' government, the world of socialism—in the Soviet Union; the world of the bourgeoisie, the world of profit hunting, the world of unemployment and hunger—in all other countries. The banner of the workers of the U.S.S.R. carries the slogan: "Those who do not work shall not eat." On the banner of the bourgeoisie could be inscribed: "The worker shall not eat." It is clear that the conscious workers of the entire world consider the Soviet Union their socialist fatherland.

But the capitalist system of violence and oppression will not vanish by itself. It will perish only as a result of the *struggle of the working class.* Only the revolutionary struggle of the conscious proletariat will push capitalism, which has become unbearable to the great masses of workers, into the grave.

Capitalism or socialism? With the establishment of the Soviet Union this question arose in its full import. Capitalism or socialism? This question becomes more acute with the growing successes of the U.S.S.R. and the growing disintegration of capitalism.

The road to socialism lies through the dictatorship of the proletariat

In all capitalist countries power is in the hands of the bourgeoisie. Whatever the form of government, it invariably covers *the dictatorship of the bourgeoisie.* The purpose of the bourgeois state is to safeguard capitalist exploitation, safeguard the private ownership of the plants and factories by the bourgeoisie, the private ownership of the land by the landlords and rich farmers.

For socialism to triumph, the rule of the bourgeoisie must be overthrown, the bourgeois state must be destroyed and the *dictatorship of the proletariat* must be substituted in its place. The transition from capitalism to socialism is possible only by means of an unremitting class struggle of the proletariat against the capitalists, by means of a *proletarian revolution* and the establishment of a proletarian state. Only by establishing its own state can the working class proceed with the building of socialism and create a socialist society.

There is only one road from capitalism to socialism—and that is the one pointed out by the Communists—the road of proletarian revolution, of the destruction of the bourgeois state machinery, of the dictatorship of the proletariat.

> "Between capitalist and communist society," says Marx, "lies a period of revolutionary transformation from one to the other. There corresponds also to this a political transition period during which the state can be nothing else than the *revolutionary dictatorship of the proletariat.*" *

It was this road, the only correct, the only possible road to socialism, that the proletariat of Russia took in 1917.

In the Soviet Union the working class won political power for itself. The October Revolution established the *rule of the proletariat,* the dictatorship of the working class. The working class strives to capture state power not merely for power's sake. State power in the hands of the proletariat is a means for building the new, socialist society.

> "Its purpose is to create socialism, to do away with the division of society into classes, to make all members of society workers, to take away the basis for the exploitation of man by man. This purpose cannot be realized at once, it requires a fairly long transition period from capitalism to socialism, because the *reorganization* of production is a difficult matter, because time is required for all the radical changes in every field of life, and because the enormous force of petty-bourgeois and bourgeois habits in economic management can be overcome only by a long, persistent struggle. That is why Marx speaks of the entire period of the dictatorship of the proletariat as the period of transition from capitalism to socialism." **

The transformation from capitalism to socialism cannot be accomplished at once. A fairly long *transition period* is unavoidable. During this period state power is in the hands of the working class, which is building socialism.

* Marx, *Critique of the Gotha Programme,* p. 44, International Publishers, New York, 1933.

** Lenin, *Collected Works,* Vol. XXIV, "Greeting to the Viennese Workers," p. 314, Russian ed.

The dictatorship of the bourgeoisie means the repression of the vast majority of the population in the interests of a handful of parasites. The dictatorship of the proletariat means the repression of a small group of exploiters in the interests of the vast majority of the population, in the interests of the entire mass of toilers. The proletariat uses its dictatorship to destroy all vestiges of exploitation of man by man. On capturing political power the proletariat becomes the ruling class: it manages all socialized production, crushes the resistance of the exploiters, guides the intermediate, vacillating elements and classes. Having become the ruling class, the proletariat begins the work of creating a system of society without classes, either ruling or subordinated, since there will be no classes or class distinctions whatever.

Under socialism the division of society into classes is done away with, abolishing class contradictions and the class struggle, doing away with the division into exploiters and exploited. But the road to classless, socialist society lies through a period of the *bitterest class struggle.*

Lenin has incessantly stressed the fact that the dictatorship of the proletariat is a period of long, persistent class struggle against the exploiters, against the remnants of the former ruling class. He wrote:

> "Socialism is the abolition of classes. The dictatorship of the proletariat has done everything possible to abolish these classes. But it is impossible to destroy classes at once. Classes *have remained* and *will remain* during the period of the dictatorship of the proletariat. The dictatorship becomes unnecessary when classes disappear. They will not disappear without the dictatorship of the proletariat. Classes have remained, but *each of them* has changed its aspect under the dictatorship of the proletariat; also their interrelations have changed. The class struggle does not disappear under the dictatorship of the proletariat, it only assumes other forms." *

Having assumed other forms, the class struggle under the dictatorship of the proletariat becomes more persistent. And this is

* *Ibid.*, "Economics and Politics in the Epoch of the Dictatorship of the Proletariat," p. 513, Russian ed.

only to be expected: the former ruling classes will do anything to win back their lost position. The exploiters stop at nothing, are ready to commit the worst crimes against the interests of the vast majority of the toilers in order to prevent the end of their rule.

> "The abolition of classes is a matter of a long, difficult and stubborn *class struggle,* which, *after* the overthrow of the rule of capital, *after* the destruction of the bourgeois state, *after* the establishment of the dictatorship of the proletariat, *does not disappear,* but only changes its form, becoming, in many respects, more bitter." *

The entire history of socialist construction in the U.S.S.R. brilliantly illustrates the truth of this principle expressed by Lenin. The tremendous victories of socialist construction have been achieved in the process of an unremitting and most bitter struggle against all the remnants of the old order of exploitation. The Soviet Union achieved most important and decisive victories over all the forces of the bourgeoisie. But the resistance of the latter grows stronger. Their methods of struggle against socialism become more vile. Having suffered total defeat in open battle, the kulaks, traders, all the remnants of the previous exploiting classes, try to sneak into Soviet enterprises and institutions and attempt to undermine the powerful socialist structure by means of sabotage, thievery, etc. The most wide-awake vigilance on the part of the proletariat, the utmost strengthening of the proletarian dictatorship are therefore essential.

> "A strong and powerful dictatorship of the proletariat—that is what we must have now in order to shatter the last remnants of the dying classes and to frustrate their thieving designs." **

Classless society cannot come of itself. It must be won. For this purpose it is necessary actively to overcome the tremendous difficulties on the road to socialism. It is necessary to crush the re-

* *Ibid.*, "Greeting to the Viennese Workers," p. 315, Russian ed.

** Stalin, "Results of the Five-Year Plan," in the symposium: *From the First to the Second Five-Year Plan*, p. 54, International Publishers, 1933.

sistance of all the relics of the old exploiting system. It is necessary to mobilize the energy and activity of the millions of builders of socialism. It is necessary to resist any and all deviations from the general line of the Party. Unfailing alertness is necessary with respect to all attempts at distorting the Marxist-Leninist teaching.

The dictatorship of the proletariat is that power which accomplishes the building of classless socialist society. The dictatorship of the proletariat is the leading force in the society that builds socialism. Therefore, in studying the transition from capitalism to socialism, in studying the structure of socialism, the dictatorship of the proletariat is the centre of attention of political economy.

Political economy—a militant, class science

The bourgeoisie is interested in hiding the laws of the inevitable decline of capitalism and victory of communism. Bourgeois professors of economics—these "learned henchmen of the capitalist class," as Lenin expresses it—serve capitalism truly and faithfully, glossing over and embellishing the system of oppression and slavery. Bourgeois economists mask and befog the real laws governing capitalist production. They try to perpetuate capitalism. They depict capitalism as the only possible order of social life. According to them the laws of capitalism are eternal and immutable. By such falsehoods they try to save capitalism from its inevitable destruction.

At the head of the revolutionary struggle of the working class stands the *Communist Party*. Only firm leadership on the part of the Communist Party ensures the victory of the proletariat. All the enemies of communism venomously hate the Communist Party. They strive in every way possible to split it, to destroy its unity, and rejoice at any deviation from its general line within the ranks of the Party.

Political economy is a sharp weapon in the struggle against capitalism, in the struggle *for communism*. Political economy, like all sciences, and primarily sciences dealing with human society and the laws of its development, is a *class* science.

The proletariat is surrounded by hosts of enemies. A bitter class struggle is in progress. In this struggle all attacks upon the general line of the Communist Party, all attempts to undermine it either in theory or in practice bring grist to the mill of the enemy. That is why a vigilant and unrelenting struggle must be maintained against all deviations from the general line of the Party, a struggle against open Right opportunism as well as against all kinds of "Left" deviations.

Counter-revolutionary Trotskyism is of special service to the bourgeoisie in its struggle against the revolution, in its preparations for a new intervention against the U.S.S.R. As one of the varieties of social-democracy, Trotskyism particularly furnishes the imperialist bourgeoisie with all sorts of slanderous fabrications about the revolutionary movement in various countries and about the Soviet Union. Trotskyism is an advance post of the counter-revolutionary bourgeoisie.

Stalin in his letter of the autumn of 1931 to the editors of the Russian magazine, *Proletarskaya Revolyutsia,** entitled "Questions Concerning the History of Bolshevism," ** called the attention of the Communist Party to the necessity of a relentless struggle against all the attempts of an ideology hostile to Leninism to penetrate into the Communist Party, and particularly to the necessity of a determined resistance to all sorts of attempts "to smuggle the disguised Trotskyist rubbish into our literature." The representatives of trends hostile to the proletariat now try to smuggle in their views subtly, unnoticeably. All such attempts must be vigorously resisted. Any show of toleration towards these hostile views, any rotten liberalism with respect to them, is a direct crime against the working class and its struggle for socialism.

The class enemies of the proletariat try in every way to misconstrue political economy and to adapt it to serve their own interests. Bourgeois and Social-Democrat economists trump up all sorts of concoctions in an attempt to save capitalism. They also try to make use of political economy for their own ends in their struggle against the Soviet Union.

One of the most important tasks in the study of political economy, therefore, is to conduct a relentless struggle against all anti-Marxian and deviationist trends.

* *The Proletarian Revolution.*

** See Stalin, *Leninism,* Vol. II, pp. 446-458.

Review Questions

1. What aim does Marxism-Leninism set before the proletariat?
2. How do the productive forces of society change?
3. In what way do the various systems of social production differ?
4. What are classes?
5. How does the abolition of classes take place?
6. What is the subject of study of political economy?
7. Of what importance is the study of revolutionary theory to the proletariat?
8. Why is political economy a class science?
9. Of what does the Party character of political economy consist?

CHAPTER II

How Did Society Develop to Capitalism?

The Russian Revolution of October (November) 1917 opened up a new chapter in the history of mankind. It set as its aim the building of socialism. Under socialism, the exploitation of man by man is done away with. The task of the second five-year period, upon which the U.S.S.R. entered in 1933, is the building of a classless, socialist society.

Our goal—a classless socialist society

In his speech to the congress of collective farm shock-brigade workers in February 1933, Comrade Stalin said:

> "The history of nations knows not a few revolutions. But these revolutions differ from the October Revolution in that they were one-sided revolutions. One form of exploitation of the toilers made way for another form of exploitation, but exploitation, as such, remained. Certain exploiters and oppressors made way for other exploiters and oppressors, but exploitation and oppression, as such, remained. The October Revolution alone set itself the aim—of abolishing *all* exploitation and of liquidating *all* exploiters and oppressors." *

In order to understand thoroughly the full significance of the struggle for a classless, socialist society, it is necessary to know the essence of class society. It is necessary to remember of what classes society is constituted under capitalism. One must keep in mind what classes are and clarify the question as to whether classes have always existed. One must understand in just what way capitalist society differs from all other forms of class rule. Finally, one must thoroughly master the questions as to what course the struggle of the working class must follow in order to destroy capitalist slavery,

* Stalin, *Speech at the First All-Union Congress of Collective Farm Shock-Brigade Workers*, p. 8, Moscow, 1933.

and as to what the laws of development and decay of the capitalist system are.

Have there always been classes?

The menials of capitalism do their utmost to prove that the division of society into classes is inevitable. It is important to the defenders of the moneybags to depict things as if the existence of exploiters and exploited were an eternal and necessary condition for the existence of any society. As far back as in ancient Rome, when the exploited rebelled against their masters, a certain defender of the ruling class told a fable in which he compared society with the organism of an individual; just as in the individual, presumably, hands exist to do the work, and the stomach to take food, just so must society have people to do all the work and others to take the fruit of the workers' labour. As a matter of fact all the later apologists of the rule of the exploiting classes, in their struggle against the destruction of the system of exploitation of man by man, have not gone very much further than this miserable fable.

In reality it has been incontrovertably proven that the human race lived for many thousands of years without class division, class rule or exploitation. As is well known, man evolved from the animal kingdom countless ages ago. Man has never lived segregated, by himself, but always in groups. During the first stages of human development these groups were small. What united the individual members of such groups? It is clear that what united them was their common struggle for existence, their common labour in obtaining food.

Primitive clan communism

Man had to conduct his struggle with nature during the primitive stages of development under exceedingly difficult conditions. A stick and a stone were all the "instruments" man was limited to for many thousands of years. Numerous dangers surrounded him at every step. He was almost powerless against the tremendous forces of nature, about whose laws he knew nothing at all.

Under these circumstances men lived in small communities, clans. They worked in common and used the fruit of their joint labour in common also. There could be no inequality at these low stages of human development since people got only enough products by hunting, herding cattle or very primitive agriculture for a bare existence.

All peoples lived in such primitive clan communities during the first periods of their development. Such primitive clan communities, or communes, continued to exist even up to very recent times in many remote corners of the earth which remained uninfluenced by the more developed countries. The pressure of the European bourgeoisie, which grabbed all these corners of the earth, of course worked havoc with such organization. A thousand or fifteen hundred years ago, however, the forefathers of some of these Europeans also lived in such a primitive clan system.

Thus we see that up to the rise of class division in society, *primtive clan communism* prevailed. There were different forms of this system among different tribes and peoples. But, irrespective of these differences, the primitive stage of development of all peoples shows a complete similarity in the principal features of social organization.

The first stages of social development, in which primitive communism existed, proceeded at an exceedingly slow rate of evolution. During hundreds, even thousands of years, conditions of life practically did not change or changed extremely slowly. Man took the first steps in his development with tremendous difficulty Generation followed generation and social conditions did not change noticeably. Very slowly indeed man learned to perfect his tools and his methods of work.

What were the social relations under primitive communism? The primitive community or clan was usually small in numbers: with the technical development existing at the time a large clan could not hope to feed all its members. Labour in such a community was organized more or less according to a plan. All members of the community had definite occupations. The men, for instance, hunted. The women stayed at home with the children and also had to till the soil. Upon returning from the hunt the game was divided according to established, time-honoured custom.

"The population was very small in numbers. It was collected only on the territory of the tribe. Next to this territory was the hunting ground surrounding it in a wide circle. A neutral forest formed the line of demarcation from other tribes. The division of labour was quite primitive. The work was simply divided between the two sexes. The men went to war, hunted, fished, provided the raw material for food and the tools necessary for these pursuits. The women cared for the house, and prepared food and clothing; they cooked, wove and sewed. Each sex was master of its own field of activity: the men in the forest, the women in the house. Each sex also owned the tools made and used by it; the men were the owners of the weapons, of the hunting and fishing tackle, the women of the household goods and utensils. The household was communistic, comprising several, and often many, families.* Whatever was produced and used collectively, was regarded as common property: the house, the garden, the long boat." **

Under conditions of primitive communism there could be no place for social groups living on unearned income. There was no exploitation of one part of the community by another in the framework of primitive communism. At that stage of human development, the instruments of labour were very simple, so that there could be no question of private property in tools: everyone was able, without much labour, to prepare for himself a spear, a stone, a bow and arrow, etc. At the same time there was no private property in land, the land was the common property of the entire community, the clan. It was just this remnant of communal land ownership that proved most enduring among the peasantry even ages after the development of class division in society. During later stages of social development the village community was frequently maintained artificially by the exploiters and the class state in order to facilitate the exploitation of the peasantry, collect taxes, etc. In other cases, on the contrary, the ruling classes destroyed communal life in the village in order to clear the field for the free development of capitalism.

Communal ownership of land remained even after agriculture had become the predominant, the principal form of labour. The

* "Especially on the northwest coast of America; see Bancroft. Among the Haidahs of the Queen Charlotte Islands some households gather as many as 700 members under one roof. Among the Nootkas whole tribes lived under one roof."—*F.E.*

** Engels, *The Origin of the Family*, pp. 192-93, Charles H. Kerr & Co., Chicago, 1902.

land which was given to individual peasant families to cultivate was redistributed from time to time. It remained the communal property of the village and was frequently distributed among the various households by means of drawing lots. Communal ownership of pasture land remained even longer. A common pasture for the entire village was by no means rare even after the rule of capital had been established.

Thus, before the rise of class distinctions in society *primitive clan communism* prevailed. In this order of society also there were various features peculiar to the different peoples and tribes. However, in spite of these peculiarities, the primitive stage of development among all peoples bore the greatest similarity in the fundamental attributes of the system of society.

Bourgeois scientists, afraid of communism and the abolition of private property, try to represent things as if the existence of society and even of man himself is inconceivable without private property. The actual history of human society refutes this fabrication of the servants of capitalism most unequivocally. As a matter of fact, private property, like the division of society into classes, appears only at a comparatively late stage of social development. People lived for many thousands of years without the least conception of private property.

Under primitive communism there was no *state*. The state appeared later, with the rise of private property and the division of society into classes. Lenin in his lecture on the state said the following:

> "In primitive society, when people lived in small clans, in the lowest stage of their development, in a state near to savagery, in the epoch from which modern civilized man is separated by several thousands of years, at that time there were as yet no signs of the existence of the state." This "was the time when there was no state, when social connections, society itself, discipline and the labour distribution were maintained by the force of custom, traditions, by the authority or respect enjoyed by the elders of the clan or the women, who at that time not only had equal rights with men, but sometimes even greater rights, when there was no specific category of specialists to rule. History shows that the state is a special apparatus for the

coercion of people, coming into being only where and when there has been a division of society into classes—that is, a division into such groups of people of which one can constantly appropriate the labour of others, where one exploits the other." *

We thus see that the division of society into a class of exploiters and a class of exploited is not at all an eternal and inevitable feature of each and every social system. On the contrary, we see that society existed for a very long period of time without knowing anything of classes, or exploitation, or private property.

The decay of primitive society

In primitive times man proceeded very slowly upon the road of development, but nevertheless there was progress. Human society never remained in a totally static condition. Tools slowly but surely were perfected. People learned to use the previously incomprehensible forces of nature. The discovery of fire played a tremendous role. Then the savages learned to make a bow and arrow for hunting purposes. Having begun with a stick and a stone, man gradually learned to make the stick into a spear and to grind the stone so as to make it better adapted for hunting purposes. A new stage was reached when the art of pottery making was achieved, when man learned to make vessels from clay. The taming of the first domestic cattle and the cultivation of grain played a tremendous part. Thus cattle-raising and agriculture began. With the discovery of how to smelt iron from the ore, and the invention of writing, the primitive period ends and the era of civilization begins. In the *Manifesto of the Communist Party,* Marx and Engels have written that beginning with this point the entire history of human society is the history of class struggles.

How did classes originate? The appearance of classes is most closely connected with the entire process of social development. The domestication of cattle leads to the separation of cattle-raising tribes from the remaining masses of the clan groups in primitive society. This is the first great social division of labour. From this point on different communities have different products. The cattle-

* Lenin, *Collected Works*, Vol. XXIV, "On the State," pp. 365-66, Russian ed.

herding tribes have the products of cattle-raising: animals, wool, meat, hides, etc. A basis is established for the exchange of products among the tribes. At first the exchange is conducted by the elders of the clan communities; cattle is the main article of barter. Barter at first takes place at points where various tribes meet; barter takes place, at first, between different communities and not between separate members of the communities.

At the same time, with the growth of the population, the old methods of work prove inadequate. The ever increasing number of people cannot feed themselves by means of these methods. There is a beginning of plant cultivation—the first steps in agriculture. Tilling of the soil, under those circumstances, inevitably brings about a much closer connection of some families with their part of the cultivated land. Thus the basis for private property is laid.

> "The increase of production in all branches—stock-raising, agriculture, domestic handicrafts—enabled human labour power to produce more than was necessary for its maintenance. It increased at the same time the amount of daily work that fell to the lot of every member of a gens, a household or a single family. The addition of more labour power became desirable. It was furnished by war; the captured enemies were transformed into slaves. Under the given historical conditions, the first great division of social labour, by increasing the productivity of labour, adding to wealth, and enlarging the field of productive activity, necessarily carried slavery in its wake. Out of the first great division of social labour arose the first great division of society into two classes—masters and slaves, exploiters and exploited." *

To the extent that man masters new forms and methods of labour, a further development of the division of labour takes place. People learn to make utensils, all kinds of tools, various kinds of weapons, etc. This gradually brings about the separation of artisanship from agriculture. All this greatly widens the basis for the development of exchange.

The dissolution of primitive communism leads to the transfer of cattle from communal to private ownership. Land and tools also

* Engels, *The Origin of the Family*, p. 195.

become private property. With the inception of private ownership the basis is laid for the rise and growth of inequality.

"The distinction between rich and poor was added to that between free men and slaves. This and the new division of labour constitute a new division of society into classes." *

With the decay of primitive communism the division into exploiters and exploited arises in society. People appear who live upon the labour of others. The exploitation of one class by another—that is what characterizes the different stages of development of class society. The forms of exploitation, however, the methods by means of which one class lives at the expense of another, change with the different stages of development.

Pre-capitalist forms of exploitation

"Slavery, which reaches its highest development in civilization, introduced the first great division of an exploited and an exploiting class into society. This division continued during the whole period of civilization. Slavery is the first form of exploitation characteristic of the antique world. Then followed serfdom in the Middle Ages, and wage labour in recent times. These are the three great forms of servitude characteristic of the three great epochs of civilization. Their invariable mark is either open or, in modern times, disguised slavery." **

We have already seen that classes differ in their position within a definite system of social production, according to their relations to the means of production. Each of the three main forms of society based on exploitation—slavery, serfdom and capitalism—has, in this respect, its own individual features. Every one of these forms of the exploiting society is distinguished by its own structure of social production, its own type of production relations.

The system of slavery is met with in the most diverse epochs of the history of mankind. Slavery is the most ancient form of exploitation. It occurs upon the very threshold of the written history of human society.

* *Ibid.*, p. 198.
** *Ibid.*, p. 214.

Under slavery the exploited class is the property of the exploiters. The slave belongs to his owner just as a house, land or cattle. In ancient Rome, where slavery flourished, the slave was called a "talking tool," as distinguished from "mute tools" and "semi-mute tools" (cattle). A slave was considered a chattel belonging to his master who did not have to answer for the murder of his slave. The slave-owner considered the slave as part of his property, and his wealth was measured by the number of slaves he owned. The slave-owner made his slave work for him. Slave labour is labour performed under compulsion, under threat of punishment. Slave labour was distinguished by its low productivity. Technical improvement was exceedingly slow under conditions of slavery. The tremendous structures built with slave labour were erected by means of the muscular effort of colossal armies of slaves who worked with the simplest kind of tools. The slave-owner had no reason to try to lighten the labour of the slaves.

What is the limit of exploitation under slavery? Under slavery not only the tools and instruments of labour belong to the slave-owner, but the labourer himself. The slave is the property of his master. The slave-owner feeds and maintains his slaves because the death of a slave is a loss to him, decreases his wealth. So long as the exchange of products was undeveloped, every slave-owner made his slaves produce only the things needed within his own estate. The life of the ruling classes under slavery was characterized by an insensate luxury and waste. But however great the luxury, there were limits to slave labour, as beyond a certain definite amount excess products could not be utilized. Under slavery the growth of wealth is circumscribed within comparatively narrow limits. This is what caused the dearth of technical development under the system of slavery.

Together with class dominance the *state* comes into being as an apparatus of coercion, compelling the majority of society to work for the exploiting minority. In the slave-owning society of old the state was confined in a narrower frame than it is at the present time. Means of communication were still little developed, mountains and seas presented obstacles which were difficult to surmount. Various forms of the state—the monarchy, the republic, etc.—were already present under slavery. Nevertheless, whatever the form of the state was, it still remained an organ of the dominance of the slave-owners. Slaves in general were not regarded as members of society.

Slave-owning society, particularly in ancient Greece and ancient Rome, reached a high level of scientific and artistic development. However, it was a culture erected on the bones of countless masses of slaves.

During periods of frequent wars the number of people who were made slaves often grew tremendously. The lives of the slaves were extremely cheap and the exploiters made their conditions of life altogether intolerable. The history of slavery is one of bloody struggle between the exploiters and the exploited. Uprisings of slaves against their masters were suppressed with merciless cruelty.

Slave revolts shook slave-owning society to its very foundations, particularly in the last period of its existence. Having conquered a series of countries in the most remote corners of the world as it was then known to the Romans, the Roman Empire had attained to enormous power, when it began to totter more and more under the stress of the contradictions that were rending the whole fabric of the society of that time. Especially famous is the slave rebellion which broke out in Rome about two thousand years ago under the leadership of Spartacus, who mobilized a huge army against the regime of the slave-owners. The revolts of the slaves could not bring victory to the exploited, could not put an end to exploitation in general. The slaves were not in a position to set themselves a clearly perceived goal. They could not create a strong organization to lead their struggle. Frequently the slaves were mere pawns in the hands of the various factions of the ruling class who were fighting among themselves. Nevertheless, the civil war and the slaves' revolts dealt a severe blow to the slave-owning order of society and prepared the soil for its destruction.

However, in place of slavery a new form of the exploitation of man by man appeared. This form, which prevailed during the Middle Ages, was *feudalism,* the last stage of whose development was *serfdom*. Feudalism underwent a comparatively long process of development. Under feudalism the tremendous mass of the peasantry was exploited by a small group of feudal barons. The barons took into their own hands the supreme power over the land worked by the peasants. For the right of working the land, the peasants had to submit to a host of feudal services for their lords.

So long as natural economy prevailed, *i.e.*, production for direct use and not for exchange, feudal exploitation was circumscribed by comparatively narrow limits. The feudal lords took a certain amount of the agricultural products from the peasants for their own use. The greater part of these products were used up by the lord and his armed guard, and only a small portion went in exchange for arms, some overseas goods, etc. The development of exchange, however, led to a gradual increase in the appetites of the feudal lords. Now they not only squeezed from the peasant the tribute that went for the use of the lord and his menials, but the amount of tribute exacted for purposes of exchange for other goods continually grew. As the exchange of goods developed, the possibilities for increased exploitation of the peasantry by the feudal lord became greater. The growth of exchange destroyed the old patriarchal relations between the feudal lord and the peasants dependent upon him and led to the rise of serfdom.

Serfdom represents a form of the severest kind of exploitation of the peasantry by the landlords. Under serfdom the basic means of production—the land—is in the hands of the landlords. The landlords appropriate the land which has been tilled by a number of generations of peasants. But they are not content with this. Taking advantage of the powers of the state which is also in their hands, the landlords turn the previously free peasants into their serfs. The peasants are attached to the land and become practically the property of the landlord.

Trying in every way to augment their income, the landlords increase the exploitation of their serfs. Exchange is already fairly well developed at the time of serfdom. Overseas trade takes on considerable proportions. Merchants furnish the serf-owning landlords with all kinds of overseas goods. Money becomes more and more important. In order to get more money the serf-owner squeezes more and more labour out of his peasants. He takes away land from the peasants, limits their allotments, and, in place of these, sets up his own fields upon which he makes these same peasants work. *Corvee* service is introduced: the peasant must work the lord's field for three to four days a week and can work his own allotment only on the other days. In other cases the serf-owning landlords appropriate ever increasing parts of the harvest from the peasants' fields by the system of making the peasants pay *quit-rent.*

The exploitation of the serfs evoked the bitterest struggles of the peasants against their landlords. The history of every country shows a great number of peasant rebellions. There were peasant uprisings in many countries during the period of serfdom (in Germany, France, England, Russia). Some of these uprisings lasted for decades. For tens of years these countries were in the throes of civil war. The uprisings were suppressed mercilessly by the landlords and their governments. This struggle of the peasants against the landlords was utilized by the rising bourgeoisie in order to hasten the fall of serfdom and to substitute capitalist exploitation for serf exploitation.

Here is what Stalin says about the substitution of one social form for another:

> "The revolution of the slaves liquidated slavery and abolished the slave form of exploitation of the toilers. In its place it introduced the feudal rulers and the serf form of exploitation of the toilers. One set of exploiters took the place of another set of exploiters. Under slavery the 'law' permitted the slave-owner to kill his slaves. Under the serf system the 'law' permitted the serf-owner 'only' to sell his serfs.
>
> "The revolution of the serf peasants liquidated the serf-owners and abolished the serf form of exploitation. But in place of these it introduced the capitalists and landlords, the capitalist and landlord form of exploitation of the toilers. One set of exploiters took the place of another set of exploiters. Under the serf system the 'law' permitted the sale of serfs. Under the capitalist system the 'law' permits the toilers 'only' to be doomed to unemployment and poverty, to ruin and death from starvation.
>
> "It was only our Soviet revolution, only our October Revolution that put the question, not of substituting one set of exploiters for another, not of substituting one form of exploitation for another—but of eradicating all exploitation, of eradicating all and every kind of exploiter, all and every kind of rich man and oppressor, old and new." *

* Stalin, *Speech at the First All-Union Congress of Collective Farm Shock-Brigade Workers,* p. 8.

The rise and development of exchange

We have already seen that exchange originated in the very ancient times of human history. Together with the first steps in the division of labour in society, the foundation was laid for the rise of exchange. At first exchange took place only between neighbouring communities; each exchanged its excess products for those of the other. However, having originated at the border between communities, exchange soon exerted a destructive influence upon relations within the community. Money appeared. At first those products which were the principal objects of exchange served as money. Thus in many cases when exchange took place with cattle-raising clans or tribes, cattle served as money. The wealth of a tribe—and after the appearance of private property, the wealth of an individual—was measured by the number of head of cattle owned.

Natural production, however, prevailed for a long time after the rise of exchange. The production of goods not intended for exchange is called *natural production.* On the other hand, the production of goods for sale on the market, for exchange, is called *commodity production.*

It is natural production which prevails during slavery and feudalism. Pre-capitalist forms of exploitation arise and develop on the basis of the prevalence of natural production. Only the gradual development of exchange undermines the foundations of these forms of society. Here is what Engels says about this stage of development:

> "We all know that in the early stages of society products were used by the producers themselves and that these producers were organized spontaneously in more or less communistic communities; that the exchange of surplus products with outsiders, which is the prelude to the transformation of products into commodities, is of later date, at first occurring only between individual communities belonging to different tribes, but later coming into effect also within the community and materially helping to break them up into larger or smaller family groups. But even after this breaking up, the heads of families conducting exchange remained working peasants producing almost everything necessary to satisfy all their demands within their own economy with the help of the members of the family and obtaining only an

insignificant part of objects of necessity from outside in exchange for surplus products of their own. The family is not only occupied in agriculture and cattle-raising, it also works up the product from these into articles ready for use; in places it still grinds flour with the hand mill, it bakes bread, spins, dyes, weaves linen and wool, tans leather, erects and repairs wooden houses, makes tools and instruments of labour, often does carpentry and forge work, so that the family or family group is, in the main, self-sufficient.

"The few things such a family has to obtain by exchange or purchase from others consisted, even as late as the beginning of the nineteenth century in Germany, mainly of the products of artisans, *i.e.*, of such things as the peasant is not at all incapable of preparing himself but which he did not produce himself only because either the raw material was not accessible to him or because the purchased article was much better or very much cheaper." *

Thus natural production prevails not only under slavery and in the Middle Ages, but also under new conditions. Commodity production is by no means prevalent at the inception of capitalism. Only the development of capitalism strikes a mortal blow at natural production. Only under capitalism does commodity production, production for sale, become the decisive, the predominant form of production.

Within pre-capitalist society, commodity production develops to an ever greater extent together with an increase in the division of labour. Of particular significance is the separation of handicraftsmanship from agriculture. Whereas the peasant agriculturist conducts his husbandry mainly as natural production, the same cannot be said of the artisan. Handicraftsmanship is, from the very beginning, clearly of a commodity-producing character. The artisan producing a pair of boots or a set of harness, a plough or horseshoes, clay or wooden vessels, works from the very start for the market, for sale. But unlike commodity production under capitalism, the artisan works with instruments of labour which are his own. As a rule he applies only his own labour power. Only later, with the development of cities, does the artisan begin

* Engels, Supplement *(Nachtrag)* to Vol. III of *Capital*, German ed., 1895.

to hire apprentices and journeymen. Finally, the artisan usually works upon local raw material and sells his commodities in the local market. When things are produced for sale on the market but without wage labour we have *simple commodity production* as distinguished from capitalist commodity production.

> "Previous to capitalist production," says Engels, "that is to say, in the Middle Ages, small-scale production was general, on the basis of the private ownership by the workers of their means of production: the agricultural industry of the small peasant, freeman or serf, and the handicraft industry of the towns. The instruments of labour—land, agricultural implements, the workshop and tools—were the instruments of labour of individuals, intended only for individual use, and therefore necessarily puny, dwarfish, restricted." *

Wherein lies the difference between simple commodity production and capitalism? The artisan, handicraftsman, small-scale farmer own their tools, raw material and means of production. They work by themselves, producing their goods with the aid of these means of production. Under capitalism it is different. There the plants and factories belong to the capitalist and in them work hired labourers who do not have their own means of production. Simple commodity production always precedes capitalism. The capitalist system could not arise without simple commodity production. The latter prepares the way for capitalism.

In its turn the development of simple commodity production inevitably leads to capitalism. Small-scale commodity production gives birth to capital.

One of the misinterpretations of Marxism is the attempt to deny the existence of simple commodity production as the historical precursor of capitalism. The political significance of this distortion of Marxism is clear. The fact of the matter is that even in the period of the prevalence of capitalism throughout the world many remnants of the former system still remain, a great number of the elements of simple commodity production, many millions of small peasants, artisans and handicraftsmen. These masses of petty commodity producers, independent in appearance, but in reality groan-

* Engels, *Anti-Dühring,* p. 301.

ing under the unbearable yoke of capitalism, constitute a reserve from which the proletariat draws its allies in the struggle for the socialist revolution. The distortion of the role and significance of simple commodity production forms a basis for the negation of the role of the basic mass of the peasantry as an ally of the proletarian revolution. This distortion lies at the basis of the counter-revolutionary theory of Trotskyism.

The attempt to separate simple commodity production from capitalism by a sort of Chinese Wall is a no less crude distortion of Marxist-Leninist theory. Lenin constantly stressed the fact that small-scale commodity production daily, hourly, gives birth to capitalism. The negation of this principle leads, for instance, under conditions prevailing in the U.S.S.R., to views like those held by the Right opportunists who advocated the perpetuation of small-scale production in the village, leads to a lack of understanding of the necessity of the socialist transformation of the village on the principles of large-scale social production.

The origin of capitalist production

Capitalism originated within the feudal-serf system. The oldest forms of capital are commercial and usurer capital. The merchant played an ever more important role as exchange developed within the old natural economy. The merchant capitalist furnished the serf-owning landlords with all kinds of luxuries, making much profit thereby. Part of the tribute which the landlord squeezed out of his serfs thus found its way into the pockets of the merchant—the representative of commercial capital. With the development of commerce, usury also flourished. Great lords—landlords, kings, governments—needed increasing sums of money. The mad luxury and waste, the endless wars devoured tremendous sums of money. Thus the basis arose for the activities of money-lenders. Lending money to the feudal lords at exorbitant interest, the usurer grabbed a large share of the tribute squeezed out of the labour of the serfs.

Commercial and usurer capital taking firm root in the life of feudal society unflaggingly undermined and broke down the foundations of this society. With the growth of commerce the exploitation of the serfs by the landlords grew continually stronger. The excessive exploitation undermined the foundations of serfdom—

peasant economy. It was impoverished, the peasants became paupers leading a hungry existence, incapable of giving a large income to the landlord. At the same time usurer capital grasped the feudal estate in its tentacles, squeezing the life out of it. The decay of serfdom prepared the way for the rise of capitalist production.

Commercial capital at first engaged only in trade. Commerce was carried on with the products furnished by artisans and serfs as well as with products imported from distant countries. With the growth of commerce, however, these sources of products became inadequate. Small-scale handicraft production could supply only a limited mass of commodities, sufficient merely for the local market. When commerce began to operate in more distant markets the necessity arose for extending production.

But only capital could secure such an extension of production. Small-scale commodity production was powerless here; its possibilities were narrowly circumscribed. A transition then took place from small-scale to capitalist production, which destroyed the pre-capitalist forms of exploitation only to substitute for them the last form of exploitation of man by man—capitalist exploitation.

Here is how Lenin describes this transition from small-scale production to capitalism:

> "Under the old conditions almost all the wealth was produced by small masters who represented the overwhelming majority of the population. The population lived stationary lives in villages and produced the greater part of their products either for their own use or for a small market consisting of the surrounding villages which had little connection with neighbouring markets. These same small masters worked for the landlords who compelled them to produce products mainly for their (the landlords') own use. The home-made materials were given to be made up into articles to artisans who also lived in the villages or else travelled about the neighbourhood taking work to do.
>
> "Since the emancipation of the serfs, however, the conditions of life of the mass of the people have undergone a complete change: big factories have arisen to take the place of the small artisans' workshops and the number of these factories has grown with remarkable rapidity; they have squeezed out the small masters and transformed them into wage workers, they

have compelled hundreds and thousands of workers to work together and produce enormous quantities of goods which are sold over the whole of Russia." *

"The place of small production everywhere is taken by large-scale production, and in the latter the masses of workers are simply hired labourers who work for wages for the capitalist, who owns large amounts of capital, builds large workshops, buys large quantities of raw materials and who puts into his own pocket the profit obtained from the mass production carried on by the combined workers. Production becomes capitalist production which ruthlessly crushes all the small masters, breaks up their stationary life in the villages and compels them to wander from one part of the country to another as mere labourers, to sell their labour power to the capitalist. A continuously increasing part of the population becomes completely divorced from the country and from agriculture, and collects in the towns and factory and industrial villages and there forms a special class which owns no property, a class of proletarians who live only by selling their labour power." **

Review Questions

1. How did people live before the appearance of class society?
2. How did classes originate?
3. What are the basic historical forms of class exploitation?
4. What are the relations between the exploiters and the exploited under the system of slavery?
5. What are the relations between the exploiters and the exploited under the system of serfdom?
6. What is the distinguishing feature of capitalist exploitation?
7. How does exchange arise and develop?
8. Why does small-scale commodity production give rise to capitalism?

* Lenin, *Selected Works*, Vol. I, "Draft and Explanation of the Programme of the Social-Democratic Party," pp. 471-72, International Publishers, 1934.

** *Ibid.*, p. 473.

CHAPTER III

Commodity Production

Capitalist production has two important distinguishing features. First, under capitalism commodity production prevails. Secondly, not only the product of human labour, but labour power itself becomes a commodity.

Capitalism is inconceivable without commodity production. On the other hand, commodity production existed long before the rise and development of capitalism. However, it was only under capitalism that commodity production became universal.

Therefore, in order to study the capitalist method of production, it is necessary first to study commodity production, its peculiarities and laws.

In capitalist countries production is carried on without a plan. All the factories and plants belong to the capitalists. Every one of these enterprises produces *commodities* for sale on the market. But no one tells the capitalist what commodities or what quantities of them his enterprise must produce. The owner of the plant or factory may increase or decrease production, or altogether close his place, as he wishes. The capitalists do not care whether the population has the necessities of life: food, clothing, etc. Every plant or factory owner thinks about only one thing: how to get more profit. If an undertaking seems profitable to him he regards it with great eagerness. If there is no profit in sight he will not trouble with it.

Such a system, where production is entirely in the hands of capitalists who manage production with the sole interest of extracting as much profit for themselves as possible by exploiting the toiling masses, exists at the present time all over the world, except in the Soviet Union where the government is in the hands of the working class and where there is planned economy.

Under capitalism anarchy of production prevails; there is and can be no planned management of social production.

"Capital organizes and regulates the labour within the factory for the further oppression of the worker, in order to increase its own profit. But in social production as a whole, chaos remains and grows greater, bringing on crises when the accumulated wealth finds no purchasers and millions of workers perish or go hungry, not finding work." *

We must now try to understand the subtle mechanism which distinguishes the anarchy of production prevailing under capitalism. In capitalist society commodity production prevails. Suppose a factory belonging to a capitalist produces castor oil. Does it mean that the owner drinks all the castor oil himself? Or a capitalist shop produces coffins on a mass scale; it is clear that the coffins are not for the owner. Tremendous plants produce great quantities of steel and iron; it is clear that the owner does not want the metal for himself. All the various products manufactured in capitalist enterprises are produced for sale, for the market. All products of labour manufactured for sale and not for one's own use are called *commodities.*

What is a commodity?

We have already seen that commodity production only gradually undermines and destroys the previous natural economy under which every family or commune produced by themselves everything they needed. The system of natural economy existed for ages. The previous, pre-capitalist forms of exploitation—slavery and feudalism—existed side by side with the prevailing system of natural economy. Not so capitalism. This system is from its very inception bound up with the development of exchange, the development of commodity production.

"The wealth of those societies in which the capitalist mode of production prevails presents itself as an immense accumulation of commodities, its unit being a single commodity." **

With these words Marx's chief work, *Capital,* begins. In this work Marx set himself the aim of discovering the economic laws governing capitalist society. Marx begins his work with an analysis

* Lenin, *Collected Works,* Vol. XVII, "The Taylor System—Enslavement of Man by Machinery," p. 248, Russian ed.

** Marx, *Capital,* Vol. I, p. 1, Swan, Sonnenschein & Co., Ltd., 1908.

of the commodity, with the disclosure of the laws governing the production of commodities.

Two properties of commodities

The product of human labour must always satisfy some human want, otherwise it would not be worth expending labour on it. This property of every product of labour is called its use value. The use value of a clock, for instance, is that it tells us the time. Many things that are not at all the product of human labour have use value, like water at its source, for instance, or fruit growing wild. Use value is met with in both natural production and commodity production. The grain the peasant raises for his own use satisfies his need for food. Grain therefore has use value.

But the grain which a peasant in a capitalist country produces for sale becomes, as we have seen, a commodity. This grain continues to possess use value because it satisfies the human need for food; but if it should lose this property for some reason (if it should rot, for instance, and become unfit for use), no one would buy it.

At the same time this grain acquires another important property. This grain has become a commodity; it can be exchanged for any other commodity. What strikes one here first is that a commodity has the property of being exchangeable, that it is exchanged for a number of other commodities.

This new feature of a product, which it acquires when it becomes a commodity, *i.e.,* when it is produced for exchange, plays an enormous role in commodity economy.

> "A commodity is, firstly, something that satisfies a human need; and, secondly, it is something that is exchanged for something else. The utility of a thing gives it *use value*. Exchange value (or simply, value) presents itself first of all as the proportion, the ratio, in which a certain number of use values of one kind are exchanged for a certain number of use values of another kind. Daily experience shows us by millions upon millions of such exchanges that all and sundry use values, in themselves very different and not comparable with one another, are equated to one another." *

* Lenin, *Marx-Engels-Marxism*, "Karl Marx." p. 15.

Between the use value and the value of a commodity there is a *contradiction.* To its producer a commodity is of no use value, it has use value for others. On the other hand, to the purchaser of a commodity for use the commodity has only use value, and to him the commodity is no longer a value. When the producer exchanges his commodity he gets its value in return, but he can no longer utilize the use value of the commodity since the latter is already in someone else's hands. A commodity is a product made not for immediate use but for sale on the market. A commodity is thus the agent of a definite social connection. It is the agent of the connection existing between the producer of the commodity and society as a whole. The connection is, however, not a direct one. Society does not tell each producer just what and how much to produce. Under commodity production there is not nor can there be planned, conscious guidance of the entire process of production in society.

Value is created by labour

Upon what does the value of a commodity depend? Some commodities are dear, others cheap. What is the reason for this difference i nvalue? Use values of commodities differ so widely that they cannot be compared quantitatively. For example, what is there in common in the use value of pig iron and roast beef? Consequently we must look for the secret of value not in use value but in something else. Marx says:

> "If then we leave out of consideration the use value of commodities, they have only one common property left, that of being products of labour." *

The value of a commodity is determined by the amount of human labour expended in its production.

So long as exchange is infrequent, products are exchanged in chance ratios. When a primitive hunter met a member of an agricultural tribe or community and exchanged some meat for grain the ratio was determined by chance circumstances. But things changed radically, parallel with the development of exchange.

With the destruction of natural economy, the ratio of exchange

* Marx, *Capital*, Vol. I, p. 4.

came continually closer to the amount of labour spent on the object exchanged. When under simple commodity production a peasant exchanges some grain for an axe made by an artisan he gives the latter an amount of grain which represents approximately the same amount of labour as that spent in making the axe.

Here is how Engels pictures the exchange of commodities according to their values under conditions of simple commodity production before the rise of capitalism:

> "The peasant of the Middle Ages therefore knew fairly accurately the labour time requisite for producing the things he obtained by exchange. The blacksmith and waggoner worked in his sight, as did the tailor and shoemaker who, in my own youth, went from hut to hut among our Rhenish peasants making clothes and shoes from home-made cloth and leather. Both the peasant and also those he purchased from were themselves labourers: the articles exchanged were the products of their own labour. What did they expend to produce these objects? Labour and only labour; for the replacement of working tools, for the production of raw material and for its working up they expended nothing but their own labour power; how could they then exchange these products of theirs for those of other workers otherwise than in proportion to the labour expended on them? Not only was the labour time expended on these products the sole appropriate measure for the quantitative determination of the magnitudes involved in the exchange, but any other measure was altogether unthinkable. Or does anyone believe that the peasant and the artisan were so foolish as to exchange a thing that took ten hours' labour for something that took only one labour hour? For the entire period of peasant natural economy no other exchange is possible than that in which the quantities of commodities exchanged tended more and more to be measured by the amount of labour incorporated in them. . . .
>
> "The same is true of the exchange of peasant products for those of city artisans. At first this takes place directly, without the intermediation of the merchant, on market days in the towns where the peasant sells his products and makes his purchases. Here also the peasant knows not only the conditions under which the artisan works but the latter knows also the conditions

of peasant labour. For he is himself still a peasant to a certain extent, he not only has a kitchen garden and an orchard, but frequently also a strip of arable land, one or two cows, pigs, poultry, etc." *

A number of self-evident facts confirm the truth that commodities are exchanged according to the labour incorporated in them. Very many commodities which were once very dear become fairly cheap, because with modern technical development less labour is required to produce them. Thus, for instance, aluminium, from which kitchenware and a number of other things are now manufactured, was a few decades ago eight or ten times as expensive as silver. It cost about $225 a kilogram then. But with the development of electrotechnical science it became possible to produce aluminium with much less labour so that before the war the price fell almost to 27 cents a kilogram, a thousand times cheaper. It became so cheap only because so much less labour is now required to produce it.

Thus the value of a commodity depends upon *the amount of labour spent in producing it*. If we produce a greater quantity of commodities with the same amount of labour, we speak of the increased productivity of labour; on the other hand, when less is produced, we speak of a decrease in productivity. It is self-evident that increased labour productivity means a *decrease* in the amount of labour that must be spent in order to produce a single one of the given commodities. As a result there will be a decrease in the value, each commodity of this particular kind will be cheaper. A decrease in productivity would, on the contrary, bring about dearer commodities. It is therefore said that productivity of labour and the value of each unit of the commodities produced are in inverse proportion (*i.e.*, when one rises the other falls, and *vice versa*). That is why Marx says,

> "The value of a commodity . . . varies . . . inversely as the productiveness of the labour incorporated in it." **

The value of a commodity is given to it by the labour spent in producing it. The value of a commodity is nothing but a definite quantity of labour time congealed (or incorporated) in the com-

* Engels, Supplement *(Nachtrag)* to Vol. III of *Capital*.
** Marx, *Capital*, Vol. I, p. 7.

modity. But value manifests itself only when one commodity is compared with another. Let us assume that the same amount of labour is incorporated in one ton of iron as in one kilogram of silver. Then a ton of iron will be equal in value to a kilogram of silver. The value of a commodity expressed in comparison with the value of another commodity is its exchange value. Exchange value is the form in which value manifests itself. At the same time it must be clearly remembered that in this form we have only the value representing the labour time incorporated in the commodity.

Under developed commodity production when commodities are exchanged through the medium of money, every commodity is compared with a definite sum of money. The value of the commodity is expressed in terms of money. Exchange value becomes the price of the commodity. *Price is only the value of a commodity expressed in terms of money.*

In order to understand the contradiction inherent in commodities it is necessary to observe the peculiarities of the labour which produces commodities.

Abstract and concrete labour

In exchanging commodities people compare the most varied kinds of labour. The labour of a cobbler differs very much from the labour of a foundryman. The labour of a miner resembles the labour of a tailor very little. Every single commodity contains the labour of some particular profession or some particular branch of industry. What is common to all commodities is human labour in general, or, as it is sometimes expressed, abstract human labour as distinguished from the concrete (*i.e.*, specific) labour of each individual branch of production.

> "All the labour power of a given society, represented in the sum total of values of all commodities, is one and the same human labour power. Millions and millions of exchange transactions prove this." *

Every particular commodity represents only a definite part of this general human labour.

Concrete labour produces use value. The concrete labour of the cobbler produces boots, the concrete labour of the miner—coal,

* Lenin, *Marx-Engels-Marxism*, "Karl Marx," p. 16.

The value of these commodities, however, expresses simply human labour, the expenditures of human labour in general under commodity production.

> "On the one hand all labour is, speaking physiologically, an expenditure of human labour power, and in its character of identical abstract human labour, it creates and forms the value of commodities. On the other hand, all labour is the expenditure of human labour power in a special form and with a definite aim, and in this, its character of concrete, useful labour, it produces use values." *

The same labour is both concrete and abstract in commodity production: it is concrete in so far as it produces use value, and abstract in so far as it produces value. On the one hand, every producer produces definite use values, say, boots, coal, cloth, etc. This represents the concrete labour of the cobbler, the miner, the weaver, etc. But on the other hand, the same cobbler, miner and weaver produce the value of the boots, coal, cloth. They produce these not for their own immediate use, but for exchange on the market. They produce boots, coal, cloth, as commodities possessing value. And value is produced by abstract, universal, human labour.

From the very beginning commodities reveal their dual nature: as use value and value. We now see that labour also, the labour embodied in these commodities, the labour applied in capitalist production, has a dual character.

The difference between concrete and abstract labour appears in the contradiction between use value and value. Use value is the result of concrete labour, whereas value is the result of abstract labour.

It is perfectly evident that this division of labour into concrete and abstract labour exists only in *commodity production*. This dual nature of labour reveals the basic contradiction of commodity production. In commodity production all the work of an individual member of society becomes, on the one hand, a particle of the entire mass of social labour and, on the other hand, it is the particular work, the individual labour of different, separate workers. It is clear, therefore, that the contradiction between abstract and

* Marx, *Capital*, Vol. I, p. 14.

concrete labour arises only with commodity production and vanishes as soon as commodity production disappears.

> "A man who produces an article for his own immediate use, to consume it himself, creates a *product*, but not a *commodity*. As a self-sustaining producer he has nothing to do with society. But to produce a *commodity*, a man must not only produce an article satisfying some *social* want, but his labour itself must form part and parcel of the total sum of labour expended by society. It must be subordinate to the *division of labour within society*. It is nothing without the other division of labour, and on its part is required to *integrate* them." *

In commodity economy the work of each separate worker represents only a particle of social labour as a whole. The work of each weaver, miner or mechanic becomes part of the general chain of social production. Each separate work constitutes only one of the links in this chain. But at the same time, each separate work in commodity production is *independent*. The labour of individuals becomes social, in the sense that each producer is connected with thousands of others in his work. But the labour of separate individuals is not co-ordinated on an all-social scale. Quite the contrary, the labour of individual workers is separate, scattered.

> "The production of commodities is a system of social relationships in which different producers produce various products (the social division of labour), and in which all these products are equated to one another in exchange." **

This contradiction, consisting in the social nature of the individual labour of independent producers, arises with commodity production and disappears with it.

In natural economy this contradiction does not exist. Let us imagine a secluded peasant economy in some far away, isolated corner of the world. This economy is almost completely cut off from the rest of the world; everything needed is produced on the farm. Labour here is not a portion of the labour of society as a whole, labour here is of a distinctly separate and individual nature.

* Marx, *Value, Price and Profit*, pp. 30-31, International Publishers, 1935.
** Lenin, *Marx-Engels-Marxism*, "Karl Marx," p. 16.

Hence the contradiction characteristic of commodity production does not exist here. However, if we take socialist society, the interdependence of the labour of individual members of society is even greater in comparison with capitalism, but here also the contradiction of commodity production does not exist: the labour of each worker has become social, has become an organized part of the general labour. The separate, scattered character of the labour of each worker has disappeared. The fruit of the labour of all becomes the property of society as a whole and not of individual owners.

If the value of a commodity is determined by the quantity of labour expended upon its production, it might seem that the lazier or the more unskilful a man, the more valuable his commodity.

Socially necessary labour

Suppose there are two cobblers working side by side. One is a fast, efficient worker and makes a pair of boots in a day. The other is a lazy drunkard and it takes him a week to finish one pair of boots. Does it mean that the boots of the second cobbler have more value than those of the first? Of course not.

> "In saying that the value of a commodity is determined by *the quantity of labour* worked up or crystallized in it, we mean *the quantity of labour necessary* for its production in a given state of society, under certain social average conditions of production, with a given social average intensity, and average skill of the labour employed. When, in England, the power-loom came to compete with the hand-loom, only one-half the former time of labour was wanted to convert a given amount of yarn into a yard of cotton or cloth. The poor hand-loom weaver now worked seventeen or eighteen hours daily, instead of the nine or ten hours he had worked before. Still the product of twenty hours of his labour represented now only ten social hours of labour, or ten hours of labour socially necessary for the conversion of a certain amount of yarn into textile stuffs. His product of twenty hours had, therefore, no more value than his former product of ten hours." *

* Marx, *Value, Price and Profit*, p. 33.

It thus appears that the value of a commodity depends, not upon the labour which in each separate instance was expended upon its production, but upon the labour which is required on the average for its production, or, as it is expressed, upon the social average or the socially necessary labour.

Simple and skilled labour

We must also distinguish between simple labour and skilled labour. Let us take a mason and a watchmaker. An hour of labour of the mason cannot be equal to an hour of labour of the watchmaker. Why? To learn the trade of a mason one does not have to spend much time in preparatory training. It is a simple labour, easily learned. Anyone can easily become a mason (or, say, a common labourer). A watchmaker (or a chemist) is a different matter. In order to become a watchmaker one must spend, say, about three years in learning the trade. If the future watchmaker decides to spend a long time in learning the trade, it is only because he expects to get paid for this later. How? In that for a watch, upon the making of which he spent twenty hours, he gets on the market commodities produced by simple or unskilled labour in, say, thirty hours. In such a case one hour of skilled (or, as it is sometimes called, complex) labour is equal on the market to one and a half hours of simple labour.

What would happen if no difference were made in exchange between an hour of simple and an hour of skilled labour? Then the supply of skilled labour would be considerably curtailed. Watchmakers, chemists and other such skilled people would become fewer and fewer. Hence there would be fewer and fewer watches, chemicals, etc., on the market, and prices for such commodities would go up. Then an hour of labour of a watchmaker would once more become equal to an hour and a half or even two hours of simple labour. Then it again becomes advantageous to learn a skilled trade.

The market and competition

We have seen that the value of a commodity is determined by the socially necessary labour expended upon its production. Does this mean that in the system of commodity production every commodity can always be exchanged for its full value? Of course not. For this it would be necessary for every commodity produced to have a purchaser immediately. It would be necessary for supply and demand always to balance each other. Can this really happen?

In the system of commodity production there is no organ in society which could tell the individual producer what commodities and in what quantities he should produce. So long as the greater part of production is for immediate use and only a small share of the surplus gets to the market, the role of the market is not very great. But with the expansion of commodity production the market becomes more and more important.

Each separate commodity producer works at his own risk. Only after the commodity has been produced and is taken to the market does he find out whether there is a demand for his commodity or not.

The price of a commodity is the monetary expression of its value. But price always vacillates according to the conditions of the market. A struggle about the price of the commodity takes place at the market between seller and buyer. Competition, among the sellers on the one hand, and among the buyers on the other, decides the question of the price at which the commodity is to be sold. The price of a commodity, therefore, does not always correspond to its value. The price is sometimes higher, sometimes lower than the value of the commodity. The value, however, always remains the centre or axis about which the price oscillates.

If more of a commodity has been produced than there is a demand for, then the supply exceeds the demand and its price falls below its value. When the price falls below the value it means that the producer of the given commodity will not be repaid for all the labour he has expended on it. It will therefore pay him better to produce some other commodity for which there is more demand. The production of the first commodity will be curtailed. But then the relation between supply and demand will become more advantageous for this commodity, and after a while its price may rise again to the level of its value and even higher.

Only in this way, by means of continuous fluctuations, is the law of value realized. Commodities sell at their value only in the event of supply exactly equalling the demand. This happens, however, only as a rare exception.

"The theory of value assumes and must assume an equal supply and demand, but it does not assert that such an equality is always to be observed or can be observed in capitalist society." *

The law of value appears as *a blind force of the market.* Every individual producer must submit to this blind force. As Marx expresses it, this force acts like the falling of a house. This means that the individual producer can never know beforehand what the all-powerful market will require of him. The law of values acts behind the back of the individual producer. Commodity production is characterized, as we have seen, by anarchy, *i.e.*, by the absence of any order, any conscious plan for society as a whole. The law of values acts as an impersonal, unconscious power in a society where anarchy of production prevails.

The development of exchange and the forms of value

From the preceding chapters we already know that commodity production did not come into existence at once in its developed form. On the contrary, exchange only gradually undermines and destroys the previous natural economy. The change from natural economy to commodity economy is prolonged over many centuries.

Under developed commodity economy one commodity is not exchanged directly for another. Commodities are bought and sold, they are converted into money. The form in which their value is manifested is money. However, in order to understand the monetary form of value, we must acquaint ourselves with the less developed forms, corresponding to the earlier stages of development of commodity production and exchange.

When production still has a primarily natural character, and the exchange is effected by chance, we have the elementary, single, or accidental form of value. One commodity is exchanged for another: the skin of an animal, let us say, is exchanged for two spears. Those distinguishing features, which become prominent when exchange and commodity production have reached their utmost development and expansion, are already contained in embryo in this still completely undeveloped form of value.

In the given instance, the simple form of value serves as an

* Lenin, *Collected Works,* Vol. II, "Articles on the Question of the Theory of Markets," p. 407, Russian ed.

expression of the value of the skin, receives its expression in the form of two spears. We see that the value of the skin is not expressed directly, but only *relatively*, in relation to the value of two spears. Two spears serve here as the equivalent of one skin. The value of the skin is expressed by means of the use value of two spears.

Thus we see here that the use value of one commodity (two spears) serves as an expression of the value of another commodity (a skin). The value and the use value are *divided* as it were, the value is separated from the use value. Here the skin figures only as the value, the two spears only as the use value. The value of the skin becomes, so to speak, separated from its use value and is equated to another commodity. From this the conclusion can be drawn that the value of a commodity cannot be expressed in terms of itself alone, to express this value there must be the bodily form of another commodity, an equivalent.

Even in the simple form of value the distinguishing feature of the commodity equivalent is that the use value of this commodity serves as the expression of its opposite—value.

> "The body of the commodity that serves as the equivalent figures as the materialization of human labour in the abstract and is at the same time the product of some specifically useful concrete labour." *

Accordingly concrete labour serves here as the expression of abstract labour, individual labour—as the expression of social labour.

The simple form of value exists only so long as exchange bears an absolutely single, accidental character. As soon as exchange is somewhat more widely developed, this form of value changes into the *total* or *expanded form of value* in which not two commodities, but a much wider circle of commodities are equated to each other. In this form each commodity can be exchanged not only for another commodity, but for a series of commodities. For example, the skin can be exchanged not only for two spears, but for a pair of shoes, for an oar, for a piece of cloth, or for a sack of corn. The total or expanded form of value will, therefore, appear as follows:

* Marx, *Capital,* Vol. I, p. 27.

$$1 \text{ skin} = \left\{ \begin{array}{l} 2 \text{ spears} \\ 1 \text{ pair of shoes} \\ 1 \text{ oar} \\ 1 \text{ piece of cloth} \\ 1 \text{ sack of corn, etc.} \end{array} \right.$$

We have this form of value when some product of labour, cattle for instance, is habitually exchanged for various other commodities, not as an exception but as a general rule.

The expanded form of value is a further stage in the development of the form of value. The value of one commodity is expressed in different commodities, belonging to different owners of commodities. The division between value and use value is here made still more evident. The value of the skin is here opposed to its use value as something common to a series of other commodities.

However, even the expanded form of value does not satisfy the demand, which grows with the development of exchange.

The development of exchange makes the shortcomings of this system of exchange more and more manifest. These shortcomings are done away with by the next, more developed form of value, namely, the general form. The general form of value naturally grows out of the total, or expanded form. In the expanded form of value one commodity is most frequently exchanged, and therefore its value is expressed in a series of other commodities. Let us suppose that this commodity is cattle. Let us say that one ox is exchanged for one boat, for three pairs of shoes, for three sacks of corn, for twenty arrows, etc. We have only to reverse this series of exchange relations and we will have the general or universal equivalent form of value, as follows:

$$\left. \begin{array}{r} 1 \text{ boat} \\ 3 \text{ pairs of shoes} \\ 3 \text{ sacks of corn} \\ 20 \text{ arrows, etc.} \end{array} \right\} = 1 \text{ ox}$$

In the universal equivalent form of value, the value of all commodities finds expression in one and the same commodity. The commodity which expresses the value of the other commodities serves as the *universal equivalent*. This commodity is readily taken in exchange for any other commodity. Thus the inconvenience which accompanies the total or expanded form of value is eliminated. Here the separation of value from use value becomes still greater. All commodities express their value in a single commodity. It becomes the function of one commodity to express the value of all other commodities. The entire world of commodities is split into two opposite groups: the universal equivalent by itself makes one group, the other group consists of all the other commodities.

The *money form of value* differs only slightly from the universal form. When the precious metals—gold and silver—definitely become the fixed universal equivalent, we have the transition from the universal form of value to the money form. In the money form the particular social function, *i.e.*, the expression of the value of all commodities, is embodied in one particular commodity. This commodity, gold or silver, is pre-eminent in the commodity world. Before it becomes money, gold must first be a commodity. But having become money, gold acquires a number of new properties in connection with its role as money.

Value is a specific social relation between persons which is expressed as a relation between things. The value of a commodity cannot be expressed in terms of itself. It can be expressed only with the help of another commodity. The exchange relation between one commodity and another, or *its exchange value*, serves as the expression of its value. We have seen the development of the form of value from the simple to the money form. The development of the form of value is linked with the development of the contradictions which are inherent in commodities. The contradictions between use value and value emerge more and more clearly in the process of the development of exchange and the corresponding forms of value. In money this contradiction is expressed most fully. Money becomes the only and universal means of the expression of value. All other commodities counterbalance money as use values.

Commodity fetishism

Under planned socialist production it is clear to every worker that he is part of an organized body. Under socialism the production relations between people become clear and obvious. The connection between each individual worker and enterprise and all other workers and enterprises is self-evident and clear.

It is not so in a society where commodity production prevails. In commodity production the production relations between people appear as relations between things. When a cobbler sells a pair of boots he has made and with the money thus obtained buys bread at the baker's for himself and his family, we have a definite production relation, a definite connection between people according to production. The bread baked by the baker serves the needs of the cobbler, and the boots made by the cobbler will perhaps go to the baker. It follows, therefore, that the work of the baker is needed to satisfy the needs of the cobbler; the work of the cobbler is needed to satisfy the needs of the baker. Thus there is a definite connection between the cobbler and the baker, a definite relation according to production. But how is this connection revealed? In what is it expressed? We have already seen. It reveals itself in the process of exchange. Commodities are objects that change hands from one producer to another. Bread goes from the baker to the cobbler. Boots go from the cobbler to the merchant and from the merchant to the same baker. However, commodities do not simply change hands. Everyone knows that the cobbler gives up the boots he has made only after he has received a corresponding amount of money for them—their price. The baker acts in exactly the same way. Thus, under the system of commodity production, production relations among people are revealed as the movement of things—commodities.

Value is the relation between persons who produce commodities. But this relation presents itself as a relation between things—commodities. This production relation is concealed by a material cover, hidden behind the movement of things. The value of a commodity seems just as natural a property of the commodity as, say, its colour or weight; it is said, for instance: this bread weighs half a pound and is worth five cents. A commodity becomes a very puzzling thing. The fate of the producer is closely tied up with that of his product. If our cobbler cannot sell the boots he will remain without bread. If the price of boots falls—he can buy so much less bread. Why cannot the cobbler sell the boots, or why does he get less for them this time than he got before? The cause lies in the changes which have taken place in the economic life, in the production relations of people in capitalist society, say a crisis has come, or the workers are buying boots more seldom because of a reduction in wages. The real cause will, however, long remain unknown to the cobbler and when he does find it out it will generally be in a distorted way. For the connection between the cobbler and the rest of the producing world is centred in his commodity—boots, in their value which is realized on the market.

The fact that under commodity production the relations between persons according to production acquire the appearance of relations between things—commodities—and that commodities, hence, acquire peculiar social properties, we call *commodity fetishism* (fetishism generally is the worship of imaginary, supernatural properties ascribed to an object—a fetish). Under capitalism all production relations between persons in society are hidden under a cover of things. All production relations between persons under capitalism appear as relations between things, as relations connected with things. This masks the real meaning of capitalist relations, veils them, hides their real character, gives them an illusory appearance. That is why it is very important to unmask, to understand, the puzzle of commodity fetishism that permeates all relations under capitalism.

Marx was the first to solve the riddle of commodity fetishism. Marx was the first to reveal the social relations between persons, where up to his time only the mysterious properties of things had been seen. He was the first to show that value is a social relation between people in the commodity production system.

> "Political economy begins with *commodities*, begins with the moment when products are exchanged for one another—whether by individuals or by primitive communities. The product that appears in exchange is a commodity. It is, however, a commodity solely because a *relation* between two persons or communities attaches to the *thing*, the product, the relation between producer and consumer who are here no longer united in the same person. Here we have an example of a peculiar fact, which runs through the whole of economics and which has caused utter confusion in the minds of the bourgeois economists: economics deals not with things but with relations between persons and in the last resort between classes; these relations are, however, always *attached to things* and *appear as things*. This inter-connection, which in isolated cases it is true has dawned upon particular

economists, was first discovered by Marx as obtaining for all political economy, whereby he made the most difficult questions so simple and clear that now even the bourgeois economists will be able to grasp them." *

The role of money in the system of commodity production

Nowadays it seldom happens that one commodity is directly exchanged for another. The producer usually *sells* the commodities he produces for money, and for the money realized *buys* the commodities he needs. Why then do we speak of the exchange of commodities? The fact is that money here really acts as an intermediary in the exchange of commodities. The capitalist sells his products and gets a definite sum of money for them. But he is not interested in this money as such. He needs this money to buy new raw material and machinery, to hire workmen, to expand production.

The exchange of commodities through the medium of money is, however, radically different from the direct exchange of commodities. The introduction of money leads to a further growth and development of the contradictions inherent in commodities.

Money is not introduced by consent or agreement, it comes into use spontaneously. Only with the aid of money can the all-sided social connection established between the separate individual producers under the commodity production system be realized.

The contradiction between concrete and abstract labour, as we have seen, is expressed in the contradiction between the use value and the value of a commodity. With the introduction of money a further development of this contradiction takes place. The commodity acquires the twofold character of commodity and money. When exchange takes place by means of money, the owner of the commodity receives in exchange for it money which incorporates the value of the commodity.

The value of the commodity is now expressed in its price, *i.e.*, in a definite amount of money. It is not enough that the commodity has been produced—it must be exchanged for money. It must be sold, its price must be realized. If it cannot be sold—it means the producer has laboured in vain.

* Engels, *Ludwig Feuerbach*, Appendix, pp. 99-100, International Pub., 1934.

Money is a universal commodity, the universal equivalent. Money is the embodiment of value, the embodiment of abstract labour. Money is the stamp with which the market puts its label of social recognition on commodities, transforming them from products of private labour to those of social labour.

But in this there already lies the danger that the products of one or another producer may not be converted into money. If it proves impossible for the commodity producer to convert his commodity into money it means his private, individual labour has not become a part of social labour. This means that due to the anarchy prevailing in production he has futilely spent his labour, raw material and tools on the production of a commodity which cannot be sold. It is clear that in money, commodity fetishism is even more acutely apparent. In capitalist commodity production all social production relations are, as Marx points out, gilded or silvered. Supernatural powers are ascribed to money. Being a product of social development money acquires an altogether extraordinary force and power in this society.

> "Being the highest product of the development of exchange and of commodity production money masks and hides the social character of individual labour, the social tie between the various producers whom the market brings together." *

Money plays an important part in the transition from small-scale commodity production to capitalism. The bosses who have grown rich, acquiring their wealth by hook or by crook, amass it in the form of money. Capital first originates in the form of money.

The functions of money

Money has a number of functions in commodity economy. Every commodity is sold for a definite sum of money. This sum of money is called the *price of the commodity*. Thus, price is value expressed in terms of money. The value of a commodity is measured by money. The measurement of the value of a commodity in money is the premise of the exchange of the commodity, its purchase or sale. Before a commodity can be bought or sold, it is essential to know its price. Thus money plays the role of a *measure of value*.

* Lenin, *Marx-Engels-Marxism,* "Karl Marx," p. 17.

The value of a commodity is determined by the working time spent on its production. However, value cannot be expressed by the socially necessary working time. In buying or selling a pair of boots, for example, it is not said that the boots cost twenty hours of labour, but that they cost, let us say $10. We have explained this previously. The value of a commodity x can be expressed only through the medium of another commodity. It is not known beforehand whether the time spent on the production of the boots will actually be taken into account. Perhaps, if the market is flooded, the boots will be sold not for $10, but only for $5. This would mean that the twenty working hours actually spent on the production of the boots would have to be exchanged for a product of only ten working hours. The price of a commodity is constantly fluctuating round its value, these fluctuations manifesting themselves in the fact that the cost of a commodity may be first above, then below the value, or *vice versa.*

To be a measure of value, money itself must be a commodity and possess value. One cannot, for example, measure weight by means of an object which has no weight. But must money actually be present when the value is measured? Obviously not. We can evaluate an enormous number of commodities without having a cent in our pockets. Money fulfils its function as a measure of value theoretically, as *ideal* money. From this it is clear that the question of the amount of money also plays no part in this function.

The decisive moment for a commodity comes after it is priced in money. It must be sold, *i.e.*, exchanged for money. An exchange of goods accomplished by means of money is called the circulation of commodities. It is clear that the circulation of commodities is inseparably linked up with the circulation of money itself. When a commodity goes out of the hands of the seller into the hands of the buyer, money goes out of the hands of the buyer into the hands of the seller. Here money plays the part of the means of circulation, or the means of commodity turnover.

To fulfil the role of the means of circulation, money must actually be present. Here it emerges not as ideal money, but as real money. Everybody knows that you cannot buy a pinch of snuff with "ideal money." You can imagine a million dollars but you will not be able to buy anything with your imaginary million.

whereas with every really existing dollar you can obtain a commodity of corresponding value.

In one important respect the requirements for the means of circulation are different from the requirements for the measure of value. To be the means of circulation, money must not necessarily possess a value of its own. In all probability the seller of the commodity takes money in exchange not for the sake of any value of its own, but in order to change it in its turn for another commodity, *i.e.,* to buy another commodity. While it is serving as the means of exchange, money does not lie in the pockets of individual persons, it continues its uninterrupted movement in the direction of the inverse movement of commodities. Consequently, money here plays only a transient part. This is precisely why full value money—gold—can be replaced in this function by its substitutes, or symbols of itself. Such substitutes for gold are bank notes, paper currency, silver and copper coins without full value, etc. These substitutes for gold (or tokens of value) have either no value at all, or much less than that which they represent. As the moon shines with the reflected light of the sun, so they reflect the value of the real money—gold.

To fulfil the function of the means of circulation a definite amount of money is required. In order to sell a commodity worth a thousand dollars, there must actually be not *any* sum of money, but precisely the thousand dollars. On the other hand, this same thousand dollars which is paid for the given commodity can afterwards serve as the circulating medium for other commodities worth a thousand dollars. But commodities are bought and sold in many places simultaneously. Therefore, the amount of money necessary at a given moment depends on the sum total of the prices of all the commodities in circulation; the sum total of the prices in its turn depends on the quantity of commodities in circulation and on the price of each individual commodity.

The amount of money that will be needed, for example in the course of a year, depends not only upon these two quantities, but also upon the rapidity of the currency of money; if the circulation takes less time, less money is needed for the process of circulation, and *vice versa.*

The twofold nature of commodities—as goods and as money—opens the way for the further development of the contradictions of commodity production. When commodities are exchanged directly for each other a sale is at the same time a purchase. Money makes it possible to separate the sale from the purchase. The commodity producer can sell his goods and for a time keep the money realized. However, when many producers try to sell without buying, this results in an obstruction in the market. Money thus already opens the way for crises, while the further development of commodity production and its transformation into capitalist production make crises inevitable.

When the commodity owner has sold his commodity, he often puts aside the money he has received. Money is the "universal representative of material wealth." * In the capitalist world, money can be converted at any moment into any commodity. The difficulty is to convert the commodity into money and not the money into a commodity. Therefore money is the best means of accumulation, or the means for amassing great wealth. Under capitalism the passion for profit knows no bounds. The thirst for enrichment acts as a spur towards the accumulation of the greatest possible amount of money.

In its role as the means of amassing wealth, money must be money in the full sense of the word. For this it must possess value of its own, just as for the fulfilment of its function as a measure of value. At the same time it must always be present in its real aspect: one cannot accumulate money which is merely ideal, one can only accumulate that money which really exists. Thus it must also possess that property which it possesses in its function of circulating medium.

In developed capitalist society a man who accumulates money merely out of a passion for accumulation is rarely met with. The man who hoards money or simply amasses wealth in its money form is characteristic of the earliest stages of capitalism. The capitalist entrepreneur is no longer blinded by the golden glitter of money. He knows that in order to increase his wealth he must extend his production, his turnover, he must extract more unpaid labour from his workers. However, even modern capitalism (or the bank that serves it) must from time to time engage in the accumulation of money. To extend production it must have

* Marx, *Capital*, Vol. I, p. 109.

a definite sum of money which it must spend all at once. In the course of a certain time it accumulates this sum.

Moreover, money functions also as a means of payment. Selling and buying are frequently accomplished on credit. The purchaser buys a commodity and pays its price only after a fixed time. This function of money reflects a further wide development in exchange. The link between individual commodity producers becomes stronger. Their interdependence increases. Now the buyer becomes the debtor, the seller is transformed into the creditor. When the time approaches for payment the debtor must obtain the money regardless of all else. He must sell his commodity so as to be able to pay his debt. What will happen, if he cannot find a buyer and he cannot clear his debt? This will deal a blow not only to his own production, but also to the production of his creditor, who will not receive back that which he gave on credit. In this way the possibility of crises, which is already inherent in the function of money as a means of circulation, becomes still more acute.

The function of money as a means of payment introduces new conditions into the law which determines the quantity of money needed for circulation. To those trends which ensue from the function of money as the circulating medium are added new trends arising from its function as a means of payment. Formerly, the quantity of money needed to serve for circulation depended on the sum total of the prices of the goods in circulation, and the rapidity of the currency of the money. Now the following new circumstances are added. First of all, from the total prices of the commodities in circulation, it is necessary to subtract the sum total of the prices of those commodities which are sold on credit. On the other hand, we must add the sum total of the prices of those commodities which were sold on credit but for which payment is due. Furthermore, we must take into cognizance the sum total of the payments which balance each other because the sellers and buyers of the various commodities are interconnected.

Finally, money plays the part of *universal money*. In the trade between individual states, gold is a commodity differing from all other commodities only in that it is accepted by everyone. Therefore the equilibrium in the trade between various countries is maintained by means of gold. Let us suppose, for example, that

England has exported commodities to America to a greater value than she has imported from America. Then America must transfer a quantity of gold to England to compensate for the difference.

It is customary to replace gold by bits of paper which represent it. If this paper money is issued in quantities not greater than is necessary for commodity circulation, if it can be freely exchanged for gold, then its purchasing power is stable. Capitalist governments, however, often issue a greater amount of paper money to cover their needs, particularly during wars and all kinds of catastrophes. Then money is devaluated. At the present time, when capitalism is experiencing the severest crisis, a number of bourgeois governments have taken this step. At first money was inflated in a number of secondary countries but soon the greatest capitalist governments, England and the U.S.A., went the same way.

The law of value—the law of motion of capitalist commodity production

The social connection between individual producers of capitalist commodity-producing society is veiled, befogged. This social connection is manifested in the exchange of commodities. In commodity production labour acquires the form of value. Commodities are exchanged according to their value, *i.e.*, in accordance with the amount of the socially necessary abstract labour embodied (congealed) in them. All the contradictions inherent in capitalist commodity production are to be found in embryo in commodities, in their value, in the exchange of commodities.

"Marx, in his *Capital*, at first analyses the simplest, the most ordinary, fundamental and commonplace thing, a *relation* that has a mass appearance and is to be observed billions of times in bourgeois (commodity) society: the exchange of commodities. In that simple phenomenon (in that 'cell' of bourgeois society) the analysis reveals *all* the contradictions (respectively the embryos of *all* contradictions) of modern society. The subsequent exposition shows the development (*both* growth and movement) of those contradictions and of this society in the Σ * of its parts, from beginning to end." **

* Mathematical symbol denoting summation.
** Lenin, *Marx-Engels-Marxism*, "On Dialectics," p. 209.

The law of value is the *law of motion* of capitalist commodity production. This motion appears in the form of a further development of the contradictions, the germs of which are inherent in value. These contradictions are manifested most sharply during crises. Anarchy of production, characteristic of the capitalist commodity producing system, appears in its most naked form during crises. The contemporary capitalist crisis bears the most eloquent evidence of this. During a crisis, the contradictions between the productive forces and the production relations, contradictions which draw capitalism towards its inevitable doom, stand out sharply.

With the historical development of commodity production and its transformation into capitalist production, as capitalism develops further, the contradictions inherent in commodities and their value grow and become more complex. The growth of the contradictions inherent in commodities reflects the gigantic historical stride of capitalist development.

> "Marx traced the development of capitalism from the first germs of commodity economy and simple exchange, to its highest forms, to large-scale production." *

Showing how Marx traces this great historical process of development, embracing many centuries, Lenin also shows how the contradictions originate, the germs of which already exist in commodities:

> "Where the bourgeois economists saw a relation of things (the exchange of one commodity for another) Marx revealed a *relation between men.* The exchange of commodities expresses the connection between individual producers by means of the market. *Money* signifies that this connection is becoming closer and closer, inseparably combining the entire economic life of the individual producers into one whole. *Capital* signifies a further development of this connection: the labour power of man becomes a commodity. . . .
>
> "Capital, created by the labour of the worker, presses upon the workers, ruins the petty owners and creates an army of unemployed. . . .

* *Ibid.*, "The Three Sources and Three Component Parts of Marxism," p. 53.

"By beating petty production, capital leads to the increase of the productivity of labour and to the establishment of a monopoly position for associations of the biggest capitalists. Production itself becomes more and more social; hundreds of thousands and millions of workers are linked up in a systematic economic organism, but the product of the collective labour is appropriated by a handful of capitalists. Anarchy of production, crises, a furious hunt after markets, and the insecurity of existence for the masses of the population are on the increase." *

The development of the contradictions of capitalism, at the same time, lays a basis for the final triumph of the proletariat.

"Capitalism has been victorious all over the world," writes Lenin, "but this victory is only the eve of the victory of labour over capital." **

Review Questions

1. What is the difference between natural production and commodity production?
2. What determines the value of a commodity?
3. What labour is called socially necessary labour?
4. What is the difference between concrete and abstract labour?
5. What is the role of the market in the commodity production system?
6. How does the law of value act?
7. How does capitalism differ from simple commodity production?
8. Can commodity production exist without money?

* *Ibid.*, pp. 52-3.
** *Ibid.*, p. 53.

CHAPTER IV

The Essence of Capitalist Exploitation

The exploitation of the working class by the bourgeoisie prevails in all capitalist countries. The working class and the bourgeoisie—these are the two basic classes facing each other in every capitalist country. We must study the conditions that make it possible for the bourgeoisie to appropriate the fruits of the labour of the worker. We must understand the secret of capitalist exploitation, which was revealed by the great teacher of the proletariat—Marx.

How the workers are exploited by capital. Labour power—a commodity

What is the secret of capitalist exploitation? How does it come about? What is the secret of the enrichment of the capitalists? By what invisible chains is the worker fettered to his exploiter? Why does one class grow rich on the impoverishment of the other?

Marxian theory gives a clear and precise answer to every one of these questions. The Marxian teachings explain to us the inner structure of the capitalist world, uncover all the inner springs of its development and its inevitable collapse.

In a previous chapter we have studied simple commodity production and its basic law—*the law of value.* Simple commodity production inevitably produces *capitalist elements* in its midst. Simple commodity production grows into, is transformed into, capitalism. The law of value is the law of the development of commodity production. This development leads to capitalism. Together with this development also grows the power of the elemental law of value.

What is capitalism? Lenin answers this question as follows:

> "Capitalism is commodity production at the highest stage of development, when labour power itself becomes a commodity." *

* Lenin, *Imperialism, the Highest Stage of Capitalism,* Chap. IV, p. 59, Moscow, 1934.

Under commodity production things are produced not for immediate use but for exchange, for the market, for sale. The law of value governs production and exchange of commodities. Commodities are exchanged in accordance with their value, *i.e.,* in accordance with the quantity of socially necessary labour needed to produce them.

Capitalism does not abolish commodity production and its laws. On the contrary, under capitalism commodity production reaches its *highest stage* of development. Under capitalism the laws governing commodity production enforce their rule to an even greater extent. Hence the laws of capitalist production are based upon the laws of commodity production and primarily upon the law of value.

"Capitalist production is marked from the outset by two peculiar traits," says Marx. "1) It produces its products as commodities. The fact that it produces commodities does not distinguish it from other modes of production. Its peculiar mark is that the prevailing and determining character of its products is that of being commodities. This implies, in the first place, that the labourer himself acts in the role of a seller of commodities, as a free wage worker, so that wage labour is the typical character of labour. . . .

"2) The other specific mark of the capitalist mode of production is the production of surplus value as the direct aim and determining incentive of production. Capital produces essentially capital, and does so only to the extent that it produces surplus value." *

The framework of commodity production expands under capitalism. *A new commodity* appears, which did not exist under the system of simple commodity production—*labour power*. What sort of commodity is this?

Marx answers this question as follows:

"By labour power or capacity for labour is to be understood the aggregate of those mental and physical capabilities existing in a human being, which he exercises whenever he produces use value of any description." **

* Marx, *Capital,* Vol. III, pp. 1025-26, Charles H. Kerr & Co., 1909.
** *Ibid.,* Vol. I, p. 145.

In other words, labour power is man's capacity for labour, his capacity for productive activity.

Marx says:

> "The capitalist buys labour power in order to use it; and labour power in use is labour itself." *

Under capitalism labour power becomes a commodity. But is labour power always a commodity? By far not always, of course. Take the petty producer. He works on his own strip of land or in his own workshop himself. He sells his produce, but he does not sell his labour power. He uses his labour power himself. It is clear that he can do this only so long as he possesses his own strip of land or workshop. Take away his tools or bench from the artisan, take away the strip of land from the petty farmer—and they can no longer apply their labour power in their own undertaking. What then remains for them to do? In order not to starve they are compelled to apply for work to the capitalist who owns the factory, the land, the plant or the railroad. But what does hiring out to a capitalist mean? It means—selling one's labour power.

We thus see that definite *conditions* or prerequisites are necessary for the rise of capitalism. It is necessary for some members of society to have in their hands all the means of production (or sufficient money for the purchase of these means) and, on the other hand, it is necessary that there should be a class of people who are forced to sell their labour power.

> "The historical prerequisites to the genesis of capital are: first, accumulation of a considerable sum of money in the hands of individuals under conditions of a comparatively high development of commodity production in general, and second, the existence of workers who are 'free' in a double sense of the term: free from any constraint or restriction as regards the sale of their labour power; free from the land or from the means of production in general, *i.e.*, of propertyless workers, or 'proletarians,' who cannot maintain their existence except by the sale of their labour power." **

* *Ibid.*

** Lenin, ***Marx-Engels-Marxism***, "Karl Marx," p. 18.

Capitalism arises on the ruins of the preceding social order—landlord (feudal) economy. Capitalism grows on the soil of petty commodity production. Capitalism effects a radical transformation in the previously existing social relations.

Primitive accumulation

How did the capitalists really get rich? At the beginning of the capitalist era, some three or four hundred years ago, the then foremost European countries (Spain and Portugal, Holland and England) had developed a wide overseas trade. Intrepid travellers discovered routes to the distant and rich countries of the East—India and China; America was discovered. The invention of gunpowder made it easy for the Europeans to overcome the resistance of the native populations of these countries. All America was turned into a series of colonies. The robbing of the richest overseas countries was one of the most important sources of primitive accumulation of European capital, especially British. Another source was war among the countries of Europe itself, and the pillage of the vanquished countries. Finally the robbing of the people of their own country by means of usury, robbing by means of overseas trade at usurious prices, and partly direct robbery (especially piracy) are not the least important methods employed in the history of the birth of capital.

But the accumulation of wealth is only half the problem the solution of which is necessary for the appearance of capitalist production. The second half is the obtainment of a sufficient number of *free hands.*

No one will go to work for a capitalist so long as he has the possibility of working independently. It is necessary to take away the means of production from the petty producer in order to compel him to take to the market all that remains to him—his labour power. Another necessary condition for wage labour is that people must be personally free so that they can move freely from place to place, so that they can freely dispose of their labour power.

These conditions did not exist under serfdom, which prevailed everywhere in Europe. That is why capitalism destroys the previously existing serfdom.

But it is not enough for the interests of capital to free the peasant—he must also be placed in a position where he is compelled *to look for work* at the enterprises of the *capitalist.* True, capital obtains a certain number of wage labourers from among the artisans and handicraftsmen it ruins, but this number is insufficient—new enterprises demand vast masses of workers. Moreover, capital must always have a reserve of a certain number of workers, as we shall see later.

Hence, simultaneously with the "liberation" of the peasantry from serfdom, another, no less important "liberation" is effected. The peasant is "liberated" from the land on which he worked. To the peasant is left (and generally he must buy it, at that) only that portion of the land which fed him under the landlord. Insufficiency of land drives the peasantry into the clutches of capital. "Excess" labour leaves the village and constitutes the reserve army of wage labourers at the disposal of capitalist industry.

Thus primitive accumulation creates the *necessary prerequisites* for the rise of capitalism. It creates the necessary *conditions* without which capitalism cannot exist. We have already seen what these conditions are. They are, on the one hand, accumulation of wealth in the hands of a small portion of society and, on the other hand, the transformation of a vast mass of workers into proletarians having no means of production and therefore compelled to sell their labour power. Primitive accumulation thus effects the *separation of the producer from his means of production.* This separation is brought about by the cruellest methods of robbery and plunder, murder and violence. After these conditions for the rise of capitalism have been created they further entrench themselves by the very process of capitalist production. When workers bend their backs at a capitalist factory they multiply the wealth of their exploiter. But they themselves remain the same dispossessed proletarians compelled to sell their labour power.

The transformation of money into capital

At first capital emerges in the form of money. Therefore money plays a prominent part in the transition from small-scale production to capitalism. At a certain stage of the development of commodity production money is transformed into capital. The formula for commodity circulation used to be C (commodity)—M (money)—C (commodity), *i.e.*, the sale of one commodity for the purchase of another. The general formula for capital is the reverse of this, M—C—M, *i.e.*, buying for the purpose of selling (at a profit).

What is the difference between these two formulae? The formula C—M—C is characteristic of simple commodity production. Here one commodity is exchanged for another. Money serves only as a medium of exchange. Here the purpose of the exchange is clear—the shoemaker, let us say, exchanges his boots for bread. One use value is exchanged for another. The commodity producer hands over the commodity which he does not need and receives in exchange another commodity which he needs.

The formula for the circulation of capital is of an entirely different character. The capitalist goes to the market in possession of a certain sum of money. The point of departure here is not the commodity, but money. With his money the capitalist buys certain commodities. However, the movement of capital does not end with this. The commodity of the capitalist is converted into money. Thus the starting point and the finishing point of the movement of capital coincide: the capitalist had money in the beginning and he has money in the end. But, as is well known, money is always the same, it does not differ qualitatively, it differs only quantitatively. Money is unlike other commodities which are distinguished by their great qualitative diversification. Thus the entire movement of capital would be quite absurd if at the end of the movement the capitalist had only as much as he had at first. The whole reason for the existence of capital, the whole meaning of its movement, is that at the end of this movement more money is withdrawn from circulation than was put in at the beginning. The goal of capital is the extraction of profit. Its formula is not selling in order to buy again, as in the case of the simple commodity producer, but buying in order to sell and extract profit.

But in what way is this profit obtained? If the capitalist buys any ordinary commodity with his money and then sells it above cost price, he enriches himself, but only at the expense of other capitalists—either at the expense of those whom he tricks by buying the commodity and not paying its actual price, or at the expense of those to whom he sells the commodity for more than its price, or at the expense of both. But the capitalist class cannot prosper by cheating itself, by the mutual trickery of the individual capitalists. Then how is profit obtained? Obviously, the capitalist who goes to the market with his money must find a commodity of a special kind.

It must be a commodity that creates value while it is being used. And under capitalist conditions there is such a commodity. This commodity is labour power.

Buying and selling of labour power and its value

Under commodity economy every commodity is sold at its value. What does the worker sell? He sells his labour power, which is essential for the capitalist to conduct his enterprise. But we know that every commodity has its value and that this value is determined by the labour time necessary to produce this commodity. What is the *value* of that commodity which the worker sells—the commodity, "labour power"?

It is perfectly evident that a person can work only when he is able to maintain his existence: feeds and clothes himself, and has a place to rest his head. It is understood that a human being can perform work only when he satisfies his requirements, at any rate his most elementary needs. If a worker is hungry, if he has no clothes, he becomes unfit for work, he loses his labour power. It can therefore be considered that the production of labour power consists in the satisfaction of the most elementary needs of the worker.

But we also know that all those things which go to satisfy the needs of man (food, clothing and shelter) are *commodities* under capitalism and cannot be obtained free of charge. A definite quantity of labour is spent in producing them and this determines their value. Thus the value of the commodity called "labour power" is equal to the *value of those commodities the worker must consume* in order to maintain his existence and that of his family, in order to recuperate his labour power and to secure future labour power for the capitalists.

> "The value of labour power is determined by the value of the necessaries of life habitually required by the average labourer." *

But the value of these commodities depends on the labour necessary to produce them.

In other words, the value of the commodity called labour power is determined by the quantity of labour necessary to produce this

* Marx, *Capital*, Vol. I, p. 527.

peculiar commodity, while this commodity, as we have already said, consists of the food, clothing, etc., consumed by the worker. It is this value of the commodity called "labour power" that is paid for by the capitalist in the form of wages.

The capitalist owns a plant: buildings in which there is machinery, warehouses in which there are raw material and fuel, all kinds of auxiliary material. All this is dead without human labour. Therefore a capitalist hires workers. With this he buys the last commodity necessary. Now everything is in order. Production can begin. The workers begin to work, the enterprise is started, the machinery is in motion.

Having hired the labourer, bought his labour power for a definite time, the capitalist makes him work. In this lies the entire purport of his purchase of labour power.

One must not confuse labour power with labour. *Labour power and labour are not one and the same thing.* Labour power is the ability of people to work. Labour is the creator of value, but it cannot itself become a commodity. *The commodity is labour power.*

We know that there is a distinction between, say, a locomotive and the motion of the locomotive. The locomotive may stand still at a station. In this case there is a locomotive but there is no motion. But the locomotive possesses the ability to move; when necessary it begins to move. In the same way labour power may remain unused, if its owner is unemployed, for instance. But inasmuch as the unemployed worker still has labour power, provided he has not fallen ill or does not drop from hunger, he may at a suitable moment begin to work just as the locomotive may begin to move after a long stop.

The price of a commodity, as we have already seen in a previous chapter, may be above or below its value. However, unlike most other commodities, with respect to labour power there is always a tendency for the price to stay *below* its value. This means that the worker does not get a sufficiency of the means of subsistence necessary to cover all his wants. If we say that the value of labour power is determined by the value of the means of subsistence necessary to maintain the existence of the worker, we do not at all mean to assert that the worker always receives for his labour power its full value. On the contrary, in the vast majority of cases he is compelled to sell his labour power at a price *below* its value. However, even when the worker receives the full value of his labour power, the capitalist gets surplus value from production and this serves as a source of enrichment to him.

We have already seen how commodities are exchanged at their value. Now let us see how the value created by some people goes into the pockets of others. Starting in business the capitalist purchases everything necessary for production: machinery, raw material, fuel. He also buys the necessary labour power by hiring workers. Production begins at the factory: fuel is burned, the machinery operates, the workers labour, the raw material is transformed into commodities. When the commodities are ready, they are sold and with the money obtained the capitalist can begin the cycle all over again.

What is the source of the capitalist's profits?

What is the value of the commodities thus produced? Their value consists, first of all, in the value of the commodities spent in their production: the wear and tear of machinery, the fuel consumed, and the raw material used up. Let us assume that the value of all this was 3,000 hours of labour. Then a new value enters, created by the workers at the particular factory. Let us assume that 20 men worked 10 hours a day each for 5 days. It is easy to see that by this they have created a value of 1,000 hours of labour. Thus the full value of the new commodity which the capitalist has is 3,000+1,000=4,000 hours of labour.

The question now arises, what did this cost the capitalist himself? It is quite evident that for the wear and tear of machinery, for the fuel burned and for the raw material, the capitalist had to pay their full value, *i.e.*, a sum of money equivalent to 3,000 hours of labour. But in addition to this 3,000 hours of labour, 1,000 hours of labour spent by the wage workers also entered into the value of the new commodity. Did the capitalist also pay out to his workers the equivalent of 1,000 hours of labour? Herein lies the solution of the whole secret of capitalist exploitation.

The capitalist pays the 20 workers the value of their *labour power* for 5 days. That is, he pays them a sum sufficient to produce their labour power for 5 days. It is easy to understand that this sum amounts to less than 1,000 hours. The amount of labour the worker spends at the factory is, of course, one thing; while the value of the commodities needed to maintain his capacity to work is quite another.

> ". . . the value of labour power and the value which that labour power creates in the labour process are two entirely different magnitudes," * says Marx.

To return to our example, we may assume that the value of the labour power of one worker amounts to 5 hours of labour. Then the capitalist will pay his workers a sum of money equivalent to 500 hours of labour.

Let us now total up. The capitalist's expenditures then amount to 3,000+500=3,500 hours of labour. But the value of the commodities, as we have seen, was 3,000+1,000=4,000 hours of labour.

Where does the capitalist's profit come from? It is now easy to answer this question. The profit is the fruit of the unpaid labour of the workers. This profit is the fruit of the additional or, as it is called, the *surplus labour* of the workers, who during 5 hours of the day produce a value equal to their wages and during the other 5 hours produce *surplus value* which goes into the pockets of the capitalist. The unpaid portion of labour is the source of surplus value, the source of all profit, all unearned revenue.

Surplus labour and surplus value

> "The wage labourer sells his labour power to the owner of land, of factories and instruments of labour. The worker uses one part of the labour day to cover the expenditure for the maintenance of himself and his family (wages), and the other part of the day he toils without remuneration and creates *surplus value* for the capitalist which is the source of profit, the source of wealth of the capitalist class.
>
> "The doctrine of surplus value is the corner-stone of the economic theory of Marx." **

The Marxian doctrine of surplus value discloses the secret of capitalist exploitation. That is why this teaching is an invaluable weapon in the hands of the proletariat struggling for the destruc-

* *Ibid.*, p. 174.
** Lenin, *Marx-Engels-Marxism*, "The Three Sources and Three Component Parts of Marxism," pp. 52-3.

tion of capitalism, for the creation of the new communist society. That is why the bourgeoisie and its "learned" henchmen rage against the Marxian doctrine of surplus value. That is why they are continually trying to "refute" and to "destroy" this teaching.

The Marxian doctrine of surplus value is based, as we have seen, on his teaching of value. That is why it is important to keep the Marxian teaching of value free from all distortion, because *the theory of exploitation* is built on it.

We can now sum up our investigation of the sources of enrichment for the capitalists. This summary can best be made by citing the concise and clear exposition of the teaching on surplus value which we find in the works of Lenin:

> "Surplus value cannot arise out of the circulation of commodities, for this represents only the exchange of equivalents; it cannot arise out of an advance in price, for the mutual losses and gains of buyers and sellers would equalize one another; and what we are concerned with here is not the individual but the mass, average, social phenomenon. In order that he may be able to receive surplus value, 'Moneybags must . . . find . . . in the market a commodity whose use value possesses the peculiar property of being a source of value' *—a commodity, the actual process of whose use is at the same time the process of the creation of value. Such a commodity exists. It is human labour power. Its use is labour, and labour creates value. The owner of money buys labour power at its value, which is determined, like the value of every other commodity, by the socially necessary labour time requisite for its production (that is to say, the cost of maintaining the worker and his family). Having bought labour power, the owner of money is entitled to use it, that is, to set it to work for the whole day, twelve hours, let us suppose. Meanwhile in the course of six hours ('necessary' labour time) the labourer produces sufficient to pay back the cost of his own maintenance; and in the course of the next six hours ('surplus' labour time) he produces a 'surplus' product or surplus value, for which the capitalist does not pay him." **

* Marx, *Capital,* Vol. I, p. 157.
** Lenin, *Marx-Engels-Marxism,* "Karl Marx," pp. 17-18.

In ancient times, when people had not yet emerged from a state of savagery, primitive man spent all his strength and energy to obtain the bare necessities of life. The savage just managed to keep himself from dying of hunger by means of the things his labour brought him.

When primitive man struggled against hunger with difficulty there could be no social inequality among people, as there is none, say, among animals. The introduction of surplus labour creates the possibility for the rise of inequality, the possibility for the exploitation of man by man. The surplus labour of some people goes for the benefit of others: the product of this surplus labour falls into the hands of the higher class in society which exploits the lower classes.

Such a situation persists up to and including the capitalist era. True, the forms of exploitation change. Exploitation has different aspects in the slaveholding, feudal and capitalist systems, but in essence it remains the same. It consists of the appropriation of the surplus labour of the entire society by the ruling class.

> "The essential difference between the various economic forms of society, between, for instance, a society based on slave labour, and one based on wage labour, lies only in the mode in which this surplus labour is in each case extracted from the actual producer, the labourer." *

Capital did not invent surplus labour, Marx pointed out. Everywhere, wherever society consists of exploiters and exploited, the ruling class extracts surplus labour from the vast masses of the toiling and exploited population. Under capitalism, however, the thirst for surplus labour assumes a more insatiable character than under any previous form of class society.

Under slavery and serfdom, while natural production predominated, there were definite limits to the amount of surplus labour appropriated. The slaveholder or feudal lord squeezed as much labour out of the masses exploited by him as was necessary to satisfy his needs or desires. Under capitalism, on the contrary, there are no limits to the thirst for surplus labour. The surplus labour which the capitalist squeezes out of the worker is transformed into ringing coins, which can again be set to work as new,

* Marx, *Capital*, Vol. I, p. 200.

supplementary capital, bringing new surplus value. The capitalist method of production is distinguished by its insatiable thirst for surplus labour. Under capitalism the tendency to increase the exploitation of the worker knows no bounds. The capitalists neglect no means to increase the exploitation of their wage slaves.

It is perfectly clear that with the destruction of the capitalist system, with the abolition of capitalist exploitation, the extraction of surplus labour from the workers for the benefit of the capitalist stops. An end is put to the division of the working day into necessary and surplus hours, in the sense in which it is divided under the domination of capital. Here is what Marx says about this:

"Only by suppressing the capitalist form of production could the length of the working day be reduced to the necessary labour time. But, even in that case, the latter would extend its limits. On the one hand, because the notion of 'means of subsistence' would considerably expand, and the labourer would lay claim to an altogether different standard of life. On the other hand, because a part of what is now surplus labour would then count as necessary labour: I mean the labour of forming a fund for reserve and accumulation" * (a reserve of the means of production and subsistence which will permit of the expansion of industry and recompense for possible losses, among others, those due to accidents).

These words of Marx give the key to an understanding of the state of things in the socialist economy of the U.S.S.R. where exploitation of the workers no longer exists.

In the socialist enterprises of the U.S.S.R. class exploitation has been torn up by the roots for the first time in history. In Soviet enterprises there are no two classes with opposing interests, as there are in capitalist enterprises. The enterprises are the property of the Soviet state, of the proletarian dictatorship. The class owning the plants and factories, and the class labouring at these enterprises is one and the same class. Under Soviet conditions the worker does not sell his labour power to a representative of an alien and hostile class. There is not and there cannot be any production of surplus value in the socialist economy of the U.S.S.R. The excess created by the labour of the worker over and above his

* *Ibid.*, pp. 539-40.

earnings goes to cover the collective requirements of that same working class and its dictatorship: for the general needs of the country, for socialist accumulation, for defence requirements, etc.

The inventions of the Trotskyists to the effect that the industries of the U.S.S.R. presumably are state capitalist and not socialist are therefore nothing but malicious counter-revolutionary slanders. With these slanders Trotskyism tries to cover up its traitorous attempts to undermine the work of socialist construction in the U.S.S.R.

What is capital?

We have analysed the production of surplus value. We have studied the dynamics of the appropriation of the unpaid labour of workers by the capitalists. We have seen that the only source of unearned revenue for the capitalists is the labour of the proletarians. Now let us take a closer look at the invisible force which compels millions of people to submit to the caprices of a handful of capitalists. We must more closely examine the power of capital, analyse what capital is.

The exploitation of the workers by the capitalists is possible only because, under capitalism, all wealth is concentrated in the hands of the bourgeoisie. The capitalists own all the means of production and subsistence, the workers have neither the one nor the other. The bourgeoisie has monopolized (that is, taken exclusive possession of) all the wealth of society.

> "The characteristic features of capitalist society which arose on the basis of commodity production are the monopoly of the most important and vital means of production by the capitalist class and big landlords; the exploitation of the wage labour of the proletariat which, being deprived of the means of production, is compelled to sell its labour power; the production of commodities for profit and, linked up with this, the planless and anarchic character of the process of production as a whole." *

This is how the capitalist system is characterized in the *Program of the Communist International.*

* *The Programme of the Communist International,* p. 11, Workers Library Publishers, New York, 1936.

Under capitalism the proletariat is deprived of the means of production. By *means of production* we understand those things that are of prime necessity for man to work with. It is easy to note that the means of production consist of several most important parts. These are, first of all, the *instruments of labour*, from the cobbler's simple awl to the most complex and intricate machines in modern plants and factories. Further, there is the *raw material* which must be used. The raw material for boots is leather; for the smelting of iron, iron ore is the raw material; for the weaving of calico, cotton is the raw material. Finally, there are a number of accessory materials needed for work, such as oil, sand, lime, etc.

The lot of these different elements of the means of production in work is not the same. The instruments of labour last a long time. In a textile mill the same looms will weave many pieces of fabric. The materials used have quite a different fate. The raw material disappears in the process of production—it is transformed into an entirely new product. The leather in the hands of the cobbler becomes boots, cloth in the hands of the tailor becomes a suit, ore at a metallurgical plant is made into iron; the accessory materials are also completely used up in the process of work: fuel vanishes in heating the factory boilers, oil disappears in the machinery.

Under capitalism these means of production, without which no work is possible, are in the hands of the bourgeoisie. This gives the bourgeoisie tremendous power over society. In the hands of the bourgeoisie the means of production become means of exploitation because they are concentrated in comparatively few hands while the vast mass of the population is deprived of them and must therefore sell its labour power.

Capital is not a thing, but a definite *social relation*, said Marx. Things—means of production and all other kinds of commodities—in the hands of the bourgeoisie in themselves are not capital. Only a definite social system makes these things into means of exploitation, converts them into carriers of that social relation which we call capital. *Capital is "a special, historically definite, social production relation."* (*Lenin.*) It is the social relation between the class that owns the means of production and the class which, deprived of the means of production, is therefore compelled to undergo exploitation.

Since in capitalist society the means of production are bought and sold, they are commodities. And as commodities they have value and can be converted into money (*i.e.,* sold); in its turn, for money one can always obtain means of production (purchase them). Hence, to put it differently, *capital* can be defined as value which brings *surplus value* (by squeezing it out of wage labour) But value is nothing but crystallized labour. Value is the result of labour. Value is expended, dead labour. That is why Marx says that "capital is dead labour, that, vampire like, only lives by sucking living labour. . . ." *

In order to understand capitalist exploitation fully, it is necessary to distinguish between constant and variable capital.

Constant and variable capital

We have already seen that the full value of a commodity includes the value of the raw material and fuel used as well as a part of the value of the machinery, etc. The quantity of the value does not change: as much value is carried over into the new commodity as represents the original value of this part of the expended capital. Hence we call this part of capital—factory buildings and machinery, raw material and fuel—*constant* capital.

But we also know that another very important element enters into the value of the new commodity—the value produced by the workers at the factory. If there are 100 workers at an enterprise working 10 hours a day each, and an hour's work has a value of, say, 50 cents, then the entire new value produced by them each day is equal to $500.

We already know that the wages which the workers receive are less than the new value which they produce. The size of the wages corresponds only to that part of the newly created value which is represented by the labour necessary to maintain the workers, while the additional labour produces surplus value which goes into the pockets of the capitalist.

If the necessary labour amounts to 5 hours a day, then the capitalist pays $2.50 a day to the worker, or $250 to the 100 workers. Thus the part of the capital which the capitalist used to purchase labour power amounts to $250, while the value created by that

* Marx, *Capital*, Vol. I, p. 216.

labour power amounts to $500. We thus see that part of the capital has been doubled in the process of production, doubled, of course, not by itself, but because of the appropriation of the unpaid surplus labour of the workers. Hence we call the part of the capital used for the purchase of labour power (*i.e.*, for the payment of wages to the workers) *variable* capital.

For the capitalist there is another distinction in capital. He keeps close track of that part of his capital which has a quick turnover, distinguishing it from that part which turns over slowly. The capitalist calls the factory buildings and machinery, which last for a long time, his *fixed capital*; on the other hand he calls that part of his capital which has a quick turnover his *circulating capital*. The latter includes the capital which is expended for raw material, fuel and wages for the workers.

In the process of production, and consequently of circulation also, these portions of capital play different parts. They last for different periods of time. The buildings of a factory can stand up for, say, fifty years. Consequently, only one-fiftieth part of the value of these buildings will be incorporated in the value of the annual production. The entire value expended by the capitalist on these buildings returns to him only in the course of fifty years. A machine will work for, say, fifteen years. Then its value returns to the capitalist in the price of the finished commodities only in fifteen years; in each one of these fifteen years the capitalist receives, through the sale of his commodities, only one-fifteenth of the value of the machine. On the other hand, the raw material and the fuel is entirely consumed in the manufacture of the commodity. If the manufacturer has converted a thousand bales of cotton into a finished product and has then sold his commodity, the entire expense for raw material is returned to him at once and in full. The same is true of labour power.

The division of capital into constant and variable capital does not coincide with its division into fixed and circulating capital.

Constant capital includes fixed capital and in addition that part of the circulating capital which goes for raw material, fuel and auxiliary materials. In general, constant capital goes for the purchase of expended (or, as it is called, dead) labour necessary for production. On the other hand, variable capital is used only for wages to the workers.

These two methods of dividing capital can be illustrated as follows:

Division According to Rate of Turnover	*Part of Capital*	*Division According to Role in the Process of Exploitation*
Fixed capital	Factory buildings Machinery	Constant capital
Circulating capital	Raw material, fuel, auxiliary material	Constant capital
Circulating capital	Wages	Variable capital

It is very important to distinguish these two methods of dividing capital. The division into constant and variable capital shows at once what the true and only source of surplus value is. The division into fixed and circulating capital confuses the real creator of surplus value—labour—with other elements which add no new value. Thus the method of dividing capital which is customary in capitalist practice masks, befogs the essence of capitalist exploitation.

In our example the workers produce $500 worth of new value a day and receive in the form of wages only $250. It is evident that the other $250 are appropriated by capital in the form of surplus value.

Rate of surplus value

It is very important to know what part of the labour of the worker gets to the pockets of the capitalist. Then we shall have a definite measure to show the degree of capitalist exploitation.

Such a criterion is the *rate of surplus value*. By the rate of surplus value we mean the ratio of surplus value to variable capital, or, in other words, the ratio of unpaid labour to necessary labour. In our example, the rate of surplus value will have the following appearance:

$$\frac{\$250 \text{ surplus value}}{\$250 \text{ variable capital}} = 100 \text{ per cent}$$

If the rate of surplus value is equal to 100 per cent, it means that the worker's labour is equally divided into necessary and surplus labour, that surplus value is equal in magnitude to variable capital, that the worker is paid for only half his labour and that the other half is appropriated by the capitalist.

It is perfectly evident that every capitalist tries to get as much surplus value as he possibly can. How does he achieve his purpose? The simplest way would be to hire more workmen and expand production. If 100 workers produce surplus value amounting to $250, 200 will net the capitalist $500. But to double production, additional capital is necessary. If the capitalist has such additional money, or means in general, he will naturally do so. This is very clear and simple.

Two methods of increasing surplus value

The question is, however, how to increase surplus value without increasing the amount of capital outlay. Here the capitalist has two ways.

We have seen that the working day consists of two parts—paid, necessary labour and unpaid, surplus labour. Let us assume that the working day is 12 hours, of which 6 hours are the paid part, and of which the other 6 hours consist of surplus labour. Let us represent this working day by a line divided into 12 parts, every division representing an hour, thus:

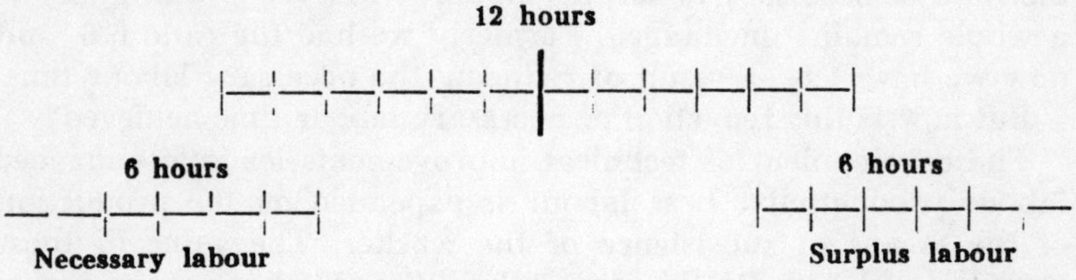

12 hours

6 hours — **Necessary labour**

6 hours — **Surplus labour**

Under these circumstances, the capitalist can increase the amount of surplus value he receives by *lengthening the working day*. Since necessary labour remains unchanged, the part falling to surplus labour will be greater. Let us assume that the working day has been increased to 14 hours. Thus we shall get the following picture:

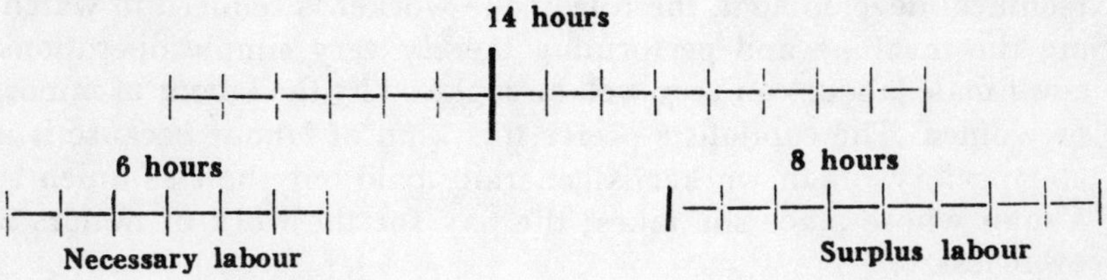

14 hours

6 hours — **Necessary labour**

8 hours — **Surplus labour**

In this case we have an increase in the *absolute* surplus value: the volume of surplus value increases because of an *absolute* increase in the working day as a whole.

There is also another way of increasing the amount of surplus value. What will our working day look like if the capitalist finds some way of reducing the amount of necessary labour? It is easy to answer this. Let us assume that the necessary labour has been reduced to 4 hours. Then the working day will look like this:

12 hours

|—|—|—|—|—|—|—|—|—|—|—|—|

4 hours |—|—|—|—| Necessary labour

8 hours |—|—|—|—|—|—|—|—| Surplus labour

In this case we have an increase of the *relative* surplus value: the volume of surplus value increases exclusively by changing the ratio of necessary to surplus labour, while the working day as a whole remains unchanged. Formerly we had the ratio 6:6, and now we have 4:8—a result of reducing the necessary labour time.

But how is this reduction of necessary labour time achieved?

The development of technical improvements leads to enhanced labour productivity. Less labour is expended on the production of the means of subsistence of the worker. The value of these means is reduced. By the same token, the value of labour power is reduced, decreasing the amount of necessary labour and increasing the relative amount of surplus value.

In order to reduce the amount of necessary labour the capitalist employs the wives and children of the workers. Then the entire family receives in wages approximately as much as was previously received only by the head of the family. When, with increased technical development, the role of the worker is reduced to watching the machine and performing merely very simple operations, adult male labour can very well be replaced by the labour of minors or women. The capitalists prefer this kind of labour because it is cheaper: a woman worker is generally paid only half as much as a man whose place she takes; the pay for the work of minors is even less.

The following method of augmenting the relative surplus value should be especially noted. Every capitalist tries in all ways to increase his profits. For this purpose he introduces all kinds of improvements which lower the cost of production. For this purpose he buys new machinery, introduces new technical improvements to increase the productivity of labour. So long as these technical innovations introduced by the capitalist remain unknown to other enterprises of the same field he receives super-profits, excess surplus value. The commodities cost him less, whereas he sells them at the same price as before or only slightly under this price.

Excess surplus value

An individual enterprise usually keeps such an advantage for only a very short time. Other enterprises also introduce technical improvements. Since the value of commodities is determined by the average socially necessary labour contained in them, the general introduction of technical improvements leads to a fall in the value of the commodity and thus the individual enterprise is deprived of its special advantage.

Under capitalism, the main driving force of technical progress is the possibility of getting super-profits. The race for excess surplus value produces an increase in relative surplus value, as it brings about a reduction in the amount of labour needed to produce the workers' means of subsistence. Excess surplus value is only another form of relative surplus value.

The struggle around the working day

It is quite evident that for the capitalist, the simplest way to augment his profits is to increase absolute surplus value. No new technical improvements are needed for this; it is only necessary to lengthen the working day. And, in fact, the capitalists always try to extend the working day to the utmost. If they could do so, they would make the worker labour more than twenty-four hours a day. Lengthening of the working day, however, has its natural physical limits. Moreover, this incurs the ever more determined opposition of the workers. That is why the capitalists cannot limit themselves altogether to attempts at increasing absolute surplus value. Together with this they also struggle for relative surplus value, which promises them unlimited possibilities.

At the dawn of the capitalist era an extremely long working day prevailed in all countries. Technical development was still weak, and most important of all, the working class was scattered and not prepared for battle; hence, the production of absolute surplus value predominated everywhere.

In some cases the working day consisted of almost the entire twenty-four hours. The worker only got a few hours for sleep, the rest of the time belonged to the capitalist. It is easy to imagine what an effect such murderous exploitation had upon the life of the workers.

A long working day is still common in many countries. In China for instance, the working day in many factories is sixteen to eighteen hours long; even in underground work, in the coal mines, the working day is as exorbitantly long. And such a long working day prevails not only for men but also for women and young children.

In capitalist society, says Marx, the free time of one class is obtained by turning the entire life of the masses into working time.

As soon as the proletarian begins to struggle for better conditions he advances the demand for *limiting the working day* as one of his first demands. Laws limiting child labour and the length of the working day appeared in the older capitalist countries (in England and then in France) only in the forties of the last century. Labour legislation everywhere appeared only after the severest struggles on the part of the working class. The bourgeois government, defending the interests of its capitalist class as a whole, consents to the enactment of such laws only under pressure of the labour movement, on the one hand, and from consideration of the necessity of preserving the lives of the working population, on the other hand, as without the workers there would be no profits for the capitalists.

In most of the highly developed countries the ten-hour day prevailed prior to the World War; the working day was shorter only in some cases of underground work (in coal and metal mines). There were some limitations on child labour and the work of women (the limitation of night work).

After the World War, when the sweep of the labour movement threatened the very existence of capitalism, the bourgeoisie in many countries made concessions. In 1919 a special proposal was even drawn up in Washington to introduce the eight-hour day on a world scale, but nothing came of this. In the following years, when capital took the offensive, most of the concessions were withdrawn. A general onslaught against the eight-hour day was made by the capitalists everywhere and in most countries the eight-hour day does not exist any longer.

Intensity of labour

One of the favourite methods of extracting more surplus value from the workers is by increasing the intensity of labour. It can be arranged that the worker shall expend more labour, expend more energy in the same interval of time. In such a case he will produce more value; hence the surplus value falling to the capitalist will also increase.

With machinery the intensity of labour is often increased by speeding up the machine. The worker must make an effort to keep up with the machine. If he fails to do so he loses his job. In other cases the capitalists try to get the workers to work more and more intensively by means of special methods of payment.

Excessive intensity of labour is just as injurious to the health and life of the worker as an excessively long working day. When the length of the working day is limited by law, the capitalists find a "way out" for themselves by an unlimited increase in the intensity of labour. In most capitalist enterprises the intensity of labour is so great that the worker prematurely loses his ability to work, ages too soon, is subject to various diseases. For the capitalists,intensification of labour is a well-tried method of augmenting the exploitation of the worker, of increasing the degree of his enslavement.

Capitalism and technical development

At the present time the decaying capitalist system, finding itself in the grip of a severe and protracted crisis, manifests itself as the foe of technical progress. The capitalists and their learned servants often try to represent machinery as being the cause of all the trouble. Too many machines, they say, too many steel monsters robbing honest people of work. Too many products produced by these machines, which then find no market. The workers know, however, that it is not the machine in itself which brings unemployment, crisis, etc. The reason for these evils is the capitalist system with its deep-rooted contradictions. It is not the machine that robs the worker of bread, but the capitalist application of the machine as a means of exploitation.

Under the conditions of the present crisis, the bourgeoisie evince a predilection for returning from machine production to hand labour. And it is not a rare thing for them to put into practice these mad schemes so inimical to progress. In America, while many steam shovels and dredges stand idle, thousands of people are made to labour with the pick and shovel on public works. Under these conditions the U.S.S.R. is the only country in the world today which continually progresses towards the adoption of the newest and most advanced technique in all fields. The country where socialism is being built holds high the flag of technical progress.

Modern technical engineering increases the productivity of labour hundreds and thousands of times.

A worker can make 450 bricks a day by hand. A modern brickmaking machine turns out about 400,000 bricks a day for every worker employed on it, *i.e.*, about 1,000 times as many.

A hand-power flour mill turns out 450-650 pounds of low grade flour. A modern flour mill in Minneapolis (U.S.A.) turns out 13,000,000 pounds of the best grade flour a day to every worker employed, or about 20,000 times as much.

A modern shoe factory can produce 83 pairs of shoes per worker every 6 days, as against 1 pair which could be produced by a worker working by himself.

Modern moribund capitalism, however, is incapable of utilizing these possibilities. Even before the present crisis the application of the newest technical developments met with tremendous difficulties even in the richest capitalist country—the United States of America.

In 1929 there were 2,730 brick-making plants employing 39,000 workers and making 8,000,000,000 bricks, whereas 6 to 7 modern plants with only 100 workers each could completely satisfy the U.S.A. market.

In 1929 there was a total of 6,500,000,000 pounds of flour produced in the United States. In order to produce this quantity of flour, with the normal production capacity of the Minneapolis flour mill mentioned above, only 17 workers would be needed.

As a matter of fact, however, there were not 17 workers but 27,028 employed in the flour-mill industry of the United States.

In the shoe industry, even in 1929, that is, in the period of greatest prosperity, 205,640 workers produced 365,000,000 pairs of shoes which gives, not 83 pairs, but approximately 35 pairs a week per worker.

An almost infinite number of such examples could be enumerated.

It is important to keep in mind that in its period of youth and prosperity capitalism brought with itself a tremendous growth of the productive forces of human society. Until the rise of capitalism no one even dreamed of modern large-scale industry, its high technical development, modern means of transport and communication. It was capitalism that brought with it machine production. It called to life the tremendous wealth that lay buried in the bowels of the earth. It evolved a tremendous advanced technique, lightening human labour considerably and increasing its power over nature.

However, capitalism places all this development of the productive forces of society at the service of the murderous exploitation of one class by another. The most perfect means of production is used by the capitalist system as the most perfect means of squeezing surplus value out of the working class. The race for gain, the race for profit—this is the motive power of capitalist industry. An increase in profit—this is the purpose for which the capitalist introduces new technical achievements.

That is why the further development of productive forces under capitalism means the further intensification of the exploitation of the working class, the further enrichment of a handful of capitalists at the expense of the impoverishment of the great masses of the people. But at the same time, by creating gigantic enterprises of a high technical order, by greatly increasing the technical powers of human labour, capitalism prepares the material basis for socialism, prepares the material conditions and the prerequisites for the realization of the aims for which the proletariat is struggling. It is in this, in the preparation of the necessary prerequisites for the triumph of the proletarian revolution. that the historical role of capitalism lies.

There is nothing more disgusting than the hypocrisy of the bourgeoisie who assert the "equality" of rich and poor, the well-fed and the hungry, the drone and the over-worked labourer. In reality the bony hand of hunger drives the worker into bondage to the capitalist more effectively than the severest legislation. Capitalism leads to a continual worsening of the conditions of life of the proletariat. Capitalism leads to ever greater *poverty* among the broad masses of workers. Hunger becomes an ever more frequent guest in working class quarters.

Wage slavery

Marx says:

> "The Roman slave was held by fetters; the wage labourer is bound to his owner by invisible threads. The appearance of independence is kept up by means of a constant change of employers, and by the *fictio juris* of a contract." *

And in fact, the worker is free to leave his employment at one capitalist enterprise only to get to another one belonging to another capitalist.

Under the pretence of fighting against forced labour the capitalists conducted a campaign against the Soviet Union. It is hard to imagine anything more base than this outburst of modern slave-drivers against the only free socialist country in the world, under the slogan of fighting for the freedom of labour. The Soviet Union is the only country in the world where wage slavery has been put to an end, where tremendous masses of workers have, for the first time in human history, acquired the opportunity of sane and free labour for themselves, for the benefit of a socialist system where there are no exploiters and no exploited.

Throughout the entire capitalist world the working masses are chained with invisible fetters to exhausting, hateful labour the fruit of which only serves to further their enslavement, to intensify capitalist bondage. Creating untold wealth for a handful of drones, the workers themselves suffer more and more from hunger and privation. "The place of the slave-driver's lash is taken by the overlooker's book of penalties," ** said Marx about capitalist en-

* Marx, *Capital,* Vol. I, p. 586.
** *Ibid.,* p. 424.

terprises. Without doubt, the fine-book of the foreman—the eternal threat of losing one's job and dying of hunger—affects the present-day worker no less than the lash of the slave-driver.

But even the lash of a foreman is by no means a rarity in modern capitalist countries. In a number of countries, especially in the colonies, the most authentic slave labour exists for the benefit of the capitalist. Capital makes sufficient profits from "free" wage labour. But where circumstances permit, it is not averse to utilizing slave labour.

Even in the most highly developed capitalist countries we may find conditions similar to slave conditions.

Under the conditions of the economic crisis the bourgeoisie gladly employs the most genuine forced labour in various forms of "labour service," primarily unemployed youth. In the German "labour service" camps, hundreds of thousands of young workers live in conditions of an army barracks regime; they receive a miserable pittance for the most arduous labour. At the same time, German fascism forces the camp inmates to go through military training, preparing them as cannon fodder for its military adventures.

In America Negro slave labour still exists. There are about 12,000,000 Negroes there, mostly workers and small-scale farmers. After the formal abolition of slavery in 1863 most of the Negro labourers were forced into a state of abject dependence upon their employers.

In the Southern states in many cases the landlord gives the Negro family a strip of land, seed, food and the necessary tools until harvest time. The tenant farmer has to turn over his entire harvest to the landowner who reimburses himself for his initial outlay. But the landlord always manages to keep the Negro in debt to him. If the Negro has, say, 100 bales of cotton which can fetch $600 on the market, the landlord will contrive to show that he has invested $800. Thus, if the Negro leaves the entire harvest in the hands of the landlord, he will still owe the landlord $200 and be compelled to renew the agreement on the same conditions. This deception is practised from year to year. If the Negro applies to a court of justice no one pays any attention to him: the word of a white man cannot be refuted by the word of a Negro. The landlords are not only masters on their own plantations, they have unlimited power in the entire community and when one of them asserts something before a "court of justice" it is law. In the South the landlord dictates the conditions under which the Negro must work. If the Negro dares to be indignant at the unlawful acts of his master and tries to run away he is immediately hunted down by the police with the help of trained police dogs. When the Negro is caught he is considered a vagrant or deserter and is returned to his landlord.

The landlord resorts to other tricks to procure cheap labour power which is applied under the most slavish conditions.

When the landlord needs labour power he calls upon the local court, and the police arrest the necessary number of workers. All kinds of fictitious charges are placed against the arrested men. The court imposes fines on the Negroes, who are unable to pay them and thus are forced into virtual slavery to the landlord who pays the fine for them, deducting it from their future wages.

Slavery in the colonies

But the most terrible form of forced labour exists in the colonies, where the imperialists turn the native population into absolute slaves. At gold and other mines, on plantations and on road work in colonial countries forced labour is employed on a broad scale.

In South Africa, according to the Masters and Servants Act if a native runs away from his master he is treated as a criminal and is forced to return. Everywhere a passport is required of him to show that he has worked for a European. If his passport is not in order he is arrested and returned to his previous employer or compelled to work for another.

In the mining industry, especially at the gold and diamond mines, the native workers live in special abodes, called compounds, surrounded by barbed wire fences. The native worker has no right to leave his prison for the entire period of his hire. No outsider is permitted to enter within the fence; armed guards stand continuous watch. His average wage is less than half a dollar a day and on this he must feed himself. For this miserable wage he must toil for twelve to fourteen hours a day.

In other African colonies the most inhuman methods of exploitation exist. The men are usually brought to the mines trussed up with ropes. Work proceeds under the supervision of armed guards. The native worker is usually forced to sign a contract after he has been made drunk, and he often does not even understand what the contract means.

Slavery is in many cases accompanied by quite open slave trading; as an instance, Portuguese Africa (Angola and especially Mozambique) or the "Independent Republic" of Liberia can be taken, the latter being entirely in the hands of United States capital.

Together with open slavery there is slavery for debt. The essence of this, as Marx explained, is that by means of loans which must be worked out, and which are transmitted from generation to generation, not only the individual worker, but his entire family become the inherited property of a proprietor and his family.

Review Questions

1. Of what does the primitive accumulation of capital consist?
2. What compels the worker to sell his labour power?
3. What determines the value of labour power?
4. What is the difference between labour power and labour?
5. What is capital?
6. Which is greater: constant or fixed capital?
7. What is the measure of the degree of exploitation of labour?
8. What are the methods of increasing relative surplus value?

CHAPTER V

Wages and the Impoverishment of the Working Class Under Capitalism

Under capitalism the worker sells his labour power to the capitalist. The capitalist hires the worker and makes him work for him. The worker receives *wages*. This constitutes the *purchase and sale of labour power*.

Value of labour power and its price

But labour power is a *commodity of a special kind*. The purchase and sale of labour power characterizes a relation between capitalist and worker—between the two basic classes of capitalist society. The value of labour power, as we already know, is determined by the value of the means of subsistence necessary for the maintenance of the worker. It must however be kept in mind that the capitalists always try to *reduce* wages below this limit. Under capitalism no one is concerned with how the worker lives. He often remains unemployed and starves to death. But even when he obtains employment his wages are not always sufficient to satisfy his most elementary needs.

The value of labour power is determined by the value of the means of subsistence of the worker. But how are the necessary means of subsistence determined? It is quite clear that the means of subsistence of the worker, their amount, their nature, depend upon a number of circumstances. Marx points out that

> ". . . the value of labour is in every country determined by a *traditional standard of life*. It is not mere physical life, but it is the satisfaction of certain wants springing from the social conditions in which people are placed and reared up."*

Unlike other commodities the determination of the value of labour power includes a *historical* or *social* element. The normal

* Marx, *Value, Price and Profit,* p. 57.

living standard of the worker is not something that is fixed and established forever. On the contrary, this standard changes with the course of historical development, and is different in different countries depending upon the historical development of the particular country. Capitalism, however, always tends to bring the living standard of the working class down to an extremely low level. The value of a commodity expressed in terms of money is its price. The price of a commodity, as we have already seen, continually fluctuates above or below its value. Wages are a special form of price for the commodity, "labour power." It is evident that the level of wages varies above and below the value of labour power. But in contradistinction to other commodities the variations here are mainly below the value.

Wages a mask of capitalist exploitation

We have seen that the labour of the wage worker in a capitalist enterprise consists of two parts: paid, necessary labour, and unpaid, surplus labour. But when the worker receives his wages, it is not at all apparent that they cover only necessary labour, whereas his surplus labour is appropriated without remuneration by the employer. On the contrary, things under capitalism are represented as if the *entire labour* of the worker has been paid for.

Let us take a miner, who is paid on the basis of piecework. For every ton of coal he mines, he gets, say, one dollar. Working his hardest, he makes barely enough each day to buy his bread. Let him try to point out to the mine owner the injustice of such exploitation. If the latter will feel kindly disposed and desire to talk to his worker at all, he will explain:

"You get a dollar a ton. No more is paid at either the neighbouring mines or elsewhere. You get a fair price. Your labour is not worth any more. Try to mine more coal and your wages will be higher."

Thus one gets the false impression that the worker receives the full value which he has earned in working.

Let us suppose that a friend of our miner works at a chemical plant near by. He works under the most injurious conditions for nine hours a day and gets, say, forty dollars a month. How does he find out that his boss is exploiting him? Let him try to speak to his boss about it, and without any hesitation he will be answered:

"You get as much as anyone else would in your place. You get a fair wage, more than this you do not earn. But if you wish, try working both shifts and you will get double wages. But in nine hours you only work out forty dollars a month. There would be no sense in paying you more."

And really, how can the worker know how much value he produces a day for his boss? The nine-hour day is not divided openly so that he can know: this part of the day I worked out my wages, and these hours I work for the boss without being paid. All hours of work are alike. And here he even gets an opportunity to increase his wages—double them, true by doubling his working day. Such a thing can really be confusing; it appears as if the capitalist really pays him as much as he produces in value.

Thus capitalist exploitation is *masked*. And here all the forces of the *ideological enslavement* of the masses come to the bosses' aid. The church asserts that the earthly system is established by god and that any thought of changing it is sinful. The capitalist press, science, the theatre, the cinema, the literature and art of the bourgeoisie—all mask the issue of exploitation, all try to make things appear as if the enrichment of the capitalists were just as natural and inevitable as the light of the sun on a clear summer day.

> "The wage form thus extinguishes every trace of the division of the working day into necessary labour and surplus labour, into paid and unpaid labour. All labour appears as paid labour. In the corvée, the labour of the worker for himself, and his compulsory labour for his lord, differ in space and time in the clearest possible way. In slave labour, even that part of the working day in which the slave is only replacing the value of his own means of existence, in which, therefore, in fact, he works for himself alone, appears as labour for his master. All the slave's labour appears as unpaid labour. In wage labour, on the contrary, even surplus labour, or unpaid labour, appears as paid." *

* Marx, *Capital*, Vol. I, p. 550.

Workers began quite early to organize into trade unions, which conducted a struggle to improve working conditions and to curb unlimited exploitation.

Wages and the struggle of the working class

Wages, as we have seen, are determined by the value of labour power. But, in the first place, wages fluctuate considerably, particularly below the value of labour power and, secondly, the value of labour power itself changes considerably dependent on a number of circumstances.

A constant struggle rages between the bourgeoisie and the working class concerning the level of wages; in this struggle much depends upon the degree of organization and unity of each side.

So long as the workers had not organized trade unions, each capitalist dealt with a scattered mass. The capitalist in such a case is in an advantageous position in the struggle about wages: if any worker does not agree to the bad conditions of employment he is discharged and the employer quickly finds someone to take his place.

Matters change when there is a trade union movement. Under such circumstances the capitalist is not opposed by a scattered mass of unorganized workers, but now has to deal with a union of all (or of the majority) of the workers, which presents uniform demands and calls for uniform conditions. Formerly the capitalist came to an agreement with individuals, now he has to come to a collective agreement with a trade union. Wages of the workers are usually determined by special rate agreements.

The capitalists, of course, find many ways of struggling against the workers even when there is a trade union. In their turn they unite in "employers' associations."

It is perfectly clear that by means of only an economic struggle on the part of trade unions the working class cannot free itself from the ever growing capitalist exploitation, from increasing poverty and destitution. For this purpose the complete victory of the proletariat, which can be won only by *revolution,* is necessary. Then, in destroying capitalism, the proletariat destroys class exploitation, the source of its impoverishment.

Marx writes as follows with regard to this:

> ". . . the general tendency of capitalist production is not to raise, but to sink the average standard of wages, or to push

the *value of labour* more or less to its *minimum limit*. Such being the tendency of *things* in this system, is this saying that the working class ought to renounce their resistance against the encroachments of capital, and abandon their attempts at making the best of the occasional chances for their temporary improvement? If they did, they would be degraded to one level mass of broken wretches past salvation. I think I have shown that their struggles for the standard of wages are incidents inseparable from the whole wages system, that in ninety-nine cases out of one hundred their efforts at raising wages are only efforts at maintaining the given value of labour and that the necessity of debating their price with the capitalist is inherent to their condition of having to sell themselves as commodities. By cowardly giving way in their everyday conflict with capital, they would certainly disqualify themselves for the initiating of any larger movement.

"At the same time, and quite apart from the general servitude involved in the wages system, the working class ought not to exaggerate to themselves the ultimate working of these everyday struggles. They ought not to forget that they are fighting with effects, but not with the causes of those effects; that they are retarding the downward movement, but not changing its direction; that they are applying palliatives, not curing the malady. They ought, therefore, not to be exclusively absorbed in these unavoidable guerrilla fights incessantly springing up from the never-ceasing encroachments of capital or changes of the market. They ought to understand that, with all the miseries it imposes upon them, the present system simultaneously engenders the *material conditions* and the *social forms* necessary for an economic reconstruction of society. Instead of the *conservative* motto: *'A fair day's wages for a fair day's work!'* they ought to inscribe on their banner the *revolutionary* watchword: *'Abolition of the wages system!'* " *

The capitalists pay the workers their wages in various ways.

Forms of wages

Of all the various forms of wages two are fundamental.

In some cases the workers receive their pay according to the

* Marx, *Value, Price and Profit*, p. 61

period of working time, when the wages may be calculated by the hour, the day, the week or month. This is called the time form of wages or time wages. In other cases the worker's pay depends upon the amount of goods he has produced; the worker is paid according to the number of tons of coal he has mined or the number of metres of calico he has woven, the number of locks he has made, etc. This is called the *piecework* form of wages. The capitalist system has invented many different forms, sometimes rather complicated ones, of paying the workers. But all these forms are based either on a time or piecework basis, and sometimes on a combination of the peculiarities of both.

It may appear at first as if there were nothing in common bebetween the method of paying by time and the method of paying by piecework—that these two forms are entirely different. In reality it is not so. In the case of timework, in granting the worker a definite weekly wage, the capitalist calculates what work his wage worker will do during that time. If he were not to estimate this, he would soon go bankrupt. It is more important, however, that, fundamentally, piecework is really the same as timework. When the rate per piece is set, the amount produced by a worker in an hour, day, or week is taken into consideration. That is why piecework also assures the average worker only the bare necessities.

Both piecework and timework are only different forms of the purchase of labour power by the capitalist. The form used depends on the circumstances prevailing in the particular industry. Each of these forms has its advantages for the capitalist, dependent upon the circumstances.

Timework

Timework is the form employed in cases where the employer has no reason for interesting each individual worker particularly in the production of as great a quantity of goods as possible. Such cases are manifold.

In many trades the skill and ability of the worker still play an important part, the quality of the commodity produced depending on this. In cases where we deal with a semi-artisan type of industry, the employer often prefers to pay his highly skilled workers by the week (by time). Not striving for quantity, the worker produces each commodity very carefully. The capitalist gains in the quality of the commodity what he loses in quantity.

In other cases, on the contrary, the worker becomes a mere appendage to the machine. The quantity of goods produced depends entirely upon the speed of operation of the machine. In such cases also the capitalist prefers timework.

Piecework

On the other hand, various methods of piecework are employed in all cases where the capitalist wants to interest the worker in producing as great a quantity of commodities as possible. Piecework saves the employer the necessity of supervising the work of his employees; making the wages depend on the quantity produced, piecework assures the most intensive labour on the part of the workers. As a rule, piecework is possible in those industries where it is easy to calculate or measure (by piece, weight, volume or length) the quantity of commodities produced.

Piecework, under capitalism, is the favourite method of increasing the exploitation of workers by increasing the intensity of their labour. Piecework rates are usually set according to the earnings of the most capable and the fastest workers. In order to make the necessary minimum wage the other workers must strain their energies to the utmost. When the employer sees that a majority of the workers have increased their pay, he reduces the rates. The workers must then work even more intensively in order to earn their former wages.

The piecework form of remuneration has an entirely different significance in the conditions obtaining in the U.S.S.R. There the worker does not sell his work to a class of exploiters, but uses it in enterprises which are the property of the proletarian state. The wage which the worker receives in the U.S.S.R. is a social allowance for labour, and is in proportion to the quantity and quality of the labour expended. Piecework remuneration in the socialist economy of the Soviet Union is the best means of establishing conformity between the quantity and quality of the labour expended and the remuneration of the individual workman, it is a powerful lever in raising the productivity of labour and in addition the well-being of the working class. Therefore, it is entirely different from piecework under capitalism.

Sometimes the capitalists pay out part of the wages in the form of a *bonus*. They figure that the bonus will stimulate special exertion on the part of the workers and make them work with the utmost intensity.

Bonuses and profit-sharing

An even greater deception is so-called *profit-sharing*. The capitalist lowers the basic wage with the excuse that the worker is supposedly also interested in having the business profitable. Then under the guise of "a share in the profits" only a part of the wages previously deducted is returned to the worker. In the end the worker "sharing in the profits" often receives less than the one working simply for wages.

By this method not only does the employer try to raise the intensity of labour to a high degree—but sometimes it induces a certain stratum of the more ignorant workers to keep away from the class movement of the proletariat and thus to serve as a support of capital.

On the basis of piecework the so-called "sweating system" exists, particularly in the needle trades industry in England and America. Work is given out to be done at home at exceedingly low rates. The tailor working under such a "sweating system" must work literally day and night to avoid starvation.

The "sweating system"

Having bought the labour power of the proletarian, the employer tries to derive the utmost possible from it for himself. Of late the cleverer and more able employers have begun to introduce the so-called "scientific organization" of labour, which in essence amounts to the following.

Scientific organization of labour. The Taylor and Ford systems

Every kind of work done at the plant is studied in detail by experts who, after long observation and research, establish the most rational methods of doing this work. Methods of work are thus established which save the worker unnecessary motion and effort, all his tools are rationally arranged, etc., so that the worker is not distracted from his main work. Under these circumstances all the energy of the worker, all the effort spent by him, goes towards useful work without any loss, is spent entirely on the operations which he has to perform. Thus the industry gets the greatest benefit from his work and the productivity of labour is greatly increased.

The scientific organization of labour is a great achievement in the rational utilization of human effort. After the overthrow of capitalism, under conditions of a proletarian government, great possibilities are opened up for the scientific organization of labour. But under the capitalist regime, the scientific organization of labour, like all scientific achievements, is used by the capitalists in their own narrow class interests. Scientific organization of labour is transformed by the capitalists into one of the means of squeezing more surplus value out of the workers.

One of the first to advocate the scientific organization of labour was an American engineer, Taylor. His system, called the Taylor system, is used in many capitalist plants, increasing the surplus value. Greatly raising the productivity of labour, turning the workers into machines executing strictly calculated motions, the Taylor system, leads to the squeezing of the last ounce of strength out of the workers, making invalids of them after a few years. The lowering of the piecework rates following the introduction of the Taylor system makes the workers' labour much harder for the same, and at times lower, wages.

During post-war years, the subtle methods of exploitation used by the American automobile king, Henry Ford, became especially famous. His methods of exploitation began to spread rapidly not only in America, but also in the capitalist countries of Europe. The basic features of the Ford system is production in a steady stream—along a conveyor. By speeding up the conveyor, the work is speeded up and the intensity of labour increased. Whoever cannot keep up with the conveyor loses his job in the capitalist plant. Thus the capitalist turns every technical improvement into an instrument for the further impoverishment and enslavement of the proletariat, into an instrument for squeezing the very life out of the workers.

Payment in kind or in money

Formerly, when a worker was hired in the village, he was seldom paid in money for his work. This was done in the following way: the worker was boarded by his employer and in addition, at the end of the summer, he received a little grain. Here the worker is paid in kind: he gets the necessary means of subsistence directly, in exchange for his labour power. Such a simple transaction is similar to the barter of products—say, an axe for bread. When trade assumes such a simple character it is perfectly evident that the value of the necessary means of subsistence is at the basis of the value of labour power.

Payment exclusively in kind is very rare in capitalist industry. But even here part of the wages is occasionally paid out in kind. This method of payment is usually merely a convenient method for the capitalist to increase his profits at the expense of the workers. The company store belonging to the employer furnishes the worker with all kinds of shoddy goods at triple prices. The workers' real wages are thus greatly reduced. Workers' organizations therefore always struggle against such a practice. Sometimes the capitalists try to achieve the same end—a decrease in the wages of the workers by making them buy goods at high prices—in a more subtle way. They assume control of all the stores in the workers' settlement or district and the workers, getting their wages in money, are compelled to buy things at high prices just the same. Workers try to struggle against such exploitation by means of organizing consumers' co-operatives.

Nominal and real wages

In developed capitalist industry, except in rare cases, wages are paid in money. The worker sells his labour power and, as with the sale of any other commodity, gets its price in the form of a definite sum of money.

However, the worker does not need the money for itself, but only as a means of getting the things he requires. Receiving his definite wages, the worker buys the things he needs; he pays the prices for them that prevail on the market at the time.

But we know that the level of commodity prices does not remain unchanged. The purchasing power of money changes under the influence of various causes. If a gold standard exists in the country, the prices may rise because gold becomes cheaper; with a decrease in the value of gold, the purchasing power of money falls. When paper currency is issued in great quantities the prices of commodities suffer great and rapid changes, following the fall in the purchasing power of money which almost always accompanies the circulation of paper currency.

Hence, if we wish to compare the wages of workers in several cases, it is not enough to know only how much money they receive in each case. It is also necessary to know how much goods can be bought with the money in each case. We must not merely compare the *nominal rates* of wages (by the nominal rate of wages we mean the amount of money received by the worker), we must also take into consideration the *purchasing power* of the money received. Only then can we establish exactly the *real* wages, which can be measured by the quantity of use values that can be purchased for the given sum of money in the given place.

Everyone knows that workers in different trades receive different rates of wages. Highly skilled workers receive much higher wages than unskilled workers who have no special technical training. Usually, the greater the skill, the higher the wages.

Wages of skilled workers

Different branches of industry require workers of different skill. Hence the wages of workers in different industries are not the same.

Besides the difference in the rates of pay for workers in different industries there is the difference in the rates of pay for workers of different skill in the same industry. The skilled worker is paid more than the semi-skilled, the semi-skilled worker more than the common labourer.

What is the reason for such differences in the rates of wages of workers according to skill? It is not difficult to understand this. Anyone can perform unskilled labour, but the skilled worker must go through a definite period of learning the trade, must spend much time and effort to obtain this skill. If there were no differences in the rates of pay no one would want to spend the time and energy to learn a trade, no one would try to obtain a definite degree of skill.

However, no amount of skill saves a worker from inhuman, incessant exploitation under capitalism.

The introduction of new machinery generally makes great numbers of highly skilled workers superfluous. What was previously done by a highly skilled master, who had spent many years in acquiring his skill, is now done by a machine. Considerable sections of skilled workers become superfluous and are thrown out of employment. In order not to starve to death they are compelled to do unskilled labour at much lower pay.

The level of wages in the various capitalist countries is not the same. There are very great differences in this between the various countries. These differences are due to many causes.

The level of wages in the various capitalist countries

It would be ridiculous to think that capitalists in one country are kinder in their relations to the workers than those in others. As a matter of fact capitalists everywhere try to lower wages to the lowest possible limits. But conditions in different capitalist countries vary considerably. Different countries have different histories. In America, for instance, capitalism developed under circumstances where a shortage of labour was experienced rather than a superfluity of it: an abundance of free land for some time gave emigrants from European countries the opportunity of settling on the land. In older capitalist countries the working class organized earlier to offer resistance to the capitalists. In the more advanced capitalist countries the intensity of labour, as well as the average degree of skill of the workers, is very high.

All these circumstances gave rise to the different levels of wages in different capitalist countries.

Thus, for instance, if we take wages in England as 100, the wages (the average hourly rate) in other advanced capitalist countries on the eve of the imperialist war were as follows:

England	100	France	64
Germany	75	U.S.A.	240

According to other calculations the average yearly wages of workers in various countries (in 1900-07, in dollars) were:

U.S.A.	463	Austria	167
England	258	Russia	97
Germany	237	Japan	55

In post-war years we also see considerably different rates of wages in the various capitalist countries. Here are figures showing the differences in *real* wages in various large cities of the most important countries. The following figures show the conditions existing in January 1929 and are based on the level of real wages in London in 1924 which is taken as 100:

Philadelphia	206	Berlin	77
Dublin	106	Madrid	57
London	105	Brussels	52
Stockholm	93	Milan	50
Amsterdam	88	Rome	44

It is understood that wages are particularly low in those countries where capitalism has only recently begun to develop. Primitive accumulation in these countries ruins the peasantry and artisans, throwing them into the army of those seeking employment. In the colonies the living standard of the proletariat is extremely low. The workers in China especially are subject to the most brutal exploitation. The Chinese coolie, feeding himself on a handful of rice, often sleeping on the streets or in the parks and clothing himself in rags, is, in the eyes of the capitalists, the most exemplary worker in the world. The more brazen capitalists tell the European workers to take an example from the Chinese coolie, to live as "economically" as he does. This kind of advice has been heard particularly often during the present times.

Growth of capitalist exploitation

As capitalism develops, the *exploitation of the working class grows.* The conditions under which the workers conduct their struggle about wages with the capitalists continually become more disadvantageous to the workers. As it develops, capitalism brings with it both a relative and an absolute *impoverishment of the working class.*

The share of the capitalists grows bigger, the snare of the workers smaller. The figures for several capitalist countries show this clearly. Let us take England. If we take the total values created in the country (the so-called national income) as 100, then the share that fell to the workers changed as follows:

Year	*Amount of national income in million pounds sterling*	*Amount of wages in million pounds sterling*	*Workers' share of national income (in per cent)*
1843	515	235	*45.6*
1860	832	392	*47.1*
1884	1,274	521	*41.4*
1903	1,710	655	*38.3*
1908	1,844	703	*38.1*

The share of the worker becomes steadily *less*.

At the same time, of course, the share of the national income of the entire country, which goes to the capitalists, grows steadily greater. What the working class loses, the capitalists gain.

In an article written before the World War, Lenin quotes the following figures showing the impoverishment of the working class. In Germany, for the period between 1880 and 1912, wages rose on an average of 25 per cent, while the cost of living for the same period rose by at least 40 per cent. Lenin notes particularly that this took place in such a rich and advanced capitalist country as Germany, where the situation of the workers was incomparably better than that of the workers in pre-revolutionary Russia, because of the higher cultural level in Germany, the freedom to strike and form trade unions and the comparative political freedom, where the membership in labour unions amounted to millions and where there were millions of readers of the labour press.

Lenin drew the following conclusion from this:

> "The worker is impoverished *absolutely, i.e.,* grows actually poorer than before, is compelled to live worse, eat more sparingly, remain underfed, seek shelter in cellars and attics. The *relative* share of the workers in capitalist society, which is rapidly growing richer, becomes ever smaller, because the millionaires grow richer ever more rapidly. . . . In capitalist society wealth grows with unbelievable rapidity alongside the impoverishment of the working masses."*

This is the situation in the richest capitalist countries of the world, where the capitalists can make concessions to the workers, since they get tremendous profits from the colonies. Of course in the more backward countries, in the colonies to which capital goes for easy profits, the exploitation of the workers increases *even more rapidly*.

We thus see that capitalist exploitation steadily increases, and that the gulf between the working class and the bourgeoisie becomes ever deeper. The opportunists in all countries continually talk of an abatement of the social contradictions, of the necessity

* Lenin, *Collected Works,* Vol. XVI, "Destitution in Capitalist Society," p. 212, Russian ed.

for civil peace between the classes, of the possibility for the working class to improve its conditions even under capitalism. The working class, however, grows poorer not only relatively (in comparison with the boundless growth of the profits of the bourgeoisie), but absolutely. Even in the richest capitalist countries the food of the workers becomes continually worse, they live in still more crowded quarters, experience ever greater want. At the same time the intensity of labour of the workers increases steadily. The worker has to spend more energy for each hour of work than he had to spend formerly. The excessive intensity of labour, the continual whipping up, rapidly exhausts the organism of the worker. There can therefore not only be no talk about an abatement of class contradictions, but, on the contrary, there is a constant *sharpening* of these contradictions, they grow inevitably.

Unemployment and the reserve army of labour

With the growth of capitalism, *unemployment* increases and the so-called "reserve army of labour" grows, furnishing hands to the capitalists in times when industry needs to be expanded, or when the older workers refuse to work under the old conditions any longer. Let us see how this takes place.

In its inception capitalism finds a sufficient supply of potential wage labourers on the market. This supply is composed of ruined farmers, artisans and handicraftsmen, who have lost their means of production. They are ready to work for the capitalist if he will only give them the means of continuing their existence. There must always be a definite reserve of free hands. Only on this condition can capitalist industry, based on the exploitation of wage labour, arise.

What does the further development of capitalism lead to?

We have already seen that developing capitalism crushes the small-scale production of the artisan and the handicraftsman by its competition. The peasants are also ruined and many of them are forced, willy-nilly, to leave their homes and to go into capitalist slavery. Capitalist industry grows, new plants and factories are opened up, absorbing new masses of workers. Ruining small-scale producers, capital attracts them to itself as wage labourers.

But together with this another phenomenon appears. There is a continual process of technical improvement in production under capitalism. And what does this technical improvement mean, what is the significance of the new inventions? Their significance is that they cheapen production, *replacing human labour* by *machine work*. Thus with the development of technical improvements fewer workers are needed to produce the same quantity of commodities. Machines *supplant* workers. Machines compel workers to labour *more intensely*. This also causes part of the workers to be thrown out of industry. Hence at the dawn of capitalism, when the workers had not yet found out who their real enemy was, they often gave vent to their rage against existing conditions by attacking the machines. During strikes and times of unrest the workers smashed machinery first of all, considering it to be the main cause for their terrible conditions.

Supplanting of workers by machinery

Introducing new machinery and throwing the workers who were supplanted by these machines onto the street, the capitalists continually create unemployment.

Raising the intensity of labour they also increase the number of unemployed. A definite number of workers becomes superfluous. These workers are unable to find any need for their labour. They constitute the industrial reserve army. The significance of this army is indeed great. The existence of a constant army of unemployed gives the capitalists a powerful weapon in their struggle against the working class. The unemployed are usually willing to go to work on any conditions: threatened with starvation they have no choice. The unemployed thus exert a downward pressure on the living standard of the proletarians who are employed. Another significance of the reserve army is that it furnishes free hands at any time when the conditions of the market require an expansion of industry. Then many thousands of unemployed find work for themselves, factories and plants increase the number of workers they employ. Unemployment temporarily decreases. But the introduction of new, improved methods throws thousands of workers onto the streets again.

Thus capitalism with one hand gives work to the masses of new workers coming from the ranks of the ruined small-scale producers, and with the other takes the last piece of bread from the mouths of thousands and tens of thousands of workers who have been supplanted by machines with the progress of capitalist technical improvements.

The general law of capitalist accumulation

This constant replacement of workers by machinery, which is a result of capitalist development, creates what is known as a "relative surplus population" in capitalist countries. Hundreds of thousands of people yearly are compelled to emigrate from their countries as they become superfluous and are left without the faintest hope of obtaining employment. During the post-war years this situation has become still worse. The countries to which these emigrants flowed have closed their doors and refuse admission.

The existence and growth of an industrial reserve army have a tremendous influence on the entire situation of the working class. Poverty increases, the uncertainty of what the next day will bring is ever present, and wages fall. The working class produces surplus value with its labour, but it goes to the capitalist class. Part of the surplus value obtained from the working class the capitalists consume and thus destroy; the rest they add to their original capital. If the capitalist originally had $100,000 and during the year he has succeeded in squeezing out of the workers $20,000 in profits, he will add about half this sum to his original capital for the next year. In this case his capital for the next year will already be $110,000. He has increased his capital, has accumulated $10,000. Accumulation of capital, therefore, is the addition of surplus value to capital. The growth of capital as a result of accumulating surplus value is enormous. The mass of surplus value squeezed out of the working class grows ever greater as capitalism develops. The mass of surplus value accumulated by the capitalists and which goes to increase their capital grows apace.

Thus accumulation of capital brings with it the growth of the wealth of a handful of capitalists. The surplus value created by the labour of the working class becomes a source of the increasing power of the exploiters. With the accumulation of capital the degree of exploitation of the workers increases. Thus, under capitalism, the working class with its own labour creates the conditions for an ever greater degree of its own exploitation.

With the accumulation of capital the living conditions of the working class become steadily worse, the degree of their exploitation increases.

All this is an inevitable result of capitalist accumulation. The more capital the capitalists accumulate, the more they expand production, introduce new machines, the more poverty and unemployment spread among the working class.

This is the general law of capitalist accumulation discovered by Marx, and it is of immense significance for an understanding of capitalism, for an understanding of the direction in which capitalism develops.

Marx defines the general law of capitalist accumulation as follows:

> "The greater the social wealth, the functioning capital, the extent and energy of its growth, and, therefore, also the absolute mass of the proletariat and the productiveness of its labour, the greater is the industrial reserve army. The same causes which develop the expansive power of capital develop also the labour power at its disposal. The relative mass of the industrial reserve army increases, therefore, with the potential energy of wealth. But the greater this reserve army in proportion to the active labour army, the greater is the mass of a consolidated surplus population, whose misery is in inverse ratio to its torment of labour. The more extensive, finally, the lazarus-layers of the working class, and the industrial reserve army, the greater is official pauperism. *This is the absolute general law of capitalist accumulation.*" *

Marx further says about this law:

> ". . . within the capitalist system all methods for raising the social productiveness of labour are brought about at the cost of the individual labourer; all means for the development of production transform themselves into means of domination over, and exploitation of, the producers; they mutilate the labourer into a fragment of a man, degrade him to the level of an appendage of a machine, destroy every remnant of charm in his work and turn it into a hated toil; they estrange from him the

* Marx, *Capital,* Vol. I, pp. 659-60.

intellectual potentialities of the labour process in the same proportion as science is incorporated in it as an independent power; they distort the conditions under which he works, subject him during the labour process to a despotism the more hateful for its meanness; they transform his life time into working time. . . . But all methods for the production of surplus value are at the same time methods of accumulation; and every extension of accumulation becomes again a means for the development of those methods. It follows therefore that in proportion as capital accumulates, the lot of the labourer, be his payment high or low, must grow worse. The law, finally, that always equilibrates the relative surplus population, or industrial reserve army, to the extent and energy of accumulation, this law rivets the labourer to capital. . . . It establishes an accumulation of misery, corresponding with accumulation of capital. Accumulation of wealth at one pole is, therefore, at the same time accumulation of misery, agony of toil, slavery, ignorance, brutality, mental degradation, at the opposite pole, *i.e.,* on the side of the class that produces its own product in the form of capital." *

Thus we see that to the extent that capital is accumulated the conditions of the working class must become worse. This general worsening of the conditions of the proletariat is brought about not only by means of lowering wages. Unemployment spreads and becomes more frequent, more often affecting each individual worker, each member of the worker's family. The labour of the worker becomes more intensive and as a result the worker ages sooner and often becomes an invalid. The age limit at which a worker is thrown out of capitalist enterprises becomes lower and lower.

Impoverishment of the working class

Capital buys out small groups of workers which it turns into its faithful servants. A privileged upper section of the proletariat is created—a workers' aristocracy. The capitalists pay certain groups of skilled workers highly, out of the tremendous profits derived from the colonies, at the expense of an even more brutal exploitation of the vast majority of the working class.

* *Ibid.,* pp. 660-61.

A great part of the highly paid sections of the workers, however, experience a constant insecurity in their positions, an uncertainty about the morrow. Capitalism inevitably leads to a worsening of their conditions.

Impoverishment of the proletariat and unemployment under conditions of crisis

The impoverishment of the working class reaches its utmost limit in times of *crisis*. A crisis exposes and *sharpens* all the *contradictions* of capitalism. The proletariat is reduced to the most extreme degree of impoverishment. Every crisis calls for a curtailment of production and throws millions of workers onto the street. The wages of those who remain at work are reduced.

The present crisis is the most profound and acute crisis ever experienced by capitalism. The capitalist system, dying, and decaying while still alive, dooms tens of millions of people to unprecedented tortures. Unemployment has reached monstrous proportions. To the unemployed we must add the vast army of those who work part time and receive a correspondingly infinitely low wage.

The present crisis brought a colossal reduction in wages in all capitalist countries without exception. Attempting to shift the entire burden of the crisis onto the shoulders of the working class, the capitalists of various countries vie with one another in reducing wages, bringing them to pauper limits, making it impossible for the worker to satisfy even his most pressing needs. The living standard of the working class, even in the richest capitalist countries, has gone down during this crisis in the most unbelievable fashion.

A tremendous number of facts bear witness to this. A journalist who investigated conditions of the miners in England, writes:

> "If you should visit the home of a miner in South Wales or Durham, you would find that all the furniture that was bought in better days has been sold. A boarder has been taken in to help meet the rent payments; but most probably this boarder has lost his job and cannot pay a farthing. If the father of the family works, the son is sure to be unemployed; or the reverse, if the son works, the father has lost his job. Everything that

could possibly be pawned has gone. There is hardly a miner who can allow himself the luxury of getting any clothes for himself, his wife or his children. They can only change their clothes if they happen to buy some old rags which the mother can somehow patch up."

Once libraries were built and theatres opened in miners' settlements with funds furnished by the miners themselves. Now the libraries can purchase no books and the theatres are closed.

In certain other branches of industry in England the workers are in a still worse state. An even more hopeless picture is presented by the textile workers of Lancashire.

Even when working at full capacity (*i.e.,* four looms to every weaver), the average wages of a weaver in the last few years did not exceed 31 shillings 6 pence a week. But in most cases a weaver works on only two looms and, in Beverley, for instance, the weekly wages of a weaver vary from 15 to 20 shillings. These wages can be made, however, only if good raw material is available. Under the conditions of the crisis, the employers use all kinds of inferior raw material. Hence, the wages of the weavers fall more because of this. Data collected in the course of many official investigations speak eloquently about the poverty of the Lancashire weavers. Thus, for example, the 1931 investigation in Wigan showed that hundreds of workers live in houses condemned by the city building commission as "unfit for human habitation." In Bolton such a commission established that most of the houses inhabited by workers are "in the immediate vicinity of the city dumps, garbage heaps, filth, or cattle yards, surrounded by mountains of manure."

In the United States in the years of the crisis the average weekly wage in industry was reduced as follows:

Years	*Wages (In dollars)*
1929	28.5
1930	25.8
1931	22.6
1932	17.1
1933	17.7

The year 1933 seems to show a certain increase in wages, but it is only an apparent increase. In point of fact the increase in the cost of living in this period was considerably higher than the increase in nominal wages. According to the greatly understated official figures, the cost of living rose by 7 per cent in 1933 in comparison with 1932, but according to the figures of the Labour Research Bureau food prices rose by 18 per cent in 1933.

In fascist Germany the conditions of the workers are going from bad to worse. Letters of German workers give an idea of the virtually penal conditions which the fascists have introduced into the enterprises. This, for example, is what one working girl writes from the factories of the famous international firm of Siemens to a German paper abroad:

> "In the press shop of the small factories of Siemensstadt the working conditions are terrible. With five working days per week, on piecework, wages reach fifteen marks at the very most. There are instances where a girl is only on four days a week and in this time draws 9 marks all told. Under such conditions there are in all only 2 marks left to live on, seeing that 5 marks go in rent and 2 marks for fares. The speed of the work is frightful. The majority of the women cannot keep up with the conditions of the piecework. The time needed for bringing and sending back material, for figuring out the work cards, for seeing to defects in the machine, for having breakfast, etc., is not taken into account."

The following figures show the degree of impoverishment of the working class in the *United States* during the crisis. The index numbers of those employed for wages in industry and the total sum paid them in wages for the years of the crisis (index number 1923-25=100) are given below.

Month and year	*Number of workers employed*	*Amount paid out in wages*
May 1929	105.3	112.9
May 1930	94.8	95.4
May 1931	80.1	73.4
May 1932	63.4	46.8

From these figures it can be seen that in May 1929, *i.e.,* before the crisis, the number of workers employed was nearly the same as in 1923-25, but that wages were somewhat higher. Then a catastrophic fall begins in which wages fall at a much more rapid rate than the number of workers employed. This means that the sum paid out in wages falls for two reasons: 1) because of unemployment, and 2) because of the reduction in the wages of those employed. For three years of the crisis the number employed was reduced 30 per cent while wages fell 60 per cent. Thus wages were cut in half during this period.

In the United States the living conditions of the millions of unemployed, who receive no help from the government, are particularly horrible. Thousands of unemployed, dispossessed for non-payment or rent, tramp the roads, erecting camps near the larger cities. These camps of the unemployed in America are called "jungles." One bourgeois magazine describes a camp located in the swamps near Stockton, California, as follows:

> "When we saw the camp," the writer says, "smoke was rising from the tents erected by various groups of unemployed. Every little group was busily preparing its food. The whole picture was fantastic: here, from where one could see the city with its stores, its grain elevators filled with grain, at one end, and the sugar refinery, at the other, with its warehouses filled with provisions all along the docks, these people, willing to work, were raking in the refuse thrown out from the warehouses, were cleaning half-rotten carrots, onions or beans and cooking them in old tin cans which they had picked up."

The authors end their description of this picture of destitution with the following words:

> "We have always been taught in the good old American way that ours is a free country. It is really free: these people are free to choose any one of three alternatives: to steal, to die of starvation or to turn into animals feeding on refuse."

The bourgeois journalist forgot one other alternative: the revolutionary struggle of the proletariat against the domination of capital.

An unprecedented increase in the number of suicides, the phenomenal spread of all kinds of diseases, innumerable cases of death from starvation—these are the results of the inhuman living conditions into which capital forces millions of people. Mortality and disease among the children proceed especially rapidly.

But whereas such is the degree of impoverishment of the proletariat in the richer capitalist countries, the conditions in the backward capitalist countries are still worse. In this respect *Poland* offers a graphic example. Recently the result of an investigation of 204 Warsaw families of unemployed was published. This investigation was conducted by a bourgeois organization that is far from sympathetic to communism. The families investigated were those of skilled workers. The report of the investigation reads:

"It must be stated that in the vast majority of cases the food was below starvation minimum. Here are examples: a moulder's family consisting of four people spends 12 zloti (about $1.50) a week on food. They eat twice a day: potatoes, cabbage, bread. They do not buy meat or milk at all. A tailor's family consisting of six persons had not eaten anything in three days at the time the commission visited it; there was also no fuel, no kerosene. In another case a family of four persons had not had a cooked meal for a period of three weeks. Their only food was bread and tea. A family of an unemployed worker lives on the earnings of the wife who peddles *pretzels* on the street. Her earnings amount to 1-1.5 zloti (about 15 cents) a day, and this is the only source of income of a family consisting of ten persons."

Summing up, the report states:

"The principal food of the unemployed is potatoes and cabbage, more rarely bread and tea, occasionally cereal, very rarely macaroni, etc., or vegetables. Of the 204 families investigated, meat is eaten by only 20 families once a week."

Matters are even worse with respect to clothing. The report says:

"The greatest shortage is felt in shoes and outer clothing. For instance, an unemployed baker's family, consisting of six persons, has no shoes whatever. When he leaves the house, the father ties a pair of soles to his feet with string; the children do not leave the house. In another case two children have one coat. The mother takes the younger one to school, takes off his coat, runs home and dresses the older boy. The same procedure is repeated when the children have to come home from school."

About the terrible housing conditions of the unemployed the report tells the following:

"Most of the homes investigated do not satisfy the most elementary requirements of hygiene."

Here are some characteristic examples:

"The home is in a cellar. Water drips down the walls. The floor of the hallway leading to the home is always under three centimetres of water. Three adults and four children live in this room. In a number of cases, more than ten persons occupy one room. Of 929 persons questioned, only 193 sleep in separate beds. This includes eleven persons who sleep on the floor, fourteen children sleeping in cribs, and nine children sleeping on trunks, benches or chairs. The majority sleeps two, three and more persons in a bed. In nine cases it was established that five persons sleep in one bed, and in three cases even six in a bed."

Despite certain increases in industrial production, the number of unemployed in Poland in the present year is higher than in the previous year. In January 1934, the number of unemployed on the register of the Labour Exchange was 410,000; in the spring of 1934 it was 350,000, but even according to the evidence of the bourgeois newspapers, the actual number of unemployed exceeded a million and a half. The total wages actually paid out to the workers in big industry amounted (according to official data) to 1,645,937,000 zloti in 1929, and to only 737,830,000 zloti in 1932, a curtailment of 55 per cent. The eight-hour day has been abolished. A series of new fascist laws have deprived the working class of its small gains in the field of unemployment and health insurance, accident and disablement benefits, etc.

Capitalist "rationalization," that is, the ruthless sweating system, encouraged by the government and introduced by the employers in the factories and mines, has resulted in an unprecedented increase of accidents in industry. It is sufficient to state that in the mining industry alone, in the years 1927 to 1932, according to official figures, 1,039 miners were killed, 97,331 sustained injuries—of which 7,471 were seriously injured—out of a total number of slightly over 100,000 men working in the coal industry in these years.

In Japan in the coal industry the daily wage of a man in 1930 was 1.72 yen, and in 1933—1.11 yen; the wage of a woman in 1930 was 1.52 yen, and in 1933—0.73 yen. Children working as helpers receive from 5 to 10 yen per month. In the textile industry of Japan, where girls often work as long as fifteen hours a day, they receive from three to five shillings a week and a place in the factory barracks.

The following eloquent item appeared in a Japanese newspaper in December 1933:

> "A group of ten girls were detained by the police. In spite of the cold they were wandering about in their summer apparel. At the examination it transpired that they had run away from a weaving mill, as they could no longer endure the arduous regime of a working day of fifteen hours without a break, and the bad conditions. When they were advised to return to the mill, the girls replied they would rather die."

Similar news items in the Japanese papers are frequently seen.

Review Questions

1. In what respect does the value of labour power differ from the value of other commodities?
2. How does the form of wages help to mask capitalist exploitation?
3. What is the significance of the struggle of labour unions under capitalism?
4. Under what conditions is it more advantageous for the capitalist to pay on the basis of timework and under what conditions on the basis of piecework?
5. How is the difference in the rates of wages in different countries to be explained?
6. What gives rise to the existence of a reserve army of labour?
7. What is the effect of the general law of capitalist accumulation?
8. What causes the impoverishment of the working class under capitalism?

CHAPTER VI

Division of Surplus Value Among the Capitalists

We already know that *surplus value* is created only by the *labour of workers*. But the various enterprises do not employ the same number of workers. Moreover, the greatest number of men is not always employed by the enterprise which has the greatest capital investments. Let us take two capitalists, each having the same amount of capital—a million dollars. One has built an electric power station equipped with all the latest improvements. The other has opened up a stone quarry where much manual labour is required. Only fifty workers are employed at the electric power station whereas five hundred are employed at the quarry. The question arises: will the owner of the quarry get ten times more profit than the owner of the electric power station?

Equalization of the rate of profit

We know that for capitalism the aim of production is to *make profit*. If operating quarries (with the same outlay of capital) were more profitable than operating electric power stations, many fortune hunters would be found who would go into the quarry business. On the other hand, few would care to invest their capital in electric power stations. But we already know now what this would lead to: the price of quarried stone would drop and the price of electric power would rise. The question may, however, be asked, what are the limits within which these prices may range?

Let us assume that prices have changed to the extent that both enterprises yield the same profits. Will prices still change? Obviously not. Therefore no owner of an electric power station will find it more profitable to go into the quarry business: both enterprises have the same advantages.

Capitalist industry consists not of one or two enterprises, however, but of a tremendous number of plants, factories, etc. The amount of capital invested in each one of them is, of course, different. But all these investments differ among themselves in their *organic composition, i.e.,* in the relation between constant and variable capital. The greater the constant capital in comparison with the variable capital, the higher the organic composition of capital. On the contrary, one speaks of a low organic composition of capital when the variable capital is greater in comparison with the constant capital.

We can therefore say that the electric power station is characterized by a *high* organic composition of capital. In other enterprises we shall find, on the contrary, a low organic composition of capital. In which cases will this be? It is not difficult to answer this question. We find a *low* organic composition of capital whenever many workers are employed while the cost of buildings, machinery, etc., is not very great. Let us take, for example, a contractor making embankments, etc., for a railroad construction job—his expenditure of constant capital is not very great: he buys some wheel-barrows, picks and shovels, and that is all. But he will employ many labourers: the greater part of his capital will go for the hiring of labour power.

Since surplus value is created only by the labour of the workers, enterprises with a low organic composition of capital appear to be the most profitable. But the struggle for profits among the capitalists leads to the equalization of profits with the same amount of capital invested. The ratio of the profits of the capitalist to the amount of capital invested is called the rate of profit. For instance, if by investing a million in an enterprise the capitalist gets profits to the amount of a hundred thousand, his rate of profit is one-tenth, or 10 per cent. Competition among the capitalists leads to the *law of the general or average rate of profit.* This law, like all the laws of the capitalist system, enforces itself amidst ceaseless fluctuations in the struggle of all against all.

We shall show in an example how the rate of profit is equalized in capitalist society. For the sake of simplicity we shall assume that there are only three capitals (or three groups of capital) in society, all of the same amount, but differing in organic composition. Let us assume the amount of capital in each to be

100 units. The first consists of 70 units of constant capital and 30 units of variable capital, the second of 80 constant and 20 variable, and the third of 90 constant and 10 variable. Let the rate of surplus value in all three enterprises or groups of enterprises be the same and equal 100 per cent. This means that every worker works half a day to earn his wages and the other half day for the capitalist. In this case the surplus value obtained by each enterprise will equal the amount of variable capital, *i.e.*, in the first—30 units of surplus value, in the second—20, in the third—10. If commodities produced in capitalist enterprises would sell at their value, then the first enterprise would get 30 units of profit, the second—20, the third—10. But the amount of capital invested in each of the three is the same. Such a situation would be very welcome to the first capitalist, but not at all so to the third. In such a case it is more advantageous for the capitalist of the third group to transfer to the first group. This leads to competition among the capitalists in the first group which compels them to lower prices and at the same time gives the capitalists in the third group the possibility of raising prices, so that the profit in all three groups is the same.

This course of equalization in the rates of profit can be shown more graphically in the following tabulation:

Capital	*Constant Capital*	*Variable Capital*	*Surplus Value*	*Value of Commodities Produced*	*Sales Price of Commodities*	*Rate of Profit (in percentage)*
I.	70	30	30	130	120	*20*
II.	80	20	20	120	120	*20*
III.	90	10	10	110	120	*20*
Total	240	60	60	360	360	*20*

Besides the difference in the organic composition of capital the amount of surplus value squeezed out of the workers also depends on the *speed of turnover of capital.* If two capitalists have the same amount of capital and if the organic composition of their capital is the same, the one whose capital turns over more quickly will be able to squeeze out more surplus value. Let one have a turnover once a year and the other three times a year. It is evident that the second one will be able to hire three times as many workers and squeeze out three times as much surplus value. On the whole, this difference is also equalized by the same law of the average rate of profit, which takes effect through competition among the capitalists.

But this means that commodities in capitalist society are sold, not at their value, but at prices which vary in some way from their value. And actually under capitalism commodities are sold at prices fluctuating about their production prices. The *price of production* of a commodity consists of the amount spent on production plus an average profit on the capital invested.

> "Profit is the ratio between the surplus value and all the capital invested in an undertaking. Capital with a 'high organic composition' (*i.e.*, with a preponderance of constant capital over variable capital to an extent above the social average) yields a less than the average rate of profit; capital with a 'lower organic composition' yields a more than the average rate of profit. Competition among capitals, their free transference from one branch of production to another, reduces the rate of profit in both cases to the average. The sum total of the values of all the commodities in a given society coincides with the sum total of prices of all the commodities; but in separate undertakings, and in separate branches of production, as a result of competition, commodities are sold, not in accordance with their values, but in accordance with the *prices of production* (or production prices), which are equal to the expended capital plus the average profit."*

Under capitalism, commodities are sold not at their value, but at the price of production. Does this mean, however, that the law of value has no force in capitalist production? Not at all. We must remember that the price of production is only a *different form of value.*

Some capitalists sell their commodities above their value, others below, but all the capitalists taken together receive the full value of all the commodities, and the total profits of the entire capitalist class are equal to the surplus value produced by all the unpaid social labour. Within the framework of the whole of society the sum total of production prices is equal to the sum total of the

* Lenin, *Marx-Engels-Marxism*, "Karl Marx," pp. 21-2.

values of the commodities, and the sum total of profits is equal to the sum total of unpaid labour of the workers. A reduction in the value of commodities leads to a reduction in their price of production, whereas an increase in their value leads to an increase in their price of production. It is in this way that the law of value has its effect through the price of production.

> "In this way the well-known and indisputable fact of the divergence between prices and values and of the equalization of profits is fully explained by Marx on the basis of the law of value; for the sum of values of all the commodities coincides with the sum total of all the prices."*

The capitalist conducts his enterprise for the sake of the profit he derives from it. Profit is the motive power of capitalist industry. The development of capitalism, however, inevitably tends to reduce the average rate of profit.

Tendency towards lower rates of profit

Profit is the mass of surplus value taken with respect to the entire capital invested in the enterprise. The rate of profit is the ratio of the gains of the capitalist to his capital. But we know that the amount of surplus value is determined by the amount of variable capital, that is, by that part of capital which goes for the hiring of labour power.

The organic composition of capital, however, is continually changing with the development of capitalism, continually becoming higher. With the growth of technical improvements, the amount of raw material, machinery and equipment of enterprises becomes constantly greater, and that part of the capital which goes to pay for *dead* labour grows at a considerably more rapid rate than the variable capital, which goes to pay for *live* labour.

But under capitalism the consequence of a higher organic composition of capital is the inevitable tendency towards a lower rate of profit. Each individual capitalist, replacing workers by machinery, cheapens production, broadens the market for his commodities and strives to obtain a greater profit *for himself*. This is self-evident, otherwise he would not install machinery. But the development of technical improvements, expressing itself in a

* *Ibid.*, p. 22.

higher organic composition of capital, calls for consequences which are *beyond the power* of the individual capitalist to remedy. This consequence is *the tendency towards a lower general* (*or average*) *rate of profit.*

"An increase in the productivity of labour means a more rapid growth of constant capital as compared with variable capital. Inasmuch as surplus value is a function of variable capital alone, it is obvious that the rate of profit (the ratio of surplus value to the whole capital, and not to its variable part alone) has a tendency to fall. Marx makes a detailed analysis of this tendency and of a number of circumstances that incline to conceal it or to counteract it."*

Among the *counteracting* circumstances comes first of all the *increase in the rate of exploitation* of the workers. It must further be kept in mind that with the increase in the productivity of labour, the *value* of machinery and equipment, etc., *falls.* If one worker used to operate two looms and now operates sixteen, it is necessary to remember that now the value of the looms is lower. Sixteen looms do not cost eight times as much now as two did formerly, but only five or perhaps four times as much. Hence, the fraction of constant capital that falls to one worker is not eight times greater than it was, but only five or four times greater. There are also other causes for the retardation of the fall in the rate of profit.

It must also be understood that the reduction in the rate of profit does not signify a decrease in the mass of profit, that is, in the full amount of surplus value squeezed out of the working class. On the contrary, the mass of capitalist profit grows steadily because capital continues to grow, the mass of workers who are being exploited increases, the degree of exploitation becomes greater.

However, the tendency towards a lower rate of profit still exists and exerts a powerful influence on the entire development of capitalism. This tendency towards a decrease in the rate of profit *greatly sharpens the contradictions of capitalism.* The capitalists try to counterbalance the falling off in the rate of profit by increasing the exploitation of the workers, which leads to a number

* *Ibid.*

of contradictions between the proletariat and the bourgeoisie. The fall in the rate of profit sharpens the struggle within the camp of the capitalists. In order to save themselves from this tendency capitalists establish enterprises in backward countries, where hands are cheaper, the rate of exploitation is higher and the organic composition of capital is lower than in the highly industrialized countries. In addition, the capitalists combine in all kinds of unions (trusts, cartels, etc.) in order to keep prices at higher levels, trying thus to increase their profits, to keep the rate of profit from falling.

During periods of crisis, when all the contradictions of capitalism grow most acute, the contradictions caused by the tendency for the rate of profit to fall become clearly apparent.

Commercial capital and its income

As we have already said, under capitalist economy things are produced not for immediate use, but for sale. Hence the troubles of the entrepreneur are not over when the commodities have been produced: they have yet to be sold. The capitalist has to sell the commodities he has produced in order to convert his capital into money again.

Under developed capitalist economy the producer does not wait for the consumer to come to him for the commodities. As a rule, the manufacturer sells his goods to an *intermediary merchant* (middleman) and the latter manages the further movement of the commodities to the consumers, to whom they will be sold.

Everyone knows that for trade, capital is necessary. Without means the merchant cannot fulfil the function of bringing the commodities to the purchaser, the consumer. If the industrialist had to sell his goods himself he would have to expend a definite amount of capital on equipping a store, hiring clerks, etc. Hence, the industrialist lets the merchant take care of this, giving him a share of the profit.

The profit of commercial capital thus consists of part of the surplus value which the industrialist concedes to the merchant. Expending a certain amount of capital, the merchant must receive the usual rate of profit on his capital. If his profit is less than the average it will be unprofitable to engage in commerce and the merchant will transfer his capital to industry.

The merchant not only serves as an intermediary for commodities produced at capitalist plants and factories, he also buys commodities from peasants, artisans and handicraftsmen.

In some village, say, the locksmith trade has flourished for ages. The handicraftsmen themselves find it difficult to locate a market for their products; their immediate region already has a sufficient supply of locks. A buyer comes, who purchases a big lot, takes it to another part of the country where he sells it advantageously. In selling the locks the buyer receives their value, while the price for which he purchased them from the handicraftsmen was very low. Part of the difference between the sales price and the purchase price goes to pay various expenses: packing, transporting, etc. The remainder constitutes his profit, the gain received from the trade. Thus commercial capital exploits the small independent commodity producers, gradually transforming them into its workmen, working at home. In this way the merchant exacts his profit from simple commodity production.

Forms of commerce, speculation

Under modern capitalist economy trade is not carried on only with articles of consumption. On the contrary, a tremendous number of commercial deals are transacted with commodities which are needed for further production or for transport.

A textile mill buys cotton, coal, machinery, looms, dyes. A machine-building plant buys coal, iron and machinery. Railroads buy vast quantities of rails, ties, railroad-cars and locomotives.

It is necessary to distinguish between wholesale and retail trade. The manufacturer customarily sells his goods to a wholesaler. The wholesaler resells the goods to smaller tradesmen who, in their turn, sell them retail to the consumer.

The structure of the trade apparatus in capitalist countries is very complex. Big deals are transacted at produce exchanges. Some commodities pass through a number of hands before coming to the ultimate consumer. The participants in these deals and resales often do not even see the commodities: usually only warehouse receipts are sold which merely confirm the presence of the commodities and confer the right to receive them. It is clear that not all goods can be dealt with in this way; for this it is necessary that the goods be of strict uniformity, that the quality be easily established and noted in the corresponding warehouse documents.

Frequently, merchants buy goods at the produce exchange not for the purpose of selling them to the consumer but only because they expect a rise in the market price so that it will be possible for them to exact a profit on the resale of these goods. Actually, prices fluctuate, dependent upon a number of causes which it is difficult or simply impossible to foresee. Let us say that at the beginning of the summer a good harvest is expected and the price of grain falls; if later the harvest suddenly seems to be worse than was expected, there is usually a sharp rise in grain prices.

This creates the opportunity for speculation. Speculation is inseparably bound up with the whole nature of capitalist commerce. The gain which falls to the share of the speculator is the loss of hundreds and thousands of people who take part in the production of or in trade with the commodities which are the subject of speculation.

Loan capital and credit

In capitalist society it is not only the capitalist who owns an industrial or commercial enterprise who receives an unearned income. Under capitalism a continually increasing number of parasites crop up, who receive tremendous incomes without doing any work whatsoever, merely because they are in possession of an enormous capital, possess a great amount of money.

How does the money of these capitalists increase?

The owners of money capital usually keep their money in a *bank*. The bank pays a definite rate of *interest* on deposits.

But where does the bank get the means with which to pay out this interest? Money that lies in the vaults of the bank in the form of gold or bills does not increase of itself.

Capitalism knows only one source for the increase of capital; this source lies in production: in the plant, in the factory, the mine, the agricultural enterprise, etc.

Therefore, a modern bank does not hide away and hold on to the money which is deposited with it. It leaves only enough money in the vaults to meet the usual demands of the depositors. Experience has shown that in ordinary times only a small proportion of the depositors call for the return of their money daily. The money which they withdraw is usually covered by new incoming deposits. Of course, things take a different turn in case of any unusual event, as in times of crisis, war, etc. Then the entire mass of depositors suddenly, all together, demand the return of their money. If the bank cannot make adequate preparations for this attack and gather into its vaults a sufficient amount of money by means of borrowing from other banks, from the government, etc., and if it does not succeed in abating the "run" on the bank, it "fails." This means that it declares itself unable to pay back its depositors. A bank failure means the ruin of many capitalists, the wiping out of the savings of the petty bourgeoisie, etc. A bank failure thus only aggravates the crisis.

Under ordinary circumstances, however, the bank can keep comparatively little money in its vaults and yet be able to satisfy the demands of all the depositors who wish to withdraw their money. The bank lends the remaining money to capitalists who are in need of funds.

We already know for what purposes the capitalist needs money. He needs it to use as *capital*, to be used for production. It makes no difference that he does not get the money permanently, but only for a definite period of time. In the production and sale of his commodities, he realizes various sums of money at various times. From the money thus received the capitalist can repay the bank loan. It must also be remembered that, under developed capitalism, banks not only grant loans to capitalists for more or less short terms, but that they also invest vast sums of money in industry for very long terms.

The industrial capitalist uses the money received from the bank as capital. With the help of his capital he expands production on a much wider scale than he could have done if he had not obtained the loan. The distinguishing feature of loan capital thus consists in the fact that it is applied in production not by the capitalist to whom it belongs, but by another. By using the loan obtained from the bank in his enterprise the industrial capitalist who received the loan can hire more workers: hence obtain more surplus value.

The industrial capitalist has to pay *part of this surplus value* to the bank for the capital it put at his disposal. If he borrowed

$1,000 and must repay $1,070 at the end of a year, it is said that the bank charges 7 per cent on money loaned.

In this case the bank will pay its depositors a somewhat smaller interest—say, 5 per cent—on money deposited. This means that, of the $70 that the bank received from the industrialist, the bank must pay $50 to the people who deposited the $1,000. The bank's profit will amount to $20 on this deal.

Anyone can see that this transaction is very similar to any other ordinary commercial transaction. If a merchant bought a horse for $50 and sold it for $70, he made $20. The bank also paid $50 and received $70, making $20 profit. The only difference is that the commodity which the bank dealt with was not a horse nor an ordinary commodity generally, but a commodity of a very special nature. What this commodity is we have already seen: $1,000 converted into capital and used as capital for the period of one year. The banks trade in capital; a bank is a *merchant dealing in capital.*

Rate of Interest

Capital is thus converted into a commodity with which transactions are carried on in various ways. In these transactions the *price of capital is established.* In our case $70 was the price paid by the industrialist for the use of $1,000 worth of capital for a period of one year. This price was paid by the entrepreneur to the merchant of capital—the bank. In its turn the bank paid the owners of this capital $50 for the right to use it for one year.

The question now arises, what does this price depend on, what determines *the rate of interest* paid for capital?

This rate is subject to frequent change. Capitalists often say: money is cheap now, or: money is dear now. In the first case this means that money can be borrowed at low rates of interest, in the second case, on the contrary, a high rate of interest must be paid. As in every commercial transaction, the price in this case is ultimately determined by supply and demand. If in a given month very many capitalists need additional money and determine to get it at any cost, then the demand on money for loans is great. Let us see, however, to what extent this cost can increase.

In our example the industrial capitalist paid the bank $70 for the use of capital amounting to $1,000 for one year. Why was such a transaction advantageous to him? Because he very probably made 15-16 per cent profit on the capital invested in his enterprise. This means that on every $1,000 invested, the entrepreneur realized $150-160 in profit. After paying the bank $70 he still had $80-90 left. This is the difference between the rate of profit obtained in industry and the rate of interest paid to the bank.

Should the rate of interest rise because of the demand for loans, this rise evidently has its limits. The bank may demand $80-90 instead of $70. It will still be of advantage to the industrialist to take the loan. But if the bank demands $150-160 he will refuse. Under these terms he would get no profit but only much trouble.

Thus, in rising, the rate of interest is limited by the average rate of profit of the entrepreneur. It is usually considerably less than the average profit. Only in rare cases (during crises) does it reach this level. On the other hand, with an increase in the supply of money over the demand the rate of interest paid for its use will fall.

Depending on circumstances, the rate of interest in this case may fall exceedingly low, although, of course, no one will lend money gratis.

Review Questions

1. How is the difference in the organic composition of capital in various branches of industry to be explained?
2. How is the rate of profit equalized?
3. What determines the price of production?
4. Does the sale of commodities at the price of production contradict Marx's teaching on value?
5. What are the causes of the tendency for the fall in the rate of profit?
6. Where does the profit of commercial capitalists come from?
7. How does a bank trade in capital?

CHAPTER VII

Capitalism in Agriculture

Until capitalism became widespread there was no such thing as modern industry. There were no gigantic metallurgical plants employing thousands of workers, there were no oil derricks, no textile mills with their hundreds of thousands of humming looms and shuttles. Before capitalism there were no railroads or steamships. Large-scale industry was created by capitalism: previous to large-scale industry there were only artisans and handicraftsmen in its place.

Antithesis between city and village

It is different with agriculture. Long before capitalism, people occupied themselves with tilling the soil, cattle-breeding, raising all kinds of animals and plants useful to man. When capitalism arose agriculture was in the state of feudalism. The development of capitalism rapidly began to destroy the former basis of agriculture, but in many countries, nevertheless, remnants of the feudal system proved very vital and survived even after the triumph of capitalism. The most important survival is the retention of land in the hands of landlords, in the hands of private owners generally.

Capitalism effects the *separation of industry from agriculture*. Under the former pre-capitalist relations, clothes, shoes, and a number of other articles for everyday use were produced within the peasant family or by peasant artisans. Capitalism creates textile and shoe industries, which because of the low cost and superior quality of their production supplant peasant production.

But capitalism not only separates all new branches of industry from agriculture. Capitalism *creates a gulf between city and village,* creates and continually deepens the antithesis between industry and agriculture. In industry the development of capitalism brings with it a rapid growth of technical improvement; every decade, sometimes every year, brings new methods of production, new improvements, new machinery. Agriculture, even in the most advanced capitalist countries, lags behind this tempestuous growth of industry. Dragging agriculture out of its previous narrow limits of natural economy and freeing it from the trammels of serfdom, capitalism at the same time brings with it the ever-growing oppression of exploitation for the broad masses of the village, condemning them to ignorance, backwardness and poverty. The many millions of the village population, the peasants, even in the most advanced countries, are cut off from city civilization, live in a state of ignorance and backwardness.

The rapid growth of industry and the extreme backwardness of agriculture—this is one of *the deepest contradictions* of the capitalist system, giving rise to all kinds of upheavals and crises, foreshadowing and preparing the inevitable *downfall of capitalism.*

> "Agriculture lags behind industry in its development—this is a phenomenon inherent in *all* capitalist countries and is one of the most deep-seated reasons for upsetting the proportion among the different branches of the national economy, for crises and high prices.
>
> "Capital has freed agriculture from feudalism, dragged it into commercial traffic and together with this into the economic development of the world, it has torn it away from stagnation, the barbarism of the Middle Ages and patriarchalism. Nevertheless, capitalism has not only failed to remove the oppression, exploitation and poverty of the masses, but, on the contrary, it creates these miseries in a new form and re-establishes their old forms on a 'modern' basis. Not only is the contradiction between industry and agriculture not removed by capitalism, but, on the contrary, it is widened and sharpened to an ever greater extent. The pressure of capital, which grows principally in the spheres of commerce and industry, falls more and more heavily upon agriculture." *

Ground rent

The prime prerequisite for production in agriculture is land. In all capitalist countries land is the *private property* of individual landowners. In almost all of these countries tremendous tracts of land are in the hands of the *landlords*—large-scale owners who do not work the land

* Lenin, *Collected Works,* Vol. XVII, "New Data on the Laws of the Development of Capitalism in Agriculture," p. 639, Russian ed.

themselves, but *rent* it out. The landlords have retained their large estates from the days of serfdom. They live as before on the fat of the land at the expense of the labour of others. Merely the form in which they exploit the peasants, squeeze out their income, has changed. Only in the Soviet Union has the land been *nationalized, i.e.,* taken away from the landlords and all other private owners, and ownership has been vested in the proletarian state which turns part over to the toiling peasantry, giving land to all toiling peasants without charge, and employing part for the organization of large-scale state farms which raise produce for supplying the workers and to satisfy the requirements of state industries serving these same workers.

Under capitalism the owner of the land receives *rent*. Anyone who wants to engage in agriculture and has the necessary capital for it must first of all rent a piece of land, at a definite rental and for a definite period of time, from the one who owns this land. The owner of the land exercises his rights of ownership to collect tribute from all those who need land. This tribute received by the landowner is called ground rent.

It is necessary to discriminate between *differential* rent and *absolute* rent. First, let us take differential rent. We know that in industry the value of commodities and their cost of production are determined by the average conditions of production. This is not so in agriculture. Land area is limited and cannot be increased as needed. Different pieces of land are not of the same fertility. An important part is also played by the distance of the land from large cities, rivers and oceans or the railroads. From better soil with the same expenditure of capital a better harvest is obtained. Land which is advantageously located saves the husbandman expenses which are required to transport products when the land is located in isolated districts. The price of production of agricultural products is determined by the conditions of production on the worst soil, otherwise capitalist entrepreneurs would not work the worst soil but would transfer their capital to industry. But if such is the case those working the better soil realize an excess income. Who gets this income? It is clear that it falls into the hands of the landowner.

But besides this differential rent the landowner also gets absolute rent. Land is under the monopoly control of private owners.

This monopoly of land ownership prevents the free transition of capital from industry to agriculture. In order to work the land, the permission of the landowner must be obtained. Technically, agriculture is on a lower level than industry. Therefore the organic composition of capital in agriculture is lower than in industry. This means that with the same capital invested, more surplus value is produced in agriculture than in industry. If there were a free flow of capital between agriculture and industry the rate of profit would be equalized by means of competition. But such freedom does not exist because of the private ownership of land. Hence agricultural products are sold at prices above the price of production. The excess thus obtained goes into the pockets of the landowner and is called absolute ground rent. Marx says that absolute ground rent is tribute paid to the landowner.

Lenin gives the following concise characterization of the conditions which give rise to differential and absolute rent.

> ". . . in the first place, we have the monopoly of the use (capitalist) of the land. This monopoly originates in the limitedness of land, and is therefore inevitable in any capitalist society. *This* monopoly leads to the price of grain being determined by the conditions of production on the worst land; the surplus profit, obtained by the investment of capital on the best land, or by a more productive investment of capital, forms differential rent. This rent arises quite independently of private property in land, which simply enables the landowner to collect it from the farmer. In the second place, we have the monopoly of private property in land. Neither logically nor historically is this monopoly inseparably linked up with the previous monopoly.
>
> "This kind of monopoly is not *essential* for capitalist society and for capitalist organization of agriculture. On the one hand, we can quite easily imagine capitalist agriculture without private property in land, and many consistent bourgeois economists demanded the nationalization of land. On the other hand, even in practice we have capitalist organization of agriculture without private ownership in land, for example, on state and communal lands. Consequently, it is absolutely essential to draw a distinction between these two kinds of monopolies,

and consequently, it is also necessary to recognize that absolute rent, which is *created* by private property in land, exists side by side with differential rent." *

Source of ground rent

The Marxian theory of rent, explained above, issues from the following premises. The landowner leases his land. The lessee is a capitalist who works his land by means of wage labour. In such a case it is not difficult to understand the source of the ground rent that goes to the pockets of the landowner. The wage workers produce surplus value with their unpaid labour. This surplus value first gets to the capitalist-lessee who divides it into two parts: one part he keeps—this is his entrepreneur's profit, the profit on his invested capital—and the other part, a definite excess over and above this profit, he is forced to give to the landowner. This part of the surplus value is the rent. It is perfectly evident that absolute and differential rent, like any other income derived without labour under capitalism, can have only one source—*surplus value* produced by the labour of the working class.

"All ground rent is surplus value, the product of surplus labour," ** says Marx.

"The theory of rent presupposes that the entire agricultural population has been split up completely into landowners, capitalists and wage labourers. This is an ideal of capitalism but by no means its reality," *** says Lenin.

In reality matters are much more complicated. Nevertheless the theory of rent maintains its full force even under the more complicated circumstances. It often happens in capitalist society that the landowner does not rent out his land but hires labourers himself to work on it. Then he is at once landowner and capitalist entrepreneur. As landowner he gets rent and as capitalist he gets profit on his invested capital. In this case rent and profit get to one and the same pocket.

Very frequently the landlord's land is rented not by capitalist

* Lenin, *Collected Works,* Vol. IV, Book I, pp. 199-200, International Publishers, New York, 1929.

** Marx, *Capital,* Vol. III, p. 743.

*** Lenin, *Collected Works,* Vol. II, p. 415, "Once More on the Problem of Realization," Russian ed.

entrepreneurs but by peasants who work the land themselves without employing wage labour. Peasants pressed by the dearth of land are compelled to rent land from the landlords under the most enslaving conditions. In this case also it is clear that the landlord obtains rent in the form of money payments, in the form of labour rent (work done for him), in the form of payments in kind, by which he enslaves the peasant. Where does the rent come from in this case, since there is no wage labour creating surplus value?

It is quite evident that in this case the source of ground rent is the *exploitation of peasant labour.* The peasant gives part of the products of his labour to the landlord as rent. This part taken away by the landlord is often so great that the peasant is doomed to a half-starved existence while doing the most difficult and exhausting work. That is why Marx says about the peasantry under capitalism, *"their exploitation differs only in form from the exploitation of the industrial proletariat."* *

However, in capitalist countries the peasant often works on his own strip of land. How does the matter of rent work out here?

Purchase and sale of land

Under capitalism the land is privately owned It is subject to *purchase and sale.* The peasant under capitalist conditions must buy the strip of land he wants to own. Let us see how the price of the land is determined.

The landowner has a plot of land which he leases. The lessee pays him $5,000 a year in rent. He has grown rich and asks the landowner to sell him the land. What price will the landowner ask? He will figure in this way: if I do not sell the land, it will bring me $5,000 in rent every year. Under all circumstances I must not lose by the sale. I must get such a sum of money as will bring me $5,000 in interest annually if I deposit it in the bank. Let us assume that the bank pays 4 per cent for money deposited with it. Then our landowner will easily figure out that he must get $125,000 for the land, since if $125,000 are deposited in a bank which pays 4 per cent interest on deposits they will bring $5,000 annually. In this case the price of the land will be $125,000.

* Marx, *The Class Struggles in France,* p. 120, International Pub., 1934.

Sometimes the value of land is spoken of. This is incorrect. If we do not take into account improvements made by human labour (for instance, buildings, water pipes and irrigation), the land by itself does not and cannot have any value. Land is not a product of human labour. But land, although it has no value, can have (and under capitalism always has) a price. This price ensues from the fact that the land has been usurped by the landowners as private property.

We thus see that the price of land is determined by the income which it can bring annually. The sum of money is fixed at the amount which would bring an equivalent income when deposited in a bank at a set rate of interest. This way of figuring is called *capitalization.* That is why Marx says that "the price of land is nothing but the capitalized . . . rent." * Thus by purchasing a strip of land the peasant pays the rent for a period of years in advance.

Ground rent and the backwardness of agriculture

Ground rent is a heavy weight which hampers the development of agriculture under capitalism. A considerable proportion of the surplus value produced in agriculture falls into the hands of large landowners who do not reinvest it in improvements, but who spend it in the cities. Things are no better when land is purchased. The agricultural producer then sinks most of his capital into the purchase price and very little is left with which to buy machinery and equipment. Ground rent is a sort of pump which pumps great riches from agriculture into the pockets of parasite landlords. In this way ground rent aggravates the age old *backwardness* and barbarism of agriculture. Thus ground rent, a result of the private ownership of land under capitalism, helps to *increase the antithesis* between city and village.

With the development of capitalism there is a very rapid *growth of the amount of ground rent.* This is easily understood. Absolute rent grows with the increase of the area brought under cultivation. Differential rent, however, grows very rapidly, as with every new piece of land brought under cultivation the difference in the fertility of the land and its location, as well as the difference in the

* Marx, *Capital,* Vol. III. p. 939.

productivity of various investments of capital on one and the same land, grow apace. Ground rent is also very much increased by the circumstance that the quality of land long under cultivation is improved by the investment of tremendous amounts of labour in the manifold improvements (irrigation, fertilization, road building, stump clearing, etc.). Ultimately, the fruit of all this labour goes to the landowner.

The constant rise in ground rent leads to a continuous increase in the price of land. Not to speak of large cities and their immediate environs, where every square foot of land goes up to exorbitant heights, the price of land in the villages also rises. Thus, the value of all farm property in the U.S.A. increased in ten years, from 1900 to 1910, by more than $20,000,000,000. Of this amount only $5,000,000,000 are due to the rise in value of equipment and buildings, the other $15,000,000,000 being due to increases in the price of land.

The growth in the amount of ground rent, a growth which keeps pace with the development of capitalism, means an increase in the tribute which society pays to the parasite landlords. The increase in ground rent makes the development of agriculture even more difficult, still further perpetuates its backwardness, still further widens the gulf between industry and agriculture.

The development of agriculture under capitalism is held back not only by ground rent. Production for the sake of profit, the general planlessness and anarchy of capitalist production lead to a piratical exhaustion of the soil. Capitalist crises, shaking the entire economy, often have the most ruinous consequences in the sphere of agriculture. The growth of capitalist contradictions embraces agriculture as well as industry.

Large and small scale production in agriculture

Capitalism brings with itself *the victory of large-scale over small-scale production.* Large-scale production possesses tremendous advantages. Large-scale production opens up opportunities for the application of machinery on a broad scale. Large-scale production can vastly increase the productivity of labour over that of small-scale production. Capitalist industry thus continually pushes out the artisan and the handicraftsman. Among capitalist enterprises themselves there is a constant struggle which leads to the victory of a few of the larger enterprises in every field.

The victory of large-scale production over small-scale production in industry is indisputable. The victory of big capital over the small producer, the triumphant progress in the concentration and centralization of capital evoke an enormous *increase in the class contradictions.* The middle section is gradually being wiped out, the intermediate section between the bourgeoisie and the proletariat, consisting of a mass of small producers, artisans, traders, etc., disappears. The petty bourgeoisie is ground down, a rare individual rising to the capitalist class and many thousands sinking into the ranks of the working class. Two opposite classes—a small handful of the bourgeoisie and the tremendous mass of the proletariat—face each other grimly; this is the result of the triumphant progress of large-scale capitalist production.

Unable to deny the expropriation and ruin of small industry, the defenders of capitalism assert that small-scale production is firmly entrenched in agriculture. There, according to them, large-scale production does not have the advantages it has in industry.

The defenders of capitalism persist in this assertion. As a matter of fact, however, large-scale production in agriculture is incalculably more advantageous than small-scale production. In the Soviet Union the growth of large state farms (*sovkhozes*) and collective farms (*kolkhozes*), which have an immeasurably greater productivity than the scattered small farms, prove this better than any words can. But even in the capitalist world the *advantage of large-scale production* in agriculture is indisputable.

It is self-evident that the advantages of large-scale production under capitalist conditions and under conditions prevailing in the U.S.S.R. are entirely different in character. Under Soviet conditions the advantage of large-scale production in the collective and state farms consists in the fact that the farms are conducted on socialist principles, bringing untold benefits to the broad masses of the toilers, constituting a highroad to socialism for them. Under capitalist conditions, however, large-scale production gives the capitalist an advantage over the small producer, helps to enslave the toiling masses.

Only large-scale production can afford to employ expensive machinery, tractors, combines, etc., which multiply the productivity of labour many-fold. Only large-scale production can freely obtain credit from capitalist banks and on immeasurably easier terms than the small farmer gets. A large undertaking can organize the sale of its products as well as the purchase of necessary material, etc., more advantageously. Only in large-scale agriculture is the application of science possible. The tremendous advantages of large-scale production in agriculture are thus evident.

Despite the backwardness of agriculture as compared with industry, the application of machinery and artificial fertilizers is gaining headway in capitalist countries. The application of complex machinery to advantage is possible only on large farms. The number of tractors in the U.S.A. increased from 80,000 in 1918 to 1,000,000 in 1930, the number of combines—from 3,500 in 1920 to 50,000 in 1930. In Germany the use of nitrogenous fertilizers increased two and a half times between 1913 and 1928-29, the use of potash—one and a half times. In France the use of nitrogenous fertilizers has doubled, potash is used five times as much, superphosphates twice as much. A large part of the bigger farms in Germany use machinery; small farms cannot afford machinery, of course. The small farms cannot afford to have their own tractors, auto trucks, or electric motors. The majority of the larger farms have these. Thus in Germany in 1925 electric motors were used on 70 per cent of the farms having over 200 hectares each, tractors on 14.5 per cent, steam engines on 60 per cent, trucks on 8 per cent. Capitalist private ownership, however, places insurmountable obstacles in the way of increasing the size of farms to a point where modern technical improvements could really be wisely utilized. Even the comparatively large farms of capitalist countries are seldom big enough to fully exploit the modern powerful tractors and combines. Even on large farms these machines are not utilized to full capacity. Only the socialist revolution, tearing down all the barriers of private property, creates the conditions for the full utilization of modern technical improvements in agriculture.

Capitalism leads to the *victory of large-scale production in agriculture* as well as in industry, and to the displacement of small-scale by large-scale production. Due to the backwardness of agriculture, however, this general law of capitalist development manifests several peculiarities with respect to agriculture. Because of the *backwardness* of agriculture, the introduction of machinery is comparatively slow. That is why there are still many *small peasant farms* even in the most advanced capitalist countries, farms in which there is a brutal abuse of labour power and a spoliation of nature. The small farmer under capitalism will bear every sort of privation just to keep his strip of land, his seeming independence. The small farm maintains itself only by means of the most exhausting labour of the farmer and his entire family. At the same time, the small farm leads to the land being robbed of its fertility: it is poorly fertilized, improperly tilled. The quality of cattle becomes lower. The small farmer and his family lead a half-starved existence while performing almost inhuman labour. He lives in constant fear of the next day. Every increase in taxes, every fall in the price of his products, every rise in the prices of industrial goods raises the question of the possibility of his further independence. Masses of small farmers are ruined every year in spite of their almost superhuman efforts to save their independence.

Often a large landowner finds it to his advantage to preserve the petty farms of the surrounding peasantry. Having a tiny strip of land the farmer cannot make a living on it. He is compelled to sell his labour power to the neighbouring large landowner. If the farmer did not have his tiny strip of land to tie him down to the place, he would probably go to the city to find work and the landlord would lose this *cheap labour power*. The farmer becomes a "wage-labourer with an allotment," as Lenin called such peasants.

> "We thus see that the principal and basic tendency of capitalism is to crowd out small-scale production by large-scale production both in industry and in agriculture. But this crowding out must not be understood only as immediate expropriation; this crowding out also includes the ruin and the worsening of conditions of the small landowner, which may last for years and decades. This worsening of conditions is evidenced by the excessive labour, the insufficient nourishment received by the small farmer and by his encumbrance with debts, by the inferior fodder and poorer general upkeep of his cattle, by the deteriorated conditions of his land with respect to tilling, fertil-

ization, etc., by the stagnancy with respect to technical improvements, etc." *

The defenders of capitalism consciously obscure all these circumstances when they assert the advantages of small-scale over large-scale farming. They praise the patience and endurance of the small farm owner to the skies. But they consciously avoid all reference to the privations which fall to his lot.

We have already mentioned that in capitalist countries by far the greatest part of the land is in the hands of a small group of large landlords and capitalists. In capitalist countries, the vast majority of small farmers taken together have less land than the small handful of large landowners. Most of the land is concentrated in the hands of the *large landowners.*

Distribution of land and the conditions of farmers in capitalist countries

In Germany, according to the census of 1925, 60 per cent of the farms having an area of up to 2 hectares each constitute only 6.5 per cent of all the land, while 11.5 per cent of estates of over 10 hectares each constitute 67 per cent of all the land. This means that a handful of large estates (about one-tenth of all the farms) have two-thirds of the entire land while the overwhelming majority of small farmers have only one-sixteenth part of all the land. In France, in 1908, farms of less than 1 hectare constituted 38 per cent of all the farms; their total landholdings amounted to only 2.5 per cent of all the land. Thus two-fifths of the farmers had only one-fortieth of the land. But estates of over 10 hectares constituting 16 per cent of all the farms had 74.5 per cent of the land, that is, approximately three-quarters of all the land. In Poland, in 1921, farms of less than 2 hectares made up 34 per cent of all the farms; these had only 3.5 per cent of the land. But estates of over 100 hectares each, making up only 0.5 per cent of all the farms, owned almost half (44 per cent) of the land. In Hungary half the land is owned by 99 per cent of all the farms (small and middle-sized farms) while the other half is owned by only 1 per cent—large landowners. In other words

* Lenin, *Collected Works,* Vol. XVII, "New Data on the Laws of the Development of Capitalism in Agriculture," p. 619, Russian ed.

10,000 landlords have as much land as almost 1,000,000 small farmers.

Before the revolution in Russia also the greater part of the land was in the hands of landlords, the royal family, the monasteries and the kulaks (rich, exploiting peasants). Thirty thousand of the largest landowners of pre-revolutionary Russia held 70,000,000 dessiatins* of land. Ten million of the poorest peasant farms also held about 70,000,000 dessiatins of land, thus making a proportion of about 324 poor peasant farms to each large estate owned by a landlord. A large landlord's estate consisted of 2,300 dessiatins on the average, a peasant farm—of 7 dessiatins of land. Insufficient land or no land at all—that was the lot of the village poor. Only the October Revolution drove the parasites off the land and turned it over to the working peasantry.

Such a distribution of landownership leads to the *enslavement* and *impoverishment* of the farmers. The toiling farmer is forced to rent land from the landlord under the most enslaving conditions. In addition to the disadvantages of small-scale farming with its technical backwardness, a number of other circumstances press upon the small farmer. He must give up the lion's share of his products to the landlord in the form of ground rent. The government taxes him. In America, for instance, taxes eat up two-thirds of the farmer's income. If, in case of a crop failure or some family disaster, the farmer is compelled to take a loan from the bank, he can never extricate himself from the interest payments. The middleman also victimizes the small farmer and entangles him in all kinds of enslaving conditions.

The 1930 census data for the U.S.A. graphically picture the impoverishment of the American farmer. For the ten years of 1920-30 the total value of farm lands has fallen from $55,000,000,000 to $35,000,000,000. The average value of the land and buildings of each farm has fallen from $10,000 to $7,500. The number of farms has decreased from 6,400,000 in 1920 to 6,300,000 in 1930. The number of farmers who have rented land has increased from 2,455,000 to 2,664,000 during this period. The area under cultivation on owned farms decreased from 637,000,000 to 618,000,000 acres; at the same time the area under cultivation on rented farms

* One dessiatin equals 2.7 English acres.

increased from 225,000,000 to 306,000,000 acres. These figures bear eloquent witness to the impoverishment of the bulk of the American farmers, to the decrease in the land owned by the farmers, to the increase in rented land, to the decline in individual small-scale farm economy.

In Japan, according to official data of the Ministry of Agriculture for 1932, of 5,576,000 peasant families 1,478,000 have no land whatever and rent land from the big landowners; 2,500,000 have less than one-half hectare each of their own land; 1,240,000 —from one-half to one hectare. Of both these categories of "owners," 2,360,000 are compelled to rent additional land in order to be able to exist. The landlords, as a general rule, parcel out their land for renting in small strips, because even the most intense exploitation of cheap labour power brings in less than rent does. For these small strips of land rented out to peasant families (about 70 per cent of peasant farms till less than 1 hectare per farm) the landlord collects in rent as much as 50 per cent and over of the gross rice harvest.

Differentiation of the peasantry under capitalism

Under capitalism the peasant is doomed to a bitter struggle for existence. He works himself to exhaustion in an attempt to preserve his "independent" farm. The soil is depleted, the condition of the cattle becomes worse; the living conditions of the peasant and his family sink steadily lower. Taxes engulf him, he has to pay rent for the land. He easily falls into bondage to the usurer, who sucks the last ounce of strength out of him. He usually sells his grain and cattle to a middleman since he cannot bring his produce to distant markets. The usurer and the middleman hold the peasant tightly in their clutches. The pressure of capital on the village grows continually stronger.

The development of capitalism leads to the enrichment of a very small number of peasants. They buy up land, lend money at usurious rates; others become rich by engaging in trade. At the same time the great mass grows ever more impoverished. Many are forced to sell first their cow, then even their horse Without a horse the peasant immediately becomes a victim of the rich. In order to earn a living he has to become either a hired hand or go away to the city.

Thus one section of the peasantry becomes bourgeoisie (*kulaks*) and the other—wage labourers. This constitutes the *differentiation of the village* under capitalism.

Between these two extreme strata there remains a broad section—*the middle peasantry.*

> "Their distinguishing feature is that commodity farming is *least* developed among them. Only in good years and under particularly favourable conditions is the independent husbandry of this type of peasant sufficient to maintain him, and for that reason his position is a very unstable one. In the majority of cases the middle peasant cannot make ends meet without resorting to loans to be repaid by labour, etc., without seeking 'subsidiary' earnings on the side, which partly also consist of selling labour power, etc. Each time there is a failure of the harvest, masses of the middle peasants are thrown into the ranks of the proletariat." *

In many countries great masses of middle peasants still exist. For the majority of the middle peasants capitalism holds out only one course: falling to the ranks of the village poor and then becoming agricultural wage labourers. A small minority climbs up, becomes exploiters. The 1930 census data of the U.S.A. are evidence of the gradual wiping out of the middle farmer. The census data show a growth in the number of small farms (less than 20 acres) and large farms (over 500 acres). The number of middle farms (20-500 acres) has fallen off considerably.

Impoverishment of the peasantry in capitalist countries

Capitalism brings great misery to the broad masses of toilers in the village. Capitalism digs a chasm between industry and agriculture. The village is doomed to age-long backwardness, the small peasant farm—to a miserable existence. The peasant groans under the weight of taxes, insufficient land and ruinous prices for agricultural products. The concentration of the land in the hands of small groups of large landowners condemns the peasant masses to continuous

* Lenin, *Selected Works*, Vol. I, "The Development of Capitalism in Russia," p. 235.

slavery and dependence so long as capitalism exists. Competition of the more profiitable large-scale production forces the poor peasant to superhuman labour in order to preserve his puny farm. The differentiation of the peasantry throws great masses of poor peasants into the ranks of agricultural labourers, who are subjected to the most severe exploitation.

Crises sharpen all the contradictions of capitalism to the utmost. The present crisis, the most acute and severest crisis that ever shook the capitalist world, increased the want and poverty of the broad masses of the peasantry to the extreme. This crisis led to a further deepening of the antithesis between city and village. The crisis also aggravated the backwardness of the village. Unbelievably low prices on agricultural products ruined masses of middle peasants. At the same time, the worker-consumer pays just as high prices for the means of subsistence as ever.

The peasantry an ally of the proletariat in the revolution

It is clear, therefore, that the proletariat finds friends and allies in the village in its revolutionary struggle against capitalist domination. The village wage labourer is also a proletarian; the only difference is that the one operates a machine for the manufacturer, the other follows a plough for the landlord or rich peasant. The ruined *village poor* is a reliable support and a firm ally of the working class. It has nothing to lose by the destruction of capitalism because it has nothing to gain by its continued existence. Finally, the *middle peasant,* who often plays an important role, can help the proletariat if the policy of the latter is correct. At the time of struggle for power it is exceedingly important to neutralize the middle peasant, that is, to prevent his going over to the enemies of the proletariat. After victory is won, the proletariat effects a permanent *union with the middle peasantry.* With a firm hand the working class leads the middle peasant with it in the building up of the new life.

A determined and unrelenting struggle against the kulaks—the village bourgeoisie—is the only basis upon which a permanent union can be effected between the proletariat and the basic mass of the middle peasantry. Only the proletarian revolution opens up before the poor and middle peasants a way out of the hopeless condition in which they find themselves under capitalism. Under capitalism only rare individual middle peasants climb up and become rich peasant exploiters. The great mass of them, however, have to make superhuman efforts merely to keep afloat. The threat of ruin, destitution, the loss of their ephemeral independence and the eventuality of their being forced down to the ranks of the poor, the proletariat—this is what constantly faces the middle peasantry under capitalism. Only the proletarian revolution opens up another vista for the middle peasant, gives him a road of escape from this hopeless condition.

The proletarian revolution cuts the roots from under capitalist exploitation both in the city and in the village. Doing away with the parasitic proprietorship of bankers, landlords and manufacturers, the proletarian revolution at once frees the poor and middle peasant from the age-old fetters that have them bound hand and foot: the bondage of the tenant system, debts to banks, usurers, etc., are abolished. The proletarian revolution further opens up before the poor and middle peasantry the door to large-scale socialized agriculture, thus avoiding ruin and impoverishment which are inevitable under capitalism.

Review Questions

1. Of what does the antithesis between city and village consist under capitalism?
2. What is the source of absolute and of differential rent?
3. How is the price of land determined?
4. What are the advantages of large-scale over small-scale production in agriculture?
5. How is landed property distributed in capitalist countries?
6. How does the differentiation of the peasantry take place under capitalism?

CHAPTER VIII

Reproduction and Crises under Capitalism

If we take any country we can see that from year to year definite quantities of the most diverse products are produced: bread, calico, locomotives, ploughs, dwelling houses, coal, machinery, sugar, rubbers, etc. The ultimate destination of these products of human labour is also different. Bread, sugar and meat are consumed by people, cloth serves to clothe people, houses are used to live in. A host of other products of human labour have an entirely different fate: the plough goes to the agriculturist for tilling the soil, machines and factory buildings serve for the further production of commodities; locomotives and railroad cars serve to transport goods and people.

Means of production and means of consumption

Those products of human labour that serve for the immediate satisfaction of human requirements, the personal needs of food, clothing, amusement, shelter, etc., are called *means of consumption*; those products of human labour that serve for the further production of goods are called *means of production*. It is important to remember that ultimately all products of human labour are called upon to satisfy one or another want of an individual or of a social group. The only difference is that some things serve this purpose directly—these are objects of personal use—whereas other things serve only for the *production* of the things that go for direct use—to this category belong the means of production.

There are also a number of things that can serve both as articles of direct consumption and as means of production. The simplest example of this is coal, which is used in the steam boilers at plants and electric power stations as a means of production, and in fireplaces in homes as an article of consumption. Everyone can easily think of a number of other things that serve both purposes.

Under capitalism the management of production is in the hands of individual entrepreneurs or groups of them. The manufacturer conducts his enterprise, as we have already seen, with only one end in view—profit, personal gain. It is therefore a matter of complete indifference to him whether he produces locomotives or cigar-lighters, plain calico or fine perfumes. He is after only one thing: more profit. It is perfectly evident that capitalists do not make any distinction between the production of articles of consumption and means of production. Whether the manufacturer will produce rubbers or rubber belting depends only on one thing—which will be more profitable to him?

What is reproduction?

The mass of goods produced in any country is in continual motion. Articles of consumption move from the manufacturer to the consumer. There they disappear: some serve for a comparatively long time in satisfying human needs (as clothing or books, for example), others disappear fairly rapidly (as food). Means of production produced at plants and factories or obtained from the bowels of the earth are also put to use. Some of these products are also short-lived (coal or oil, for instance), others, on the contrary, are used up very slowly and need to be replaced only after a long period of time (machinery, for example).

One thing is clear. In order for society to exist, for the economic system to be preserved, it is necessary that definite quantities of goods be produced not only once, but continuously, *over and over again*. This everyone knows to be a fact.

Shirts are worn out, but new shirts are produced at factories. Bread is consumed, but at the same time fresh grain is ripening in the fields. Coal is burned, but all the time new coal is being mined. Locomotives wear out, machines become antiquated, but human labour is constantly busy making new ones.

In all these cases, despite the big differences between these products one can observe one thing which they all have *in common*. Various kinds of commodities are produced, used and produced again. There is a constant reproduction of things.

> "Whatever the form of the process of production in a society, it must be a continuous process, must continue to go periodically through the same phases. A society can no more cease to produce than it can cease to consume. When viewed, therefore,

as a connected whole, and as flowing on with incessant renewal, every social process of production is, at the same time, a process of reproduction." *

Simple and extended reproduction

We must distinguish between simple and extended reproduction. If the same quantity of a product is produced in a society year in and year out—we have *simple reproduction*. In this case, everything that is produced in a year is consumed. But the development of capitalism implies a rapid growth of production. A greater quantity of all kinds of products is being produced from year to year. We have *extended reproduction*; reproduction takes place on an extended basis. Capitalism brings about a change from the old stagnant conditions of society to its tempestuous development. Hence extended reproduction is a characteristic of capitalism.

Reproduction under capitalism

Reproduction takes place in any society, regardless of the social system. But under different systems of society the *manner* in which reproduction takes place is *different*. Under socialism, for instance, reproduction takes place in a totally *different* manner from under capitalism. "If production be capitalistic in form, so too, will be reproduction,"** says Marx.

During the process of reproduction not only are various products of human labour reproduced, but so also are social production relations, production relations among people. And in fact, under capitalism, reproduction not only consists in new quantities of grain, coal and machinery being thrown on the market to replace what was used up, it also consists of the continual reestablishment and maintenance of the capitalist form of human relationships. From year to year workers continue to labour in capitalist plants and factories, from year to year the owners of these enterprises pocket the surplus value produced by the labour of the working class. We thus see that not only are commodities reproduced—bread, meat, metal, coal, etc.—but definite *relations* among people in the *process of production* are reproduced. The

* Marx, *Capital*, Vol. I, pp. 577-78.
** *Ibid.*, p. 578.

relation between the working class and the bourgeoisie is reproduced. Other production relations are also reproduced, as the relations between various groups of capitalists, etc.

But the *reproduction of capitalist relations* also means the *reproduction* of those exceedingly deep *contradictions* which are inherent in the capitalist system. Under capitalism *extended reproduction* does not only mean a growth in the quantity of different kinds of goods produced from year to year. Under capitalism *extended reproduction* implies also a growth in the number and scale of capitalist plants and factories, the *increased exploitation* of the workers at these enterprises. Under capitalism extended reproduction means the extension of capitalist relations based on the exploitation of wage workers, the extension of capitalism from land to land, the capture of one branch of production after another by capitalism. Thus extended reproduction under capitalism means the ceaseless growth of the acute contradictions of the capitalist system which lead this system to its doom, to its replacement by a new, socialist system. Thus the *growth of capitalism* brings with it its *own destruction*.

Capitalist accumulation

In order to produce more coal or iron, new mines and pits must be opened. In order to produce more cloth, new looms must be put to work. In general, for the expansion of production it is necessary either to enlarge the existing enterprises or to create new ones. How does this take place under the capitalist system?

In capitalist countries the means of production are owned by a small group of people: plants and factories, coal and metal mines —all are the private property of the capitalist class. In a previous chapter, when we studied primitive accumulation, we learned that capitalist private property originates in robbery, violence and lawlessness. But once it has arisen capitalist ownership of the means of production is maintained and extended from year to year.

Capital brings surplus value to its owner. We have already studied the source of surplus value. We have also seen in what forms and how this surplus value is distributed among the different sections of the ruling classes.

It may seem at first as if the entrepreneur were free to do as he pleased with his profit. And in fact capitalism knows no proscriptions in this respect. If a textile manufacturer has made $100,000 in profit in a year he can do whatever he wishes with this money. If he is a glutton—he can spend it on food, if he is a drunkard—spend it on drink. And there are many people among the capitalist class who actually spend their profits on such things. However, this is not the essence of the matter.

Notwithstanding the absence of any written laws the capitalist, with very rare exceptions, uses part of his profits to expand his enterprise. We call this addition of part of the surplus value to the original capital *capitalist accumulation.*

Of his $100,000 profit for the year our manufacturer will put $60-80,000 back into his business to expand his factory, buy new and improved machinery. Two forces compel him to do this: the desire for gain and the fear of competition. Capitalism is distinguished by just this feature—that the desire for gain knows no limits. No matter how big the capital of the entrepreneur and no matter how enormous his profits, he will continually try to increase his wealth and his profits. And there is only one way to achieve this: to accumulate capital by adding to it from his profits. Watching his competitors our manufacturer cannot calmly employ his entire profits for his personal use, for all kinds of unproductive expenditures. He sees his competitors exerting every effort in an attempt to improve their business, expand, improve the technical processes, in order to produce commodities more cheaply and of better quality and thus crush competition. If our manufacturer does not wish to be crushed, he must reinvest a large part of his profits in his business.

Thus, even though there are no laws compelling accumulation under capitalism, elemental forces effect this compulsion and make the majority of capitalists accumulate a part of their profits. The accumulation of surplus value produced by the proletariat is a necessary condition for extended reproduction.

Concentration and centralization of capital

Accumulating a part of his profits annually the manufacturer becomes the owner of ever more capital. If his enterprise was previously valued at $1,000,000, with the gradual accumulation of profits to the amount of, say, $50-70,000 a year, at the end of some ten years our manufacturer will have $1,500,000 to

$1,700,000, *i.e.,* will increase his capital one and a half or more times. The expansion of capital through the accumulation of surplus value is called the *concentration of capital.*

There is yet another method by means of which the capital of individual capitalists grows. We have already seen how the stronger enterprise crushes the weaker, the big capitalist swallows up his smaller and weaker competitors. Buying up the properties of his ruined competitors considerably below their value, or joining them to his own enterprise by some other means (in payment of debts, for instance) the big manufacturer increases his capital. Such cases of merging several capitals is the result of a struggle which brings the ruin of some and the victory of others. Often, however, the merging of capital proceeds peacefully. by the organization of stock companies, corporations, etc. Of this phase we shall speak more in detail later. *Centralization of capital* is the term given to all cases of the merging of capital by the joining of several enterprises into one.

Concentration and centralization of capital bring about the accumulation of capital in the hands of a continually smaller number of rich men. A handful of billionaires, owners of tremendous fortunes, controls untold wealth. The fate of tens and hundreds of thousands of people is in their hands. Concentration and centralization of capital thus lead to a sharpening of class contradictions, to a more marked division of capitalist society into two opposed classes: a handful of the biggest capitalists and the mass of exploited proletarians.

Concentration and centralization of capital, amassing tremendous wealth in the hands of a few persons, open the way for the creation of tremendous enterprises. As we have already seen, large-scale industry is much more advantageous than small. It is no wonder then that capitalism puts to the fore ever larger and larger enterprises in which tremendous numbers of workers are employed. Here, for instance, are the comparative figures showing the changes in the size of enterprises in the U.S.A. over a period of thirty years (average per enterprise):

	1889	*1899*	*1909*	*1919*
Workers	8.1	13.8	24.1	38.0
Capital (in thous. of dollars)	6.7	19.0	68.7	154.1
Production (in thous. of dollars)	13.4	28.1	77.2	216.9

Even more characteristic of the rapid growth of large-scale enterprises is the case of pre-revolutionary Russia, where the distribution of workers per enterprise according to size was as follows:

*Enterprise**	*1895 (Percentage)*	*1915 (Percentage)*
Large (employing more than 500 workers)	45.2	61.2
Medium (employing from 50-500 workers)	38.9	30.6
Small (employing from 10-50 workers)	15.9	8.2

In 1895 the average number of workers employed in an enterprise was 98.5, in 1915 this figure had grown to 173.4.

Here is a more detailed table showing the process of concentration of industry in Russia for the ten years from 1901 to 1910 (inclusive):

Group of enterprises	*Number of enterprises*		*Number of workers (in thousands)*	
	1901	*1910*	*1901*	*1910*
Employing up to 50 workers	12,740	9,909	244	220
Employing from 51 to 100 workers	2,428	2,201	171	159
Employing from 101 to 500 workers	2,288	2,213	492	508
Employing from 501 to 1,000 workers	403	433	269	303
Employing over 1,000 workers	243	324	526	713
Total	18,102	15,080	1,702	1,903

Using this table in one of his articles in the pre-revolutionary newspaper, *Pravda,* Lenin wrote:

"This is the usual picture for all capitalist countries. The number of small undertakings *decreases*: the petty bourgeoisie,

* Smaller enterprises, employing less than ten workers, are not taken into account.

the small manufacturers, are ruined and wiped out, become clerks, sometimes proletarians. The number of large enterprises grows rapidly and their proportion to industry as a whole grows even more rapidly. From 1901 to 1910 the number of large enterprises employing more than 1,000 workers each has grown almost one and a half times: from 243 to 324. These employed about half a million workers in 1901 (526,000), *i.e.,* less than one-third of the total number, and in 1910 they employed *more than 700,000*, more than one-third of the total. The larger factories crush the smaller ones and concentrate production to an ever greater extent. Ever greater numbers of workers are gathered in a smaller number of enterprises, and the entire profit from the labour of united millions of workers is pocketed by a handful of millionaires."

Historical tendency of capitalist accumulation

Capitalism in its development leads to an ever greater socialization of labour. All kinds of connections between separate enterprises, regions and entire countries are established to an unprecedented degree. Individual spheres of industry, previously more or less independent, are broken up, subdivided into a host of connected and mutually interdependent branches. Capitalism unites the work of different people, tying them together with invisible bonds. But socialization of production under capitalism does not proceed in the interests of society as a whole, nor in the interests of the working masses—it proceeds only in the interests of a small group of capitalists, who are trying to increase their gains. Simultaneously with the growth of the socialization of labour, the subdivision of labour among enterprises, and the struggle and competition between capitalists also increase. Only the abolition of the private ownership of the means of production and the transfer of this ownership to society as a whole, only the expropriation of the bourgeoisie and the organization of socialist production will do away with this contradiction.

The enlargement of enterprises proceeding apace with the concentration and centralization of capital *prepares* all the conditions for the socialization of the means of production, for the reconstruction of economic life on socialist principles. A large enterprise, where thousands of workers are employed, is something quite different from an artisan's workshop. Whereas society would find it difficult to take over countless numbers of small workshops, it is fully possible to socialize production when it is concentrated in a few huge plants and factories.

Marx defines the historical tendency of capitalist accumulation as follows:

> "Self-earned private property, that is based, so to say, on the fusing together of the isolated, independent labouring individual with the conditions of his labour, is supplanted by capitalistic private property, which rests on exploitation of the nominally free labour of others, *i.e.*, on wage labour.
>
> "As soon as this process of transformation has sufficiently decomposed the old society from top to bottom, as soon as the labourers are turned into proletarians, their means of labour into capital, as soon as the capitalist mode of production stands on its own feet, then the further socialization of labour and further transformation of the land and other means of production into socially exploited and, therefore, common means of production, as well as the further expropriation of private proprietors, takes a new form. That which is now to be expropriated is no longer the labourer working for himself, but the capitalist exploiting many labourers. This expropriation is accomplished by the action of the immanent laws of capitalistic production itself, by the centralization of capital. One capitalist always kills many. Hand in hand with this centralization, or this expropriation of many capitalists by few, develop, on an ever extending scale, the co-operative form of the labour process, the conscious technical application of science, the methodical cultivation of the soil, the transformation of the instruments of labour into instruments of labour only usable in common, the economizing of all means of production by their use as the means of production of combined, socialized labour, the entanglement of all peoples in the net of the world market, and with this, the international character of the capitalistic regime. Along with the constantly diminishing number of the magnates of capital, who usurp and monopolize all advantages of this process of transformation, grows the mass of

misery, oppression, slavery, degradation, exploitation; but with this too grows the revolt of the working class, a class always increasing in numbers, and disciplined, united, organized by the very mechanism of the process of capitalist production itself. The monopoly of capital becomes a fetter upon the mode of production, which has sprung up and flourished along with, and under it. Centralization of the means of production and socialization of labour at last reach a point where they become incompatible with their capitalist integument. This integument is burst asunder. The knell of capitalist private property sounds. The expropriators are expropriated." *

Reproduction and sale of commodities

We have seen that every capitalist, on starting production, buys the means of production (raw material, fuel) on the market and hires workers (*i.e.*, buys labour power). But now the capitalist has completed his annual production. The raw material and fuel have been spent, the workers have expended their year's labour, a great amount of finished commodities, shoes, let us say, lies in the manufacturer's warehouse. What is needed for the *renewal* of production? What is needed in order to *continue* the production of shoes?

It is perfectly evident that it is necessary for the manufacturer to purchase a *new* lot of raw material and fuel, to hire his workers *again* for the next year. But for this purpose he needs money. Where will the manufacturer obtain money? He may borrow it, but this only means that he will finally have to repay it. The manufacturer must obtain his money from the *sale* of (or, as is sometimes said, he must *realize)* his finished commodities. Upon selling his products the manufacturer again buys labour power and means of production and begins his next cycle of production. Thus the *realization* of the finished products is *a necessary condition* for the renewal of production, a necessary condition for reproduction. We see therefore that the process of reproduction for the individual capitalist has three stages: 1) the purchase of means of production and labour power; 2) the process of production itself; 3) the sale of the finished products. It is easy to

* Marx, *Capital,* Vol. I, pp. 788-89.

note that the second stage is the *direct process of production,* during which the workers produce surplus value for the capitalist. The first and last stages refer to the *process of circulation:* in the first stage the capitalist converts his money into commodities, in the last, on the contrary, he sells his commodities and realizes money for them. He needs this money, however, principally in order to buy the things that are necessary to continue production, for continuous production, for reproduction. Thus capital goes through its cycles.

It is well known that in capitalist society there is not one capitalist, but many capitalists who are struggling among themselves. Every capitalist deals with his capital as he finds best for himself. The acts of individual capitalists, and consequently the movements of individual capitals, conflict and intermingle with one another. The entire mass of individual capitals, taken together, constitute the social capital as a whole. It is in this intermingling of the movements of separate, independent capitals, which at the same time constitute parts of the social capital as a whole, that reproduction under capitalism takes place. For reproduction to be effected, it is necessary for not only the individual capitalist, *but for the entire mass of capitalists* to be able to realize the products of their enterprises.

> "The scientific value of Marx's theory consists in its having explained the process of reproduction and circulation of the total social capital." *

Explaining the process of reproduction and circulation of the total social capital, the Marxist-Leninist theory also discloses the deepest *contradictions* which appear in the process of capitalist *reproduction.* The theory of reproduction makes clear the complex *conditions* which are required for the realization of the entire mass of commodities produced under capitalism. The theory of reproduction shows how the very process of capitalist development constantly infringes upon these conditions and calls forth a breach in the entire process of reproduction, leading to shocks and crises.

* Lenin, *Collected Works,* Vol. II, "Once More on the Problem of Realization," p. 415, Russian ed.

Conditions of realization under simple and extended reproduction

Let us examine more closely the conditions in which realization of commodities takes place under capitalist reproduction. The value of the entire output of a capitalist country, like that of a single commodity, is made up of the following three parts: 1) constant capital; 2) variable capital; 3) surplus value. We know further that the entire mass of the various enterprises can be divided into two large groups: 1) enterprises producing means of production (machinery, raw material, fuel, etc.), and 2) enterprises producing articles of consumption.

> "The problem of realization consists in finding on the market for every part of the capitalist product another part of the product that will be an equivalent of it, in terms of value (constant capital, variable capital and surplus value) and in terms of its material form (means of production, articles of consumption, particularly articles of necessity and objects of luxury)." *

For the sake of simplicity we may assume that the entire economy of the country is conducted on capitalist principles. In reality this is not true for any part of the world; even in the most developed capitalist countries a certain degree of artisan and peasant production, which is not of a capitalist nature, persists. However, if we take such an unmixed or, as it is called, pure capitalist economy, we shall have the following situation under simple reproduction. The entire mass of products made at the first group of enterprises must be equal to that used up by both groups during the year. For example, if during the year 20,000,000 tons of coal were consumed, then the annual output of the mines must also equal 20,000,000 tons. If during the year 100,000 looms were used up, then the production of new looms must equal this number. As for the second group of enterprises, the entire mass of commodities produced by them, articles of consumption, must be equal in value to the combined income of all the workers and capitalists of both groups of enterprises. And in fact, since according to our assumption there are no other classes in this society, all the articles of consumption produced must be used up

* *Ibid.*, Vol. III, "Theoretical Mistakes of the Narodnik Economists," p. 22, Russian ed.

by the workers and capitalists. But the workers and capitalists can buy only as much as their combined income will allow: the workers to the extent of their wages, the capitalists to the extent of the surplus value.

How are the component parts of the annual product realized? The constant capital of the first group will be realized within the group since it exists in the form of means of production. The variable capital and surplus value of the second group can also be realized within the same group since they exist in the form of articles of consumption. What parts will be exchanged between the two groups? This is also not very difficult to answer. The variable capital and surplus value of the first group must be exchanged for articles of consumption, and the constant capital of the second group must be exchanged for means of production. All these parts must evidently be equal to each other for the exchange to be made without difficulty. Thus a condition of simple reproduction is the following equation: the variable capital and surplus value of the first group must be equal to the constant capital of the second group.

Marx denotes constant capital by the letter c, variable capital by the letter v, and surplus value by the letter s. The groups are denoted by Roman numerals. Then the formula for simple reproduction assumes the form—$\text{I}(v+s)=\text{II}\ c$.

Now let us see what the conditions for realization are under extended reproduction. We already know that simple reproduction is only an imaginary case and that actually the development of the capitalist system proceeds along the lines of extended reproduction. How do the conditions of realization change under extended reproduction? Extended reproduction implies accumulation. In order to expand an enterprise, it must be enlarged or a new one must be built. In any case some new means of production must be added. But these means of production must first be produced, as they do not come of themselves. This means that the first group of enterprises, which produces means of production, must have a certain excess of means of production necessary for the purpose of expansion. And this means that the sum of variable capital and surplus value of the first group must be *greater* than the constant capital of the second group. Only in this case will there be an excess of means of production necessary for extended reproduction. This means that I $(v+s)$ must be greater than II c.

We know that under capitalism constant capital grows at a more rapid rate than variable capital. A growth of the organic composition of capital takes place, the amount of machinery per worker employed increases. We also see that under extended reproduction the variable capital (plus surplus value) of the first group must grow faster than the constant capital of the second group. It is therefore clear that the increase in the constant capital of the first group must greatly exceed the growth of the constant capital of the second group. And this means that under extended reproduction the section of social production engaged in producing means of production must grow more rapidly than the section engaged in producing articles of consumption.

Let us see what the more complex conditions for realization are under extended reproduction. With simple reproduction all the surplus value is consumed by the capitalist. With extended reproduction the surplus value in each group falls into two parts: 1) the part consumed and 2) the part accumulated. The accumulated part is added to the capital. Since the capital of each group is made up of constant and variable parts, the accumulated surplus value must be divided into two parts: constant and variable. We have denoted the entire surplus value by the letter s. Let us denote the part consumed by the capitalists by the letter a; and the part accumulated, by the letter b. The part of the accumulated surplus value which is added to constant capital we shall denote by the letters bc, and the part which is added to variable capital by bv. Then the process of realization under extended reproduction will take the following form. As with simple reproduction the second group must exchange its constant capital—c—with the first group; at the end of the year, this exists in the form of articles of consumption, while for purposes of production it must be had in the form of means of production, *i.e.*, as machinery, raw material, etc. In their turn, the first group must exchange with the second their variable capital which is intended for consumption by the workers but which exists in the form of means of production. The part of the surplus value of the second group intended for consumption exists as articles of consumption; hence it does not have to be exchanged with the first group. The portion of the surplus value of the first group intended for consumption denoted by *a,* exists in the form of means of production; hence it must be exchanged for articles of consumption produced by the second group. The accumulated portion of surplus value of the first group falls into *bc*—means of production—and *bv*—articles of consumption for the workers. Evidently *bv* must be exchanged with the second group, which has all the articles of consumption. But the second group, in its turn, must exchange the part *bc,* which is to be added to its constant capital, with the first group, while the part *bv* of the second group does not have to be exchanged; this has to be articles of consumption for the workers and exists as such in the second group. Now we can see what exchange has to take place between the first and second groups for extended reproduction. The first group must exchange *a, v* and *bv;* the second group must exchange *c* and *bc.* It is perfectly evident that the exchange can take place only if these quantities are equal to each other, that is, when we have I $(v+a+bv) =$ II $(c+bc)$. This is the condition for realization under extended reproduction.

Contradictions of capitalist reproduction

The Marxian theory makes clear what conditions are requisite for the realization of commodities under simple and extended capitalist reproduction. But is does not at all assert that these conditions exist. On the contrary, the entire movement of the capitalist system proceeds by means of continuous *variations* and *deviations,* by means of a constant *infringement* of those mutual relations which should exist between the various branches of industry.

Capitalist reproduction shows up all the contradictions inherent in the capitalist system. In the process of reproduction the *basic contradiction of capitalism* stands out—the contradiction between the social character of production and the private-capitalist character of appropriation. Capitalist enterprises unite many thousands of workers. The work of each enterprise is vitally necessary to society as a whole. These enterprises employ all the forces of social development, all the forces of technical science, the forces of the united social labour of many hundreds and thousands of people. And they belong to a small handful of capitalists who conduct them for their own gain, chasing after the greatest profits.

The development of capitalism leads to a *growth in the contradictions between the bourgeoisie and the proletariat.* Reproduction and accumulation of capital lead, as we have seen, on the one hand, to the growth of the untold wealth which belongs to a small group of capitalists and, on the other hand, to an increase in the exploitation, oppression, misery and, at the same time, the indignation and the will to struggle of the broad masses of the proletariat.

The basic contradiction of capitalism—the contradiction between the social character of production and the private character of appropriation—clearly betrays itself in the *anarchy of production* (*i.e.,* in its planlessness). This anarchy of social production peculiar to capitalism is thus characterized by Engels:

> ". . . every society based on commodity production has the peculiarity that in it the producers have lost control of their own social relationships. Each produces for himself, with the means of production which happen to be at his disposal and in order to satisfy his individual needs through the medium of exchange. No one knows how much of the article he produces is coming onto the market, or how much demand there is for it; no one knows whether his individual product will meet a real need, whether he will cover his costs or even be able to sell it at all. Anarchy reigns in social production. But commodity production, like all other forms of production, has its own laws, which are inherent in and inseparable from it; and these laws assert themselves in spite of anarchy, in and through anarchy. These laws are manifested in the sole form of social relationship which continues to exist, in exchange, and enforce themselves on the individual producers as compulsory laws of competition. At first, therefore, they are unknown even to these producers, and have to be discovered by them gradually, only through long experience. They assert themselves therefore apart from the producers and against the producers, as the natural laws of their form of production, working blindly. The product dominates the producers."*

We have seen how complex the conditions for capitalist realization are. But who sees to it that these conditions are strictly ob-

* Engels, *Anti-Dühring,* p. 305

served? It is perfectly evident, that with a planless, anarchic system such as capitalist production presents, these conditions of realization are put into effect only by the *blind forces of the market.* With countless variations and deviations, with ceaseless infringements, the mutual relations between the various branches of industry which are necessary for the realization of commodities under capitalism forge a way for themselves.

The tendency towards an unlimited expansion of industry is inherent in capitalism. In the race for profits every capitalist strives to throw the greatest possible amount of commodities on the market. He tries to expand his enterprise, to increase the volume of his production. The commodities which are produced must, however, be sold to someone. On the other hand, it is in the nature of capitalism to tend *to reduce consumption* by the broad masses of the people *to the most miserable level.* Expansion of the capitalist market is to some extent due to the growth of the demand for means of production which go for the expansion of enterprises. However, ultimately the enterprises using these means of production produce ever-increasing quantities of consumers' commodities. And the market for these is limited because of the impoverishment of the working masses. Thus the *contradiction between production and consumption* inherent in capitalism reveals itself in the process of reproduction, a contradiction which is only one of the forms in which the fundamental contradiction of capitalism is expressed—the contradiction between the social nature of production and private nature of appropriation.

However, in analysing these contradictions of capitalism, it would be altogether incorrect to draw the conclusion that capitalism cannot exist in general. At the present time capitalism is living in the period of its downfall, its destruction. Nevertheless, during the course of a definite period, the capitalist system brought with itself the development of the productive forces of society necessary to prepare the ground for a higher, socialist system. The development of capitalism cannot proceed otherwise than through a series of contradictions, and to note these contradictions simply clears up for us the historically transient nature of capitalism, clears up the conditions and causes for the tendency towards the transition to a higher form.

The Marxist-Leninist theory of reproduction shatters all the subtle arguments of the defenders of capitalism. It exposes the complete untenability of the invention of the hirelings of capitalism to the effect that capitalist reproduction can, presumably, run along smoothly and evenly without any hitch, without shocks or crises. The theory also decisively shows the untenability of the opinion that capitalist reproduction cannot, presumably, take place altogether because of its inherent contradictions. The adherents of this opinion at the time when capitalism was still taking its first steps declared capitalism "impossible." Under modern conditions, the followers of this erroneous theory come to the traitorous conclusion that capitalism, because of the rending contradictions inherent in it, must inevitably perish of itself, automatically, without any revolutionary struggle on the part of the proletariat.

Marx disclosed the law of capitalist production. Marx showed how reproduction takes place under capitalism. Some critics of Marx, Rosa Luxemburg among them, tried to show that under capitalism reproduction is possible only to the point when capitalism has destroyed all the remnants of the previous system—small-scale commodity production. The adherents of this erroneous theory of Rosa Luxemburg frequently draw the most harmful inferences from it. They argue something like this: since capitalism is doomed to perish because of its inability to proceed with reproduction after the remnants of simple commodity production have been destroyed, we need not proceed with the struggle for the overthrow of the power of capitalism—and they calmly lie back to wait for the moment when capitalism will collapse of itself. It is quite evident that such a position is deeply alien to revolutionary Marxism-Leninism. Capitalism will not perish of itself, automatically. Only the revolutionary struggle of the proletariat, requiring tremendous self-sacrifice, will bring about the destruction of capitalism, slavery and oppression.

The following passage is taken from a book describing the life of miners in America:

Capitalist crises of overproduction

"A miner's son asked his mother: 'Why don't you light the fire? It's so cold.'

" 'Because we have no coal. Your father is out of work, and we have no money to buy coal.'

" 'But why is he out of work, mother?'

" 'Because there's too much coal.' " *

This conversation excellently portrays the glaring contradiction which becomes evident during every capitalist crisis. The family of the coal miner freezes because "too much" coal has been mined from the bowels of the earth. Millions of people go hungry because "too much" bread has been produced and wheat is therefore used for locomotive fuel. The unemployed and their families are without shelter because "too many" houses have been built which are therefore standing vacant.

But are "too much" bread, clothes, coal, houses, etc., actually produced? It is perfectly clear that during a crisis tremendous masses of people experience desperate need for the bare necessities of life. But they have no money with which *to buy* these commodities. And under capitalism a need for a commodity has meaning only when it is a demand *backed by cash in hand* (effective demand). The demand for bread, coal, etc., during the crisis is tremendous, but the *effective demand* is small because of the impoverishment of the masses of the people, because of the desperate poverty of the unemployed. This is the glaring contradiction which attains gigantic proportions in times of crisis.

Capitalist crises are crises of overproduction. So many commodities are produced that under conditions of the exploiting capitalist system, which limits the purchasing power of the broad masses, they can find no market. What is the root cause of crises under capitalism?

Why are crises inevitable under capitalism?

Under commodity production the individual producers are connected. But the connection is a spontaneous one. The blind forces of the market hold sway over each individual producer. Under such a system a total discrepancy between what is produced and what is needed is always possible. The production of commodities in itself already opens up the *possibility* for the advent of crises, for the complete disorganization and disruption of the process of reproduction.

Under simple commodity production, however, crises although

* A. Rochester, *Labour and Coal,* p. 11, International Publishers, New York, 1931.

possible are not unavoidable. The *inevitability* of crises arises only with capitalism. Only the contradictions inherent in capitalism make repeated (periodic) crises of overproduction inevitable.

As we have seen, capitalism leads to a broadening of the social character of labour, merging the diverse labour of individual workers into a single stream. At the same time, the products of this united labour of many thousands and millions of workers find themselves at the complete disposal of a small group of capitalists, who dictate the entire fate of industry.

> "All production thus merges into one social production process, whereas each enterprise is managed by a separate capitalist, depending on his arbitrary decisions, making the social products his private property. Is it not clear then that this form of production comes into irreconcilable contradiction with the form of appropriation?" *

It is this *fundamental contradiction of capitalism*—the contradiction between the social character of production and the private character of appropriation—that makes crises *inevitable* under capitalism. And it is this contradiction that stands out most sharply and clearly during crises.

This contradiction inevitably leads to a point where the masses of commodities produced *find no market*. It is not because no one is in need of food or clothing that they find no market; on the contrary, under capitalism the number of those in desperate need of the bare necessities of life is tremendous. The trouble is that the masses of the workers who stand in need of these necessities have no means of obtaining them. The market is curtailed, plants and factories cannot get rid of their products, overproduction overtakes one branch of industry after another. The warehouses are full of finished products, the factories cut down production, many enterprises close altogether, the workers are thrown out onto the streets. The growth of *unemployment* cuts down the consumption of goods by the working class even more, cuts down the demand for commodities. Tremendous masses of workers starving while the warehouses are full—this is the picture of capitalist crises.

* Lenin, *Collected Works*, Vol. I, "What the 'Friends of the People' Are and How They Fight Against the Social-Democrats," p. 92, Russian ed.

Describing the devastating crisis of 1901, Lenin wrote about capitalist crises as follows:

"Capitalist production cannot develop otherwise than in leaps—two steps forward and one step (and sometimes two) back. As we have already observed, capitalist production is production for sale, the production of commodities for the market. Production is carried on by individual capitalists, each producing on his own, and none of them can say exactly what kind of commodities, and in what quantities, are required on the market. Production is carried on haphazardly; each producer is concerned only in excelling the others. Quite naturally, therefore, the quantity of commodities produced may not correspond to the demand on the market. The probability of this being the case becomes particularly great when an enormous market is suddenly opened up in new unexplored and extensive territories." *

Seeking their own gain, the bourgeoisie develops the production of the most diverse commodities in a frenzied haste. To the capitalist one kind of commodity is as good as another, so long as it gives him more profit. Every entrepreneur tries to expand production: a greater scope promises greater profits. It is perfectly clear that in this race for profits, in this struggle of all against all, those complex conditions which are required for maintaining a balance between diverse branches are not adhered to.

"Gigantic crashes have become possible and inevitable, only because powerful *social* productive forces have become subordinated to a gang of rich men, whose only concern is to make profits." **

Under capitalism, production grows *spontaneously*. Industry proceeds planlessly, anarchically. The race for profits evokes a tendency towards an unlimited expansion of production. However, this tendency meets the impassable barriers of capitalist relations. These barriers have their roots in the fact that the consuming power of the broad masses is limited because of their exploitation by capital.

* Lenin, *Collected Works,* Vol. IV, Book I, pp. 171-72, International Publishers, New York, 1929.

** *Ibid.,* p. 172.

"In order that an enterprise may make a profit the goods produced in it must be sold, a purchaser must be found for them. Now the purchasers of these goods must be the vast mass of the population, because these enormous enterprises produce enormous quantities of goods. But nine-tenths of the population of all capitalist countries are poor; they consist of workers who receive miserable wages and of peasants who, in the main, live under even worse conditions than the workers. Now, when, in the period of a boom, the large industrial enterprises set out to produce as large a quantity of goods as possible, they throw on the market such a huge quantity of these goods that the majority of the people, being poor, are unable to purchase them all. The number of machines, tools, warehouses, railroads, etc., continues to grow. From time to time, however, this process of growth is interrupted because the masses of the people for whom, in the last analysis, these improved instruments of production are intended, remain in poverty, which verges on beggary." *

Thus, inherent in capitalism, there is the deepest contradiction between the colossal growth of production possibilities and the relatively reduced purchasing power of the working masses. The productive forces tend to grow without limit. In order to obtain more profits, the capitalists expand production, improve technical processes, exploit the workers more intensively. The development of credit makes it possible for individual capitalists to expand production far beyond the limits of their own capital. The constant trend towards a reduction in the rate of profit, peculiar to capitalism, spurs each entrepreneur on to greater expansion. But this tendency towards an *unlimited expansion of industry* inevitably comes into conflict with the *limited powers of consumption* of the broad masses of workers. The growth of exploitation does not only mean the growth of production. It also means a reduction in the purchasing power of the masses, a curtailment of the possibility of selling commodities. The purchasing power of the masses of workers and peasants remains at a low level. Hence the *inevitablity of overproduction crises* under capitalism.

* *Ibid.*, p. 173.

Crises accompany capitalism from its earliest beginnings. From the very outset of capitalist industry, crises shake capitalism at certain definite intervals. Crises were born together with the capitalist system. Over a period of one hundred years the capitalist world has been shaken by crises every eight to twelve years.

Periodicity of crises

The first general crisis occurred in 1825. Then there were recurrent crises in 1836, 1847, 1857, 1873 (in Europe), 1890, 1900, 1907, 1921, 1929-35. Beginning with 1825, crises began to embrace not one country alone but all countries where capitalism was developed.

As can be seen by this series of crises, they occur at definite intervals throughout the entire development of capitalism. Capitalist crises are distinguished by their periodicity (*i.e.,* they occur at regular intervals of time). Between one crisis and another, capitalist industry passes through a certain circle or, as it is called, cycle. In the period before the imperialist war, crises usually gave place to depression, then this depression passed over into a moderate revival; the revival in turn gave place to a period of boom when expansion and the race for profits reached their highest point. Then a crisis came and the cycle was begun anew.

Engels thus describes the process of development of capitalist economy from crisis to crisis:

> ". . . since 1825, when the first general crisis broke out, the whole industrial and commercial world, the production and exchange of all civilized peoples and of their more or less barbarian dependent peoples have been dislocated practically once in every ten years. Trade comes to a standstill, the markets are glutted, the products lie in great masses, unsaleable, ready money disappears, credit vanishes, the factories are idle, the working masses go short of food because they have produced too much food, bankruptcy follows upon bankruptcy, forced sale upon forced sale. The stagnation lasts for years, both productive forces and products are squandered and destroyed on a large scale, until the accumulated masses of commodities are at last disposed of at a more or less considerable depreciation, until production and exchange gradually begin to move again. By degrees the pace quickens; it becomes a trot; the industrial

trot passes into a gallop, and the gallop in turn passes into the mad onrush of a complete industrial, commercial, credit and speculative steeplechase, only to land again in the end, after the most breakneck jumps—in the ditch of a crash. And so on again and again. . . .

"In these crises, the contradiction between social production and capitalist appropriation comes to a violent explosion. The circulation of commodities is for the moment reduced to nothing; the means of circulation, money, becomes an obstacle to circulation; all the laws of commodity production and commodity circulation are turned upside down. The economic collision has reached its culminating point: *the mode of production rebels against the mode of exchange. . . .*" *

The causes of the regular appearance of crises are rooted, as we have already seen, in the fundamental contradiction of capitalism—the contradiction between the social character of labour and the private character of appropriation. Once the crisis has appeared and devastated the economic life of the country, a certain stimulus is necessary for the transition from depression to revival. Such a stimulus for the revival of the basic industries producing means of production is the *re-equipment of enterprises.* After the crisis plants and factories need new, improved equipment. They order machinery and this creates a wave of demand whose vibrations reach the most remote industries. It can be considered that the *equipment* of an enterprise *serves for approximately ten years.* Thus it is necessary to renew the fixed capital of an enterprise approximately every ten years. Therefore about every ten years industry receives the stimulus created by the necessity for renewing the equipment of enterprises.

This picture changes in the post-war period. Capitalism now lives through a decline, it decays while it is still alive. Now a crisis shakes its foundations incomparably more violently than previously. The former cyclical development of industry is shattered.

In many countries there has been no rise in industry at all, in others there was a slight rise for a short time. On the other hand, the decline during the present crisis was exceedingly great.

* Engels, *Anti-Dühring*, pp. 309-10.

The significance of crises

Crises are of great significance in the entire process of capitalist development. In times of crisis the inability of capitalism to cope with the forces which are called to life by capitalism itself is clearly manifest. The *anarchy* and the confusion of capitalist *production and reproduction* are revealed with particular clarity. The crisis further reveals the *predatory nature* of capitalism, which allows the greatest wealth to perish while even the most essential needs of the broad masses of the people are left unsatisfied.

"The crisis shows that modern society can produce immeasurably more goods than it does, which could be used to improve the conditions of life of the whole of the toiling people, if the land, factories, machines, etc., had not been seized by a handful of private owners, who extract millions of profits out of the poverty of the people." *

The crisis *sharpens class contradictions,* aggravating the conditions of the workers and increasing unemployment to a tremendous degree. The crisis compels very many workers, who formerly tended to be at peace with or indifferent to capitalism, to become active in the struggle against it. The crisis lays bare all the *contradictions* of capitalism and shows the *inevitability of its destruction.*

Crises glaringly show the deep contradiction inherent in capitalism between the productive forces and the production relations, a contradiction which is dragging capitalism to its inevitable destruction.

This role of crises is characterized by Engels as follows:

"The fact that the social organization of production within the factory has developed to the point at which it has become incompatible with the anarchy of production in society which exists alongside it and above it—this fact is made palpable to the capitalists themselves by the violent concentration of capitals which takes place during crises through the ruin of many big and even more small capitalists. The whole mechanism of the capitalist mode of production breaks down under the pressure of the productive forces which it itself created. It is no

* Lenin, *Collected Works*, Vol. IV, Book I, p. 166.

longer able to transform the whole of this mass of means of production into capital; they lie idle and for this very reason the industrial reserve army must also lie idle. Means of production, means of subsistence, available labourers, all the elements of production and of general wealth are there in abundance. But 'abundance becomes the source of distress and want' (Fourier), because it is precisely abundance that prevents the conversion of the means of production and subsistence into capital. For in capitalist society the means of production cannot function unless they first have been converted into capital, into means for the exploitation of human labour power. The necessity for the means of production and subsistence to take on the form of capital stands like a ghost between them and the workers. It alone prevents the coming together of the material and personal levers of production; it alone forbids the means of production to function, the workers to work and to live. Thus, on the one hand, the capitalist mode of production stands convicted of its own incapacity any longer to control these productive forces. And, on the other hand, these productive forces themselves press forward with increasing force to put an end to the contradiction, to rid themselves of their character as capital, *to the actual recognition of their character as social productive forces.*" *

In the *Communist Manifesto* there is the following clear characterization of the role of crises in capitalist production:

"Modern bourgeois society with its relations of production, of exchange and of property, a society that has conjured up such gigantic means of production and exchange, is like the sorcerer who is no longer able to control the powers of the nether world whom he has called up by his spells. For many a decade past the history of industry and commerce is but the history of the revolt of modern productive forces against modern conditions of production, against the property relations that are the conditions for the existence of the bourgeoisie and of its rule. It is enough to mention the commercial crises that by their periodical return put the existence of the entire bourgeois society on its trial, each time more threateningly. In these crises

* Engels, *Anti-Dühring*, pp. 310-11.

a great part not only of the existing products but also of the previously created productive forces are periodically destroyed. In these crises there breaks out an epidemic that, in all earlier epochs, would have seemed an absurdity—the epidemic of over-production. Society suddenly finds itself put back into a state of momentary barbarism; it appears as if a famine, a universal war of devastation had cut off the supply of every means of subsistence; industry and commerce seem to be destroyed. And why? Because there is too much civilization, too much means of subsistence, too much industry, too much commerce. The productive forces at the disposal of society no longer tend to further the development of the conditions of bourgeois property; on the contrary, they have become too powerful for these conditions, by which they are fettered, and so soon as they overcome these fetters, they bring disorder into the whole of bourgeois society, endanger the existence of bourgeois property. The conditions of bourgeois society are too narrow to comprise the wealth created by them. And how does the bourgeoisie get over these crises? On the one hand, by enforced destruction of a mass of productive forces; on the other, by the conquest of new markets and by the more thorough exploitation of the old ones. That is to say, by paving the way for more extensive and more destructive crises and by diminishing the means whereby crises are prevented." *

Review Questions

1. What is reproduction?
2. What are the conditions for simple reproduction?
3. What are the conditions for extended reproduction?
4. How are concentration and centralization of capital explained?
5. What is the difference between concentration and centralization of capital?
6. What are the causes of capitalist crises?
7. Of what significance are crises for the working class?
8. How can one explain the periodic repetition of crises?

* *The Communist Manifesto*, pp. 14-15, International Publishers, 1934.

CHAPTER IX

Imperialism—the Eve of the Socialist Revolution of the Proletariat

During the nineteenth century, capitalism developed and spread from country to country until it embraced the whole world. Together with the growth of capitalism its harrowing contradictions steadily became more pronounced and greater. During this period industrial capital was at the head of capitalist development. That is why we call this period the epoch of industrial capital or *industrial capitalism.*

From industrial capitalism to imperialism

The growth and development of the fundamental contradictions of industrial capitalism brought about a new stage in the development of capitalism—*imperialism.* Imperialism as a new and higher stage in the development of capitalism appeared at the beginning of the twentieth century. Under imperialism all the fundamental *contradictions* of capitalism are *sharpened* to the utmost. Imperialism is the last stage of capitalist development. Imperialism is *moribund capitalism.* Under imperialism the capitalist system becomes a hindrance to the further development of society.

Lenin's teaching on imperialism is a sharp weapon in the hands of the proletariat in its revolutionary struggle for socialism. Lenin showed that imperialism is moribund capitalism, that imperialism is *the eve of the socialist revolution of the proletariat.*

The teaching of Lenin on imperialism

In his work on the foundations of Leninism, Stalin points out that Marx and Engels lived and fought at a time when imperialism had not yet developed, in a period of the preparation of the proletariat for revolution, whereas Lenin's revolutionary activity was effected within the period of developed imperialism, the period of the unfolding proletarian revolution.

Leninism is the *further development of Marxism* under new conditions, under the conditions of the epoch of imperialism and proletarian revolutions. It follows, therefore, that at this time one cannot be a Marxist without being a Leninist. It also follows that to deny the Leninist theory of imperialism is to break away entirely from Marxism. It is clear from this that any distortion or mistake in the theory of imperialism inevitably means a break with revolutionary Marxism-Leninism.

Lenin analysed imperialism as a *special stage* in the development of capitalism, as a new stage in capitalist development, as a distinct historical epoch conditioned by radical changes in the field of economics. Lenin considered as most important those changes which have taken place in the field of capitalist production and which distinguish the epoch of imperialism from the previous epoch of industrial capitalism. In this Lenin based himself on those laws of the development of capitalism which were discovered by Marx, and indicated how those laws act in the new epoch.

Lenin pointed out all the *peculiarities* that *distinguish* this new epoch, which is the epoch of decaying and dying capitalism and the eve of the socialist revolution. Imperialism inevitably brings *devastating wars* and the *general crisis* of the entire capitalist system.

> "Imperialism emerged as the development and direct continuation of the fundamental attributes of capitalism in general." *

Imperialism is a new stage in the development of capitalism, but this new stage is the *direct continuation* of the previous stage—the epoch of industrial capitalism. The fundamental and decisive contradictions inherent in industrial capitalism—the contradiction between the bourgeoisie and the proletariat, the struggle within the capitalist camp, anarchy of production, crises—not only do not disappear with imperialism, but on the contrary, they attain their utmost acuteness.

The idea that imperialism has absolutely nothing in common with the previous era of industrial capitalism is a crass error. Such a view (the so-called "theory of pure imperialism") was

* Lenin, *Imperialism, the Highest Stage of Capitalism*, p. 84.

propounded by Bukharin and several of his adherents during the years of the imperialist war. In spite of the seeming "Leftism" of this theory (the peculiar nature of imperialism is very much stressed), it leads in practice to completely opportunist conclusions both with respect to modern capitalism and with respect to the transition to socialism.

Lenin evolved his theory of imperialism in a process of unceasing, unrelenting *struggle* against all kinds of bourgeois and petty-bourgeois views on this question, in a relentless struggle against all kinds of opportunist distortions and misinterpretations of Marxism on the question of imperialism. The Leninist theory of imperialism is inseparably bound up with the Leninist teaching on the *proletarian revolution*. Anti-Leninist views on questions of imperialism, on the other hand, are most intimately connected with counter-revolutionary political positions. All distortions and errors in the interpretation of the Leninist theory of imperialism inevitably lead to opportunist views.

Lenin begins his analysis of imperialism with an investigation of the process of *concentration of production*, which brings with it the *rule of monopolies*. Carefully tracing the steps of the capitalist development of the last epoch, Lenin reaches the conclusion that this period can be characterized, primarily, by the fact that the previously predominant, free competition is replaced by the rule of capitalist monopoly which sharpens the contradictions of capitalism to the utmost.

Five features of imperialism

Monopoly rule, penetrating the entire economic and political life in capitalist countries, is the fundamental attribute of imperialism. It is this predominance of monopoly which lays its ineradicable stamp on all phases of economic development in the era of imperialism. Lenin gives the following definition of imperialism, embracing its five fundamental features:

"1) The concentration of production and capital developed to such a stage that it creates monopolies which play a decisive role in economic life;

"2) The merging of bank capital with industrial capital, and the creation, on the basis of this 'finance capital,' of a financial oligarchy;

"3) The export of capital, which has become extremely important, as distinguished from the export of commodities;

"4) The formation of international capitalist monopolies which share the world among themselves;

"5) The territorial division of the whole world among the greatest capitalist powers is completed.

"Imperialism is capitalism in that stage of development in which the domination of monopolies and finance capital has established itself; in which the export of capital has acquired pronounced importance; in which the division of the world among the international trusts has begun; in which the partition of all the territories of the globe among the great capitalist powers has been completed." *

In another work, *Imperialism and the Split in Socialism*, Lenin gives the same list of the most important features of imperialism. In this book, pointing out the necessity of defining imperialism as precisely and as fully as possible, Lenin wrote as follows:

"Imperialism is a special historical stage of capitalism. Its special character is threefold: imperialism is 1) monopoly capitalism; 2) parasitic, or decaying capitalism; 3) moribund capitalism. The substitution of monopoly for free competition is the fundamental economic feature, the *quintessence* of imperialism. Monopoly manifests itself in five main forms: 1) cartels, syndicates and trusts; the concentration of production having reached the stage which gives rise to these monopolistic combinations of capitalists; 2) the monopolistic position of big banks: three to five gigantic banks manipulate the whole economic life of America, France, Germany; 3) usurpation of the sources of *raw material* by the trusts and the financial oligarchy (finance capital is monopolistic industrial capital merged with bank capital); 4) the (economic) partition of the world among the international cartels has begun. The international cartels which dominate the *whole* world market, dividing it 'amicably' among themselves—until war brings about a redistribution—already number over *one hundred!* The export of capital, a specifically characteristic phenomenon distinct from export of commodities under non-monopoly capitalism, is closely bound

* *Ibid.*, p. 85.

up with the economic and territorial political partition of the world; 5) the territorial partition of the world (colonies) is *completed*." *

We already know that one of the most important laws of capitalism is the law of the *concentration and centralization of capital.*

The domination of monopoly

The development of capitalism leads to the ruin of small-scale production and to the triumph of the large enterprises. In the process of competition the strong crushes the weak. In the competitive struggle all the advantages are on the side of the large enterprises. They take advantage of all the achievements of technical science, which are beyond the means of their weaker competitors.

The victory of large-scale production, the concentration and centralization of capital inevitably lead, at a definite stage of development, to *monopoly*. Monopoly is an agreement between, or union of, capitalists in whose hands the overwhelming part of the production of certain commodities is concentrated. It is easy to see the tremendous *advantages* of such a combination for the capitalists. As the entire production (or the overwhelming part) of a given commodity is in their hands exclusively, they can increase their *profits* tremendously by raising the price of this commodity. It is understood that such a combination is possible only when the greater part of production is concentrated in the hands of a small number of the biggest capitalists.

Already at the beginning of the twentieth century the concentration of production in a comparatively small number of large enterprises had gone very far in most capitalist countries. Of course, in every country there are to this very day medium and small enterprises which employ a small number of workers and produce small quantities of products. But the decisive role is played by the *biggest plants and factories* which exploit thousands of workers, possess the greater part of the mechanical power and use tremendous amounts of electrical energy. These gigantic enterprises, putting out an enormous amount of commodities, occupy dominating positions. Thus in the U.S.A., for example, at the beginning

* Lenin, *Collected Works*, Vol. XIX, "Imperialism and the Split in Socialism," p. 301, Russian ed.

of the present century almost half of the entire industrial production was already concentrated in about three thousand of the largest enterprises. These three thousand giant enterprises represented numerically only one-hundredth part of the entire number of industrial enterprises. It is clear that the other ninety-nine hundredths are represented by petty, scattered enterprises which are entirely unable to contend with the small number of huge enterprises.

The *joint-stock company form of enterprise* greatly helped the triumphant progress of big capital. Previously, plants and factories were established by individual entrepreneurs. Individual capitalists owned their enterprises, managed them and pocketed the profits. However, some enterprises which needed particularly large expenditures of capital—railroad building, for instance—proved more than an individual capitalist could manage; for such purposes joint-stock companies were formed. In a stock company the capital of many owners is joined. Every capitalist gets a definite block of stock (shares) corresponding to the amount of capital he has invested. Formally, the general meeting of shareholders decides on all fundamental questions, but in practice a small group of the *biggest shareholders* is in full control. Since the number of votes cast at the general meeting depends on the amount of stock owned, the small shareholders cannot influence the management of the business. It is sufficient to own from 30 to 40 per cent of the total stock to be in control of a stock company. Thus the stock company is a form of organization in which big capital subjects to itself and uses for its own ends the accumulated means of small and medium capitalists and to some extent even the savings of the upper strata of office employees and workers.

In modern capitalist countries the vast majority of large enterprises are stock companies. Stock companies stimulate the rapid centralization of capital and the expansion of enterprises. Stock companies build gigantic enterprises such as are beyond the possibility of individual capitalists. Modern railroads, mines, metallurgical plants, the large automobile plants, steamship lines—all these would be impossible without stock companies

Helping to enlarge enterprises, stock companies prepare the ground for monopoly corporations. Monopoly organizations first arise in the decisive and basic industries—*in heavy industry*. In this field the progress of large-scale production is particularly rapid, and here concentration proceeds apace. Oil wells, coal mines, iron mines, iron and steel foundries are concentrated in the hands of a small number of enterprises in every country. Competition among these giants assumes a particularly fierce character. The free exit of capital from these fields is exceedingly difficult. Every such undertaking requires tremendous expenditures of capital on buildings, equipment, huge machines. The utilization of this capital for the production of other commodities at disadvantageous prices is impossible. Crises are felt most keenly by heavy industry. During crises the demand for machinery, iron and coal falls faster than the demand for consumers' goods. Every curtailment of production hits heavy industry hard: million-dollar plants stand idle for lack of orders, the cost of production rises tremendously. Heavy industry is the first to fall under the power of monopoly. At the same time, having swallowed heavy industry, monopoly reaches out for the light industries also, subjugating them one after another.

Cartels, syndicates, trusts

Capitalist associations vary in form. At first there are short term agreements of a fortuitous nature on prices. These only pave the road for longer term agreements of all kinds.

There are cases when separate undertakings come to an agreement to maintain prices at a certain level. In this case each enterprise remains absolutely independent. It only undertakes not to lower its prices beyond certain limits in order not to affect adversely the other enterprises in the same field through competition. Such associations are called *cartels.*

Closer contact among enterprises is established when they unite in *syndicates.* Here the enterprises lose their commercial independence: the sale of finished products and sometimes even the purchase of raw material *pass through the hands of the general office of the syndicate.* Every enterprise carries on its production independently, only now it already has a set quota, limiting the quantity of commodities it can produce. This quota is set by the syndicate.

Even closer is the connection in the *trust.* Here the separate organizations *merge completely.* The owners of the individual enterprises become shareholders in the trust. All the enterprises embraced by the trust have one general management.

Vertical combinations

The merging of individual enterprises connected in any way in the process of production assumes a continually greater role. Thus, for instance, a metallurgical plant merges with a coal-mining enterprise which furnishes it with coal and coke. Further, this metallurgical and coal-mining enterprise often merges with a machine-building enterprise where locomotives or other machines are built. Such a merger is called a *vertical combination.*

The development of monopolies spurs many capitalists on to form combined enterprises. Let us assume that the coal-mining companies have formed a syndicate and raised the price of coal and coke. Metallurgy needs a great amount of both products. Many owners of metallurgical plants will, in such a case, try to obtain their own mines and coke ovens. Thus they avoid high payments to the syndicated coal industry and obtain the opportunity of making tremendous super-profits.

Corporations

The spread of the joint-stock company form of enterprise often brings about a close connection between separate enterprises. A complicated interlocking of the interests of different enterprises is created, by which one enterprise is linked up in some way with another, which in its turn is connected with a third, and so on. The active participation and interference of *banks* in industry greatly strengthens the spread of such financial connections among whole groups of enterprises.

It is particularly worth noting those cases in which some powerful group of capitalists buys up a large share of the stock of some enterprise. We have already pointed out that it is sufficient to own a third of the stock of a company to be in complete control of it. Owning such a number of shares (or, as it is called, *the controlling interest*), the group of capitalists subjects to its own influence one stock company after another. This absorption of individual enterprises into the sphere of influence and action of the kings of big capital takes place everywhere, and the forms this process takes are most diversified.

Usually, such forms of closely linking together separate enterprises on the basis of their *financial* interdependence is called incorporation, and the groups thus formed are called *corporations*.

Monopoly and competition

The substitution of capitalist monopolies for free competition is a fundamental attribute of the imperialist epoch. Even in his time Marx pointed out that free competition inevitably leads to the rise and domination of monopolies. But monopoly tries to destroy free competition. Monopolists try to gain control of the entire production of a commodity. The monopolist situation opens up unwonted opportunities for enrichment to the capitalists, at the expense of an increased exploitation of the broad masses of toilers.

The creation and growth of monopolies does not abolish competition among capitalists but, on the contrary, makes it even sharper and fiercer. Whereas, formerly, under free competition many separate capitalists fought with one another, now, powerful unions of capitalists enter the fight—group against group. The monopolists wage desperate battle against those enterprises (the so-called "wild" ones) that do not want to enter into alliance with them. In the struggle, all manner of underhand methods are used, even to the point of dynamiting rival enterprises. Further, when the monopolists raise the price of their commodity it arouses fierce resistance in those branches of industry which are the consumers and purchasers of this commodity. When the coal syndicate raises the price of coal, this evokes the resistance of all those owners of plants and factories who use coal in their business. Many try to substitute other fuel for coal, for instance peat or oil, or go over to the use of electric power. The metallurgical industry which uses a particularly great amount of coal and coke will attempt to obtain its own coal mines. A struggle to the death develops among whole branches of industry. The more concentrated an industry, the greater the role of monopoly in it—the more furious this struggle.

A bitter struggle develops *within the monopolist association*. The competitors and rivals of yesterday, united in a cartel, syndicate or trust, continue to struggle among themselves by other means. Everyone tries to grab a bigger share of the common monopolist gains for himself. The struggle within the monopoly is most frequently conducted in great secrecy and only in particularly severe cases does it break out openly.

We thus see that not only does competition give birth to monopoly but that monopoly, in its turn, *gives birth to competition, strengthening* and *sharpening* it to extreme limits.

> "Free competition is the fundamental attribute of capitalism, and of commodity production generally. Monopoly is exactly the opposite of free competition; but we have seen the latter being transformed into monopoly before our very eyes, creating large-scale industry and eliminating small-scale industry, replacing large-scale industry by still larger-scale industry, finally leading to such a concentration of production and capital that monopoly has been and is the result: cartels, syndicates and trusts, and merging with them the capital of a dozen or so banks manipulating thousands of millions. At the same time, monopoly, which has grown out of free competition, does not abolish the latter, but exists alongside it and hovers over it, as it were, and, as a result, gives rise to a number of very acute antagonisms, frictions and conflicts." *

Imperialism as monopoly capitalism

Lenin time and again emphasized that the replacement of free competition by the dominance of monopoly, which does not mean the abolition of competition, but which, on the contrary, is a condition for its extreme sharpening, is the *most important attribute* of the epoch of imperialism. Lenin constantly pointed out that imperialism is monopoly capitalism. Monopoly is, in the words of Lenin, the last word of the latest phase in capitalist development. The substitution of *monopoly for free competition* is a fundamental economic trait, the essence of imperialism, Lenin says. In his work on imperialism, Lenin, in characterizing imperialism as a special stage of capitalism, writes:

> "If it were necessary to give the briefest possible definition of imperialism, then we should have to say that imperialism is the monopoly stage of capitalism. Such a definition would include what is most important, for, on the one hand, finance

* Lenin, *Imperialism, the Highest Stage of Capitalism*, p. 84.

capital is bank capital of the few big monopolist banks, merged with the capital of the monopolist combines of manufacturers; and, on the other hand, the division of the world is a transition from a colonial policy, which has extended without hindrance to territories unoccupied by any capitalist power, to a colonial policy of monopolistic possession of the territories of the world which have been completely divided up." *

Elsewhere Lenin points out:

"Imperialism (or the 'epoch' of finance capital—we will not argue about words) is, economically speaking, the highest stage in the development of capitalism, namely, the stage when production is carried on on so large a scale that *free competition is superseded by monopoly*. This is the *economic* essence of imperialism. Monopoly manifests itself in trusts, syndicates, etc., in the omnipotence of gigantic banks, in the cornering of the sources of raw material, etc., in the concentration of bank capital, etc. The whole point lies in economic monopoly." **

Here the radical difference in the approach to the study of imperialism by Lenin, on the one hand, and the Social-Democratic theoretician of imperialism, Hilferding, on the other, is disclosed. Hilferding puts foremost not those changes which have taken place in the field of the industrial structure of the latest capitalism, but those changes which are taking place in the field of circulation—first of all, in the field of credit, in banking spheres. In this the exchange conception characteristic of Hilferding's falsification of Marx is apparent. Instead of the primacy, *i.e.*, predominance, decisive importance, of production he puts the primacy of circulation. The exchange concept is very characteristic of Social-Democratic theoreticians. The exchange concept, together with a number of mistakes in the theory of value, money and crises connected with it, led Hilferding, even before the war, to the opportunist conclusions noted by Lenin. In pre-war times Hilferding depicted things in such a light as if gaining control of six of the largest Berlin banks were sufficient to make one master of the

* *Ibid.*, p. 84-5.
** Lenin, *Collected Works*, Vol. XIX. "A Caricature of Marxism and 'Imperialist Economism,'" p. 207, Russian ed.

entire country. Such a way of presenting the question veils the necessity of a prolonged revolutionary struggle by the proletariat for power, for establishing and entrenching its dictatorship, for mastering production, for organizing production in both industry and agriculture. Such a way of putting the question masks the necessity of overcoming the fierce resistance which the bourgeoisie puts up against the victorious proletariat at every step. After the war, Hilferding developed the traitorous theory of organized capitalism. This theory of organized capitalism represents a further development of the same ideas that lay in the exchange concept. We shall return to this theory of organized capitalism in greater detail further on.

Monopoly associations in the most important capitalist countries

Monopoly associations spread most rapidly in *America;* that is why it is called the "land of trusts." At the beginning of the present century, American trusts had already concentrated in their hands the greater part of production. Thus the oil trust had in its hands 95 per cent of the entire oil production; utilizing its monopolist position the oil trust increased its profits from 5 per cent in 1882 to 42 per cent at the beginning of this century. The chemical trust unites 81 per cent of the production of its industry; the lead trust 85 per cent, and so on. The United States Steel Corporation is one of the most powerful organizations of capital in the world. It has increased its capital from $1,500,000,000 in 1902 to $2,500,000,000 in 1929 and has 147 plants. Up to the crisis it produced 16,000,000 tons of pig iron and 20,000,000 tons of steel, which represented 40 per cent of the entire production of these products in the U.S.A. There were 276,000 people working in the enterprises of this corporation. Approximately the same number of people was employed by another trust, the American Telegraph and Telephone Company, which has control of 80-85 per cent of all the telegraph and telephone communication in the country. Three-quarters of the steel production in the U.S.A. is concentrated in the hands of three gigantic trusts. In the electrical industry one trust (the General Electric Company) occupies a dominant position. In the sugar and tobacco industries 80 per cent of the production is concentrated in the hands of the corresponding trusts.

The American oil trust commands a capital of over $1,000,000,-000. There are altogether a score of companies in the automobile industry, and of these the five largest have control of three-fourths of the production in their industry.

Of these in their turn there are two firms conducting a fierce struggle with each other. These are the well-known Ford Company and its rival, the General Motors Corporation. Ford commands a capital of over $1,000,000,000; General Motors Corporation—$1,500,000,000. Its gross income from the sale of automobiles in 1926 amounted to $1,000,000,000, that of Ford to $750,000,000. Its net profits were $180,000,000, that of Ford $100,000,000.

The tremendous network of railroads in America is owned by a small group of billionaires. In 1927 the Morgan banking group had control of about 22,000 miles of railroad tracks, valued at $3,500,000,000.

American banks are most closely connected with industry. The banks have a tremendous number of enterprises under their influence and control. Thus it is estimated that the Morgan group of banks controls enterprises representing a total capital of $74,000,000,000.

Under the blows of the crisis even the most gigantic monopolist concerns crack. It is enough to point out that the Ford plants, which before the crisis employed 120,000 men, in the autumn of 1932 employed no more than 15,000. Other giants of monopoly capital were in a similar position. A number of the largest trusts failed altogether, like the Kreuger Match Trust. The British oil king, Deterding, who is continually trying to instigate intervention against the U.S.S.R., was faced with great difficulties.

In *Germany,* before the war the Steel Union had nine-tenths of the entire steel production under its control; in the coal industry, the Rhenish Westphalian Coal Syndicate at the time of its organization had control of 87 per cent (and later 95 per cent) of the coal production in this coal region, which is the richest in Germany.

In post-war years the Stinnes Corporation in Germany was much talked about. Stinnes accumulated a tremendous fortune on war supplies during the war. After the war, taking advantage of the inflation of the mark, he bought up all kinds of enterprises for almost nothing: coal mines, electrical supplies factories, telegraph agencies and banks, paper mills and steamship lines, metallurgical plants and newspapers. As soon as the mark was stabilized this gigantic concern, employing hundreds of thousands of workers, fell to pieces.

A new wave of concentration and the creation of tremendous monopoly associations rose in Germany in post-war years. By the end of 1928 two-thirds of all the stock companies (according to capital invested) were united in corporations. At about that time also, the two largest trusts in contemporary Germany, the chemical and steel trusts, were formed by mergers. The chemical trust commanded a capital of 1,200,000,000 marks. In its hands were concentrated 80 per cent of the dye works and 75 per cent of the nitrogen production. The German steel trust commanded a capital of 800,000,000 marks and employed (up to the time of the crisis) over 150,000 workers, producing about one-half of all the pig iron and steel in Germany.

The same thing is to be observed in other capitalist countries. In England and Japan, France and Italy, even in small countries like Belgium or Sweden—everywhere, command is in the hands of an exceedingly small number of tremendous monopolist enterprises, managed by a handful of trust directors.

In tsarist Russia there were also a number of great monopolist combines of capitalists. The Produgol Syndicate controlled more than half the coal produced in the Donets Basin. Another syndicate, Prodamet, controlled up to 95 per cent of all the iron sales on the market. One of the oldest syndicates was the sugar syndicate.

The strength and significance of monopolies is vastly increased by the new role which *banks* play under imperialism.

Finance capital

Banks were at first intermediaries in making payments. As capitalism develops the credit activity of banks increases. The bank deals in capital. It takes capital from those capitalists who cannot for the moment make use of their capital themselves, and gives capital to those capitalists who need it at the moment. The bank collects all kinds of income and places it at the disposal of the capitalists.

With the development of capitalism, banking establishments just as industrial enterprises, unite, their size and turnover continually increase and they accumulate tremendous amounts of capital. The greater part of this capital belongs to others, but the bank's own capital grows apace. The number of banks becomes less, smaller banks close or are swallowed up by larger competitors. But the size of banks, the magnitude of their capital, increases. It is sufficient to give the following example. From 1890 to 1912 the number of banks in England decreased from 104 to 44, but their capital increased from £430,000,000 to £850,000,000. Now a bank can no longer limit its activity to granting short term loans to industrialists when they need them. In order to utilize the tremendous accumulations of capital *the banks come into closer contact with industry*. The bank now invests a certain part of its deposits directly in industry by granting long term loans for the expansion of production, etc.

The joint-stock company gives the bank the most convenient form for investing its capital in industry. All the bank must do is to obtain a certain amount of stock in the enterprise. Having gained control even of only one-third of the total stock the bank acquires complete control of and unlimited power over the whole enterprise.

Joint-stock companies thus serve as links between the banks and industry. The banks, in their turn, help the growth of stock companies, taking upon themselves the reorganization (reconstruction on new principles) of privately owned enterprises into stock companies and the establishment of new stock companies. The purchase and sale of shares take place more and more through the medium of banks.

The law of concentration and centralization is manifested with particular force in banking. In the biggest capitalist countries from three to five of the *largest* banks control the entire network of banks. The other banks are either practically subsidiaries of those giants, their independence a mere outward show, or they play an entirely insignificant role. Those giant banks are closely welded to the monopolist industrial associations. A merging or *fusion of bank and industrial capital* is taking place. Bank capital fused together with industrial capital is called finance capital. The amalgamation of bank capital with industrial monopolies is one of the distinctive attributes of imperialism. That is why imperialism is called the epoch of finance capital.

The growth of monopoly and the growth of finance capital put the entire fate of the capitalist world in the hands of a *small group of the biggest capitalists.* The merging of bank capital with industrial capital brings about a situation where the biggest bankers begin to manage industry and the biggest industrialists are admitted into the bank directorates. The fate of the entire economic life of every capitalist country lies in the hands of a numerically insignificant group of bankers and industrial monopolists. And the arbiter of economic life is the arbiter of the whole country. Whatever the form of government in bourgeois countries in the epoch of imperialism, practically, a few uncrowned kings of finance capital have *full power.* The official state is only the servant of these capitalist magnates. The solution of the vital problems in all capitalist countries depends on a small group of the biggest capitalists. In their own greedy interests these magnates of capital bring about great conflicts between entire countries, incite wars, suppress the labour movements and crush uprisings in the colonies.

With the prevalence of monopoly a handful of people control the lives of the entire people. One of the leaders of capitalist Germany—the director of the A.E.G. (General Electric Company), Rathenau, once declared openly:

> "Three hundred people who know one another are masters of the economic destinies of the world and they appoint their own successors from among their own numbers."

It has been estimated, for instance, that in France 50-60 big financiers are the masters of 108 banks, 105 of the biggest enterprises in heavy industry (*i.e.*, coal, iron, etc.), 101 railroad companies and 107 other most important enterprises—421 in all, of which each one involves hundreds of millions of francs. The concentration of the preponderating part of the entire wealth in the hands of an insignificantly small group of men is proceeding at a rapid rate. Thus in England 38 per cent of the entire wealth of the country is in the hands of 0.12 per cent of private owners, and less than 2 per cent own 64 per cent of the wealth of the country.

In the U.S.A. approximately 1 per cent owns 59 per cent of all the country's wealth.

In the epoch of free competition, world trade develops. Tremendous quantities of *commodities* are shipped from one country to another. In the period of monopoly capitalism the *export of capital* acquires tremendous significance.

Export of capital

The fact that export of capital is characteristic of imperialism is closely connected with the reign of monopoly. Monopolies create an enormous "surplus" of capital in the older capitalist countries which have had a long period of capitalist development. Monopolies also cause a curtailment of the opportunities for investing capital in the home countries. The accumulated monopolist profits tend to flow out of the country in search of opportunities for profitable investment. Such opportunities for profitable investment are found in the more backward countries. Wages there are exceedingly low, the working day exorbitantly long. The sources of raw material have not yet been completely plundered by the capitalists. The market possibilities are big—capitalist products push out the products of the small artisan establishments, condemning millions of petty producers to hunger and starvation. But the monopolies seize the internal market of the country, and foreign capitalists find it continually more difficult to sell their commodities there. The import of commodities is hampered by high tariffs. At the same time the oganization of monopolies leads to a state where the internal market of the developed capitalist countries becomes continually less able to meet the requirements of the gigantic enterprises for the sale of their commodities. Monopolies inflate prices, which leads to a restriction of the internal market. They must continually throw more goods onto the external market. But how can they sell them there, when these markets are surrounded by high tariff walls?

Here the export of capital helps. The biggest capitalist enterprises export part of their capital. They organize their own branches abroad. They build plants and factories there, thus throwing their commodities onto that country's internal market.

However, capital is exported not only for the organization of enterprises. Capital is also exported in the form of various loans by means of which the richer countries enslave and subject to themselves the more backward countries.

Before the war, the foreign investments of the three most important European countries (England, France and Germany) reached colossal proportions: about 100,000,000,000 francs. The income from this capital reached about 8-10,000,000,000 francs a year.

The significance which the export of capital bears to the imperialist states is shown by the following data. In 1925 the export of British commodities—products of British industries—amounted to £700,000,000, the profits from this export amounted to about £100,000,000. In the same year, 1925, Great Britain received £420,000,000 in interest on its foreign investments. This is more than four times the profits received from the export of goods.

Capital tends to flow primarily to backward countries, where labour power is cheap, industry weak and the market for goods, therefore, still great. At the beginning of the World War, for instance, foreign capital invested in Russian industry amounted to more than 2,000,000,000 rubles. So much French and Belgian capital was invested in the Russian coal industry that the main office of Produgol, which disposed of the greatest part of Russian coal (65 per cent), was permanently located in Paris. The German A.E.G. and Siemens Schukert had almost complete control of the Russian electrical and electrical equipment industries. Tremendous British, American, and Dutch capital was invested in the oil industry in Russia.

With the export of capital *close contact* is established between the exporting and importing countries. The country exporting capital is interested in preserving the existing conditions in the country to which the capital goes. The French capitalists, for instance, were interested in preserving the tsarist regime in Russia, which is why they granted the tsar a loan in 1906, thereby helping materially to crush the first Russian revolution.

With the development of monopoly capitalism the export of capital acquires continually greater proportions and assumes greater significance.

"Under the old type of capitalism when free competition prevailed, the export of *goods* was the most typical feature. Under modern capitalism in which monopolies prevail, the export of *capital* has become the typical feature." *

Under imperialism the export of capital comes to the fore. This does not mean, of course, that the export of goods becomes less or loses its significance. The fact of the matter is that the export of capital is closely linked up with the shipment of tremendous masses of goods. If, for example, Great Britain exports capital to Argentina, it means that enterprises whose stock is purchased by British capitalists are organized there. One can be positive that the greater part of the equipment and machinery for these enterprises will be imported from England. Or the export of capital may take the following form. Say Great Britain grants some country a loan; for the money thus obtained the latter country purchases goods in England: material for railroads, military equipment, etc. Thus we see that the export of capital not only does not narrow down the export of commodities, but, on the contrary, becomes a powerful new weapon in the struggle for external markets, in the struggle for expanding the sale of goods.

Division of the world among unions of capitalists

Syndicates and trusts keep prices up artificially, securing colossal super-profits for themselves. In order to *maintain high prices* the monopoly organizations try to fence their countries off from foreign competition. For this purpose imperialist governments introduce high *tariffs* on imported goods. The tariff frequently amounts to many times more than the value of the commodity.

Already in 1927 the tariffs amounted, on an average (in percentages of the value of the commodities), to 37 per cent in the U.S.A., 20 per cent in Germany, 21 per cent in France, 15 per cent in Belgium, 29 per cent in Argentina, 41 per cent in Spain, 16 per cent in Austria, 27 per cent in Czechoslovakia, 23 per cent in Yugoslavia, 27 per cent in Hungary, 32 per cent in Poland, 22 per cent in Italy, 16 per cent in Sweden. This is the average percentage. Since on a number of things (as raw material which does not exist in the given country) the tariff cannot be very high, it must be very much higher on others (primarily industrial products, partly foodstuffs). It was during the last few years that most coun-

* Lenin, *Imperialism, the Highest Stage of Capitalism*, p 59.

tries introduced new increased tariff rates. In the summer of 1930 a new tariff was enacted in the U.S.A. which practically prohibited the import of a host of commodities. That same year Germany raised the duties on agricultural products to an unprecedented degree. In this way the East Prussian landowners got an opportunity to raise prices on their products. It is the working class that has to pay for all this in the end, as it constitutes the basic mass of consumers.

Thus the internal market is made entirely dependent on monopoly. But the internal market is limited. Under imperialism the class contradictions become more acute and the impoverishment of the masses increases. The internal market is not capable of assimilating the tremendous quantities of commodities produced by the huge enterprises. The struggle for foreign markets comes to the foreground. This struggle proceeds between the armed states of monopoly capital. Monopoly organizations of giant strength take part in this struggle. It is clear that it must become continually sharper and fiercer. It is clear that under imperialism the struggle for markets, together with the struggle for *sources of raw material*, for *markets for export capital*, for *the division of the world*, becomes the cause of inevitable armed conflicts and devastating wars.

The growth of monopolies leads to attempts on the part of monopoly organizations of various countries to come to an agreement on the question of the division of markets. When two or three of the largest trusts in different countries begin to play a decisive role in the world in the production of any definite commodity, the struggle among them becomes particularly devastating. Then an attempt at an agreement is inevitable. The agreement usually provides for a division of markets: every participant in the agreement is assigned a number of countries where he can sell his commodities without encountering the competition of the other participants in the agreement. Such *international cartels* existed in several branches of industry even before the World War. At that time the production of electrical equipment was concentrated in the hands of two tremendous trusts—American and German—closely connected with the banks. In 1907 they came to an agreement on the division of the world: each one had a number of countries put "at its disposal." An agreement existed before the war between the American and German steamship companies. There were railroad and zinc syndicates. An agreement was being negotiated among the oil trusts.

After the World War a number of cartels were formed embracing several countries in Europe. These were: the steel cartel, cartels, embracing the production of stone, chemical products, copper, aluminium, radios, wire, artificial silk, zinc, textiles, enamel ware. In most of these cartels France, Germany, Belgium, Czechoslovakia and Austria participated. Some also included Poland, Switzerland, Hungary, Spain and the Scandinavian countries. The world crisis that began in 1929 had a tremendous disruptive influence on most of these cartels. The internal contradictions grew and many of these cartels have either fallen to pieces already or are on the verge of collapse.

It would be a mistake to think that these international monopoly agreements represent a peaceful method of solving the contradictions. Quite the reverse.

> "International cartels show to what point capitalist monopolies have developed and they *reveal the object* of the struggle between the various capitalist unions." *

International agreements are distinguished by their instability and bear within themselves the sources of the fiercest conflicts. In the division of markets each side gets a share in proportion to its strength and power. But the power of individual trusts changes. Each one carries on a continuous silent struggle for a bigger share. Changes in the relative strength inevitably call for a redivision of markets and every redivision leads to the fiercest struggles. Thus the international monopolies not only do not weaken the contradictions between imperialist countries, but, on the contrary, are conducive to their extreme sharpening.

In the epoch of monopoly and finance capital the seizure of the colonies by capitalist countries is greatly enhanced.

Seizure of the colonies and the division of the world

Since ancient time Europeans have brought their commodities to the colonies and backward countries, charged them triple prices for all kinds of trash and have themselves taken most of the valuable things out of the colonies. Powerful

* Lenin, *Imperialism, the Highest Stage of Capitalism*, pp. 71-2.

countries by degrees seized vast territories having large populations. British imperialists love to brag that "the sun never sets on the British Empire." And in fact, the possessions of British imperialism are spread all over the earth so that at any one moment the sun shines on some part of them. Of the 1,750,000,000 inhabitants of the globe, about 600,000,000 live in oppressed colonies, and 400,000,000 in semi-colonies (China, Persia, etc.). Thus, more than half of the human race, about a billion people, are in the power of the great robber nations.

During the decades preceding the World War the division of the world progressed with particular rapidity. From 1876 to 1914 the so-called "Great Powers" seized about 25,000,000 square kilometres of land; they thus grabbed foreign lands having an area twice that of all Europe. Most of the land fell to the old robbers—Great Britain and France. The younger robbers like Germany, Italy, etc., got only the left-overs. All the countries which were in any way suitable for exploitation had already been seized by others; the late-comers had to make a feast of the crumbs that fell from the table, or try to snatch a fat chunk from the teeth of the others.

The fierce struggle for sales markets, for raw material markets, for markets for capital investments led to the division of the entire world among a few robbers.

There are no more "free lands." Imperialist countries can obtain new territory in only one way: by snatching some of the plunder from their competitors. The division of the world is *completed.* Fights between the imperialists for a *redivision* of the globe are now inevitable. And such a struggle inevitably leads to armed conflicts, *to war.*

Dumping

In order to capture foreign markets monopoly organizations usually widely employ dumping. Dumping is the sale of commodities on foreign markets at prices considerably below those on the internal market, in many cases below cost. The sale of commodities in foreign countries at dumping prices is necessary to the trusts for a number of reasons. Primarily, dumping leads to the capture of foreign markets. Then the sale of commodities abroad makes it possible to narrow down the supply within the country, which is necessary in order to raise and maintain high, monopoly prices. Dumping abroad makes it possible to curtail sales within the country without correspondingly curtailing production, which would increase the cost of production.

Dumping is a common occurrence under imperialism. In Germany the steel trust publishes its prices in the newspapers every month; for every commodity two prices are given—one for the internal market and the other, about one-third lower, for export. The dumping carried on at the present time by Japanese imperialism is particularly unrestrained. Utilizing the ruthless exploitation of their workers, the Japanese capitalists are flooding the world market with commodities, which they sell at throw-away prices. They are not only squeezing European and American commodities out of China, but they are deluging industrial countries with their commodities. Thus they export automobiles to America, sell bicycles at an absurdly low price in Germany, export silk shirts to the centre of the French silk industry—Lyons.

In old tsarist Russia the sugar syndicate practised the most genuine dumping. At that time not a single capitalist country raised its voice against this dumping, but since then the capitalists and their newspapers have frequently raised the cry of "Soviet dumping." This screaming was only part of the badgering of the Soviet Union and had for its purpose the paving of the ground for new attacks on the part of the imperialists against the first country in the world to build socialism. The howling to the effect that "Soviet dumping" was increasing the crisis in capitalist countries is particularly ridiculous. The Soviet Union does not sell its goods abroad at dumping prices. It exports commodities not in order to capture foreign markets, but in order to pay for the goods it needs. The advantages of socialist economy make it possible for the U.S.S.R. to produce a number of commodities more cheaply than the capitalists. The October Revolution put an end to the parasites—the landlords and capitalists—at the same time eliminating the cost of keeping them—ground rent and capitalist profits. It is thus perfectly obvious that all talk about Soviet dumping is the invention of the enemies of the U.S.S.R. and is particularly absurd because Soviet economy, having left the capitalist path, has as a consequence also freed itself from the methods of struggle bound up with it.

The law of uneven development under imperialism

In the capitalist system individual enterprises, individual branches of industry and individual countries develop *unevenly and spasmodically.* It is evident that with the anarchy of production prevailing under capitalism and the frenzied struggle among the capitalists for profits, it cannot be otherwise. This uneveness of development is manifested with *particular acuteness in the epoch of imperialism, and becomes a decisive force, a decisive law.*

> "Finance capital and the trusts are aggravating instead of diminishing the differences in the rate of development of the various parts of world economy." *

Imperialism is monopoly capitalism. The rule of monopolies increases the uneven and spasmodic development of individual countries. Monopoly associations, on the one hand, open up opportunities for the younger countries to catch up with and outstrip the older capitalist countries, and on the other, monopolies have, inherent in them, tendencies towards parasitism, decay and a retardation of technical progress: under certain conditions monopolies delay the development of some countries and thus create opportunities for other countries to forge ahead.

> ". . . under capitalism the development of different undertakings, trusts, branches of industry or countries cannot be *even.* Half a century ago, Germany was a miserable insignificant country as far as its capitalist strength was concerned compared with the strength of England at that time. Japan was similarly insignificant compared with Russia. Is it 'conceivable' that in ten or twenty years' time the relative strengths of the imperialist powers will have remained *unchanged?* Absolutely inconceivable." **

The export of capital greatly accelerates the development of some countries, retarding the further growth of others. Modern technique, the modern stage of development of productive forces open wide the door of opportunity for the younger countries: they

* Lenin, *Imperialism, the Highest Stage of Capitalism,* p. 93.
** *Ibid.,* p. 114.

have the chance of outstripping their older rivals, of leaping over in a short period of time a series of stages of technical development that took scores of years in the older countries.

The division of the world is completed under imperialism. A struggle for a redivision ensues. This impels every imperialist power to strengthen itself at a feverish rate. Each country tries to surpass its rivals.

The uneven and spasmodic development of individual countries, becoming still more pronounced under imperialism, sharpens the antagonisms between countries. The law of uneven development makes stable and lasting international alliances of imperialist powers impossible. The *relative strength* of different countries is continually undergoing *change,* and changes in the relative strength inevitably lead to all kinds of *conflicts.*

The Leninist law of uneven development under imperialism is brilliantly developed in a number of works by Stalin. In the struggle with Trotskyism which denies the Leninist law of uneven development, Stalin further developed the teaching of Lenin. Stalin thus sums up this question:

"The law of uneven development in the period of imperialism means the spasmodic development of some countries with respect to others, the rapid crowding out of some countries by others on the world market, the periodic redivision of the *already divided world* through military conflicts and military catastrophes, the deepening and sharpening of the conflicts in the camp of imperialism, a weakening in the front of world capitalism, the possibility of this front being broken by the proletarians of individual countries, the possibility of the triumph of socialism in individual countries.

"What are the basic elements of the law of uneven development under imperialism?

"First, the fact that the world has already been divided up among the imperialist groups, that there are no more 'free,' unoccupied territories in the world and that in order to capture new markets and sources of raw material, in order to expand, it is necessary to take such territory from others by force.

"Secondly, the fact that the unprecedented development of technique and the increasing uniformity of the level of development in capitalist countries have enabled and assisted some countries spasmodically to overtake others, have enabled the less powerful but rapidly developing countries to crowd out the more powerful ones.

"Thirdly, the fact that the old division of spheres of influence between individual imperialist groups is continually coming into conflict with the new relation of forces on the world market, that for the establishment of 'equilibrium' between the old distribution of spheres of influence and the new relation of forces, periodic redivisions of the world are necessary by means of imperialist wars." *

Wars of conquest, inevitable under imperialism, bring about tremendous changes in the relation of forces among the various nations. The imperialist war of 1914-18 brought about the smashing of Germany, the parcelling out of Austria-Hungary and the establishment of a number of new states on its ruins. The unevenness of development of the various countries is manifested with particular clarity and explicitness in the post-war years. America gained most by the war. It profited most from the struggle of the others. Formerly, it was indebted to other countries, especially England. Now almost the entire world, including England, is in debt to America. A number of branches of industry in America almost doubled production after the war.

Less than 7 per cent of the world's population is concentrated in the U.S.A. which occupies about 6 per cent of the earth's surface. At the same time, up to the present crisis, 40 per cent of the world's coal mines, 35 per cent of hydro-electrical energy, 70 per cent of the oil, 60 per cent of the world's wheat and cotton, 55 per cent of the timber for construction purposes, approximately 50 per cent of the iron and copper and about 40 per cent of the lead and phosphates of the world were produced there. Up to the time of the crisis, the U.S.A. consumed 42 per cent of the world's output of iron, 47 per cent of the copper, 69 per cent of the oil, 56 per cent of the rubber, 53 per cent of the tin, 48 per cent of the coffee, 21 per cent of the sugar, 72 per cent of the silk and 80 per cent of the automobiles.

* Stalin, "Once More on the Social-Democratic Deviations."

On the other hand, England, which had occupied first place in world economy before the war, declined rapidly. After the war England became a usurer-land, and a number of the most important branches of industry, particularly the coal industry, remained at the same level, while rival countries forged ahead.

The present crisis brought about tremendous changes in the relation of forces among the various capitalist robber nations. It hit different countries with different force. Thus it increased the unevenness of development still more. It affected the U.S.A. the most severely. That is why the United States does not occupy the same place now that it occupied a few years ago. Then, America was the sole "ideological ruler" of the European bourgeoisie and the leaders of Social-Democracy. Now, the crisis has exposed all the deep contradictions of American capitalism. Not a trace of the much lauded American "prosperity" has remained. Of course, the U.S.A. is still the biggest and strongest capitalist country. Its weakening, however, strengthens the contradictions which are rending the capitalist world.

The law of uneven development and the proletarian revolution

The law of uneven development, sharpened by the imperialist epoch, shatters all the utopian theories of the possibility of a lasting peaceful agreement among the monopolists of various countries. The growth of contradictions among the imperialist robbers and the inevitability of military conflicts bring about a mutual weakening of the imperialists, bring about a situation where the world front of imperialism is most vulnerable to the onslaught of proletarian revolution. On this basis, *a breach in this front* results at the point where the chain of the imperialist front is weakest, where conditions are most favourable for the victory of the proletariat. Inseparably bound up with this law of the uneven development of capitalism, which reaches its point of greatest acuteness in the epoch of imperialism, is the Leninist teaching of the triumph of the proletarian revolution and the building of socialism in a single country—a teaching that was subjected to the severest attacks on the part of Trotskyism. Lenin has written about this as follows:

"Uneven economic and political development is an absolute law of capitalism. Hence, the victory of socialism is possible, first in a few or even in one single capitalist country. The victorious proletariat of that country, having expropriated the capitalists and organized its own socialist production, would confront the rest of the capitalist world, attract to itself the oppressed classes of other countries, raise revolts among them against the capitalists, and, in the event of necessity, come out even with armed force against the exploiting classes and their states." *

Thus the Leninist law of uneven development is of tremendous significance for *revolutionary practice*. Stalin points out that even during the war, Lenin, basing himself on the law of the uneven development of imperialist countries, counterposed to the theory of the opportunists his theory of the proletarian revolution, the teaching of the triumph of socialism in a single country "even though this country is capitalistically less developed."

At the same time, the opportunists of all countries try to cover up their betrayal of the revolution by asserting that the proletarian revolution must begin all over the world simultaneously. The traitors of the revolution thus create for themselves a sort of *mutual responsibility*. The doctrine of the law of uneven development is subjected to furious attacks on the part of the Social-Democratic theoreticians and, primarily, counter-revolutionary Trotskyism, the vanguard of the counter-revolutionary bourgeoisie. Trotsky and his adherents claim that under imperialism the unevenness of development of individual countries does not increase but decreases. Trotskyism does not see those decisive contradictions which predetermine the growth of unevenness in the epoch of imperialism. Fighting against the Leninist law of uneven development, Trotskyism reaches the social-democratic conclusion that it is impossible to build socialism in a single country. The Trotskyist denial of the possibility of the victory of socialism in the U.S.S.R. is closely bound up with the Trotskyist "theory of permanent revolution," with a lack of faith in the possibility of a firm alliance between the proletariat and the masses of middle peasants, a lack of faith in the power and creative abilities of the proletariat in building socialism.

* Lenin, *Selected Works*, Vol. V, "The United States of Europe Slogan," p. 141.

Trotskyism is carrying on a desperate struggle against the Leninist policy of the Communist Party of the Soviet Union, which is bent on building socialism in the Soviet Union. A particularly prominent role in exposing the counter-revolutionary character of Trotskyism was played by Stalin. During the many years that the C.P.S.U. carried on a struggle against Trotskyism, Stalin brilliantly exposed the counter-revolutionary, Menshevik essence of the Trotskyist positions, no matter how "Left" the phrases under which they were masked.

The complete collapse of the Trotskyist positions is unequivocally shown up by the historic victories of the First Five-Year Plan. Summing up the results of the First Five-Year Plan, Stalin said:

> "The results of the Five-Year Plan have smashed the social-democratic thesis that it is impossible to build socialism in a single country taken by itself. The results of the Five-Year Plan have shown that it is quite possible to build socialist society in a single country, because the economic foundations of such a society have already been laid in the U.S.S.R." *

The theory of ultra-imperialism

In opposition to the Leninist theory of imperialism the Social-Democrats have formulated the false theory of ultra-imperialism, the author of which is Kautsky, who has enormous experience in the distortion and falsification of Marxism and who now comes out as one of the most brazen slanderers of and agitators for intervention against the Soviet Union.

The substance of Kautsky's views, against which Lenin fought determinedly, is the following: Kautsky denies that imperialism is a distinct stage, phase, or a new step in the development of capitalism, distinguished primarily by deep economic peculiarities. According to Kautsky, imperialism is not an economic system but merely a certain policy of the capitalists of certain countries. Kautsky's principal definition, against which Lenin fought determinedly, says:

* Stalin, "The Results of the First Five-Year Plan," in the symposium: *From the First to the Second Five-Year Plan*, p. 59.

> " 'Imperialism is a product of highly developed industrial capitalism. It consists in the striving of every industrial capitalist nation to bring under its control and to annex increasingly big *agrarian* regions irrespective of what nations inhabit those regions.' " *

"This definition is utterly false theoretically," says Lenin. What is false about this definition? Lenin exposes Kautsky thus:

> "The distinguishing feature of imperialism is *not* the domination of industrial capital but that of finance capital, the striving to annex, not agrarian countries particularly, but *all kinds* of countries. Kautsky *separates* imperialist politics from imperialist economics, he separates monopoly in politics from monopoly in economics in order to pave the way for his vulgar, bourgeois reformism such as 'disarmament,' 'ultra-imperialism' and similar nonsense. The meaning and the aim of this theoretical falsehood is to gloss over the *profound* contradictions of imperialism and thus to justify the theory of 'unity' with the apologists of imperialism, the frank social-chauvinists and opportunists." **

Lenin stresses the fact that Kautsky's definition is incorrect and non-Marxian. This definition is the basis of a whole system of views which completely break away from Marxism both in theory and in practice. Tearing politics away from economics, depicting imperialism as merely a policy preferred by some capitalist countries, Kautsky altogether assumes the position of the bourgeois reformists who think that it is possible to achieve more "peaceful" policies without infringing on the inviolability of the economic system of imperialism. That is why with Kautsky, as Lenin keenly points out,

> "The result is a slurring over and a concealment of the most profound contradictions of the latest stage of capitalism instead of an exposure of their depth. The result is bourgeois reformism instead of Marxism." ***

* Quoted by Lenin, in *Imperialism, the Highest Stage of Capitalism*, p. 87.

** Lenin, *Collected Works*, Vol. XIX, "Imperialism and the Split in the Socialist Movement," p. 303, Russian ed.

*** Lenin, *Imperialism, the Highest Stage of Capitalism*, p. 89.

Kautsky's counter-revolutionary, thoroughly bourgeois position becomes particularly evident in his arguments about so-called "ultra-imperialism" (*i.e.*, super-imperialism), which are based directly on his fundamentally anti-Marxian definition of imperialism.

The theory of ultra-imperialism asserts that, as a result of the growth of monopoly associations in separate countries, the contradictions and struggles among the various countries disappear, the capitalists of these various countries forming alliances among themselves; imperialist wars are relegated to the past, a united world economy results. This theory of "peaceful" ultra-imperialism is thoroughly hostile to revolutionary Marxism. It completely distorts the picture of imperialist reality. Refuting this invention of Kautsky's, Lenin writes:

> "Compare this reality, the vast diversity of economic and political conditions, the extreme disparity in the rates of development of the various countries, and the violent struggles of the imperialist states, with Kautsky's stupid little fable about 'peaceful' ultra-imperialism. Is this not the reactionary attempt of a frightened philistine to hide from stern reality? Do not the international cartels which Kautsky imagines are the embryos of ultra-imperialism . . . represent an example of the division and the *redivision* of the world, the transition from peaceful division to *violent* division and *vice versa*? Is not American and other finance capital, which divided the whole world peacefully, with the participation of Germany, for example, in the international rail syndicate, or in the international mercantile shipping trust, now engaged in *redividing* the world on the basis of a new relation of forces, which has been changed by methods *by no means* peaceful?" *

The uneven development of various countries, which becomes more pronounced under imperialism, *completely refutes* the theory of ultra-imperialism. Lenin wrote as follows in reference to this:

> "Kautsky's meaningless talk about ultra-imperialism encourages, among other things, that profoundly mistaken idea which only brings grist to the mill of the apologists of imperial-

* *Ibid.*, p. 92.

ism, *viz.*, that the domination of finance capital *lessens* the unevennesses and contradictions inherent in world economy, whereas in reality it *increases* them." *

Being a bourgeois reformist and apologist of imperialism, Kautsky tries to *gloss over* its sharpest *contradictions*. He denies the proposition that imperialism is a separate phase in the development of capitalism. This denial is necessary to him in order to slur over all the fundamental peculiarities of this newest phase by reason of which imperialism is the eve of the socialist revolution. The theory of ultra-imperialism, as a number of its later variations, is directed against the Leninist law of uneven development, which reaches its highest point under imperialism. The theory of ultra-imperialism denies the increasing unevenness in the development of capitalism in the epoch of imperialism and closes its eyes to the most obvious facts which are clear evidence of this unevenness. Kautsky denies the significance of monopoly domination as a fundamental distinguishing attribute of the new period in the development of capitalism. He denies the tendency towards decay connected with monopolies. He carefully glosses over the parasitic character of imperialism. He denies the proposition that imperialism is moribund capitalism. On the contrary, his theory of ultra-imperialism issues from the premise that imperialism is not at all the last stage of capitalism, that capitalism does not exhaust its resources in the epoch of imperialism. Here, Kautsky shares the position of all the learned lackeys of the bourgeoisie, who exert themselves to prove that capitalism is going to exist for a long time yet and that it is only now stepping into maturity.

Kautsky's position on questions of imperialism is characteristic of the ideology of international Social-Democracy. Rosa Luxemburg, whose mistakes the Trotskyist contrabandists adopted when they attempted to foist their ideas on the world under the guise of idealizing Luxemburgism, made *mistakes* of a clearly Kautskyist type on the question of imperialism. She considered imperialism not as a separate stage in the development of capitalism, but as a definite policy of the new period. In her principal

* *Ibid.*, p. 90.

theoretical work, *The Accumulation of Capital*, Luxemburg concludes that a collapse is inevitable not because the inner contradictions of capitalism become extremely acute in the epoch of imperialism, but because of the conflict of capitalism with its external surroundings, because of the impossibility of realizing surplus value under so-called "pure" capitalism (*i.e.*, a capitalist society consisting only of capitalists and workers without any "non-capitalist mass" in the form of small producers). Basing herself thus on semi-Menshevik positions, Luxemburg could not rise to the Leninist conception of imperialism, to a correct understanding of its fundamental peculiarities and distinguishing attributes. Luxemburg's mistakes in the conception of imperialism are closely allied to her erroneous positions on a number of important political questions: the question of the split in Social-Democracy, the agrarian and national questions, the role of the Party and spontaneous elements in the movements, etc. The theory of the automatic collapse of capitalism, ensuing from Luxemburg's erroneous theory of reproduction, in practice disarms the working class, spreads a mood of *passivity* and *fatalism* in its midst, stultifying its will to struggle. It is perfectly evident that the Kautskyist errors of Luxemburg on the question of imperialism kept her from severing relations with Kautsky and Kautskyism, serving as a sort of bridge connecting her to the Kautskyist centre even during the progress of the imperialist war when the absolute treachery of Kautsky and his complete desertion to the counter-revolutionary camp of imperialism became perfectly evident.

The Trotskyist position on the theory of imperialism is *only one of the varieties of Kautskyism*. During the war Lenin repeatedly established the fact that Trotsky is a Kautskyist, that he shares Kautsky's views, defending and glossing over Kautsky's distortions of Marxism. In defending the Kautskyist position, Trotskyism comes out with particular venom against the Leninist law of uneven development. And this is really not surprising. We have already seen that the law of uneven development does not leave a single stone of the whole traitorous and counter-revolutionary Kautskyist structure of "ultra-imperialism" unturned. Trotskyism builds its counter-revolutionary theory of the impossibility of building socialism in a single country on the denial of the Leninist law of uneven development.

The leaders of Social-Democracy depict matters as if the growth of monopoly leads to the replacement of capitalist anarchy by a new system—that of *organized capitalism.*

The theory of organized capitalism

The Social-Democratic theoreticians began to spread the legend about organized capitalism particularly during the post-war years of partial stabilization. The most prominent disseminator of this theory is one of the most brazen leaders of Social-Democracy—Hilferding. The Social-Democrats try to maintain that with the growth of monopoly there is an end to the blind forces of the market. Capitalism supposedly *organizes itself*, competition disappears, *anarchy* of production is *eliminated, crises* become things of the past, *planned, conscious organization* predominates. From this the Social-Democrats reach the conclusion that trusts and cartels peacefully *grow into planned*, socialist economy; supposedly, one must only help the bankers and trusts straighten things out for themselves and then capitalism will of itself, unnoticed, without any struggle or revolution "grow" into socialism!

It is quite clear that the theory of organized capitalism is a further development of Kautsky's theory of ultra-imperialism. The Social-Democratic theory of organized capitalism also *glosses over* and *befogs* the glaring contradictions of imperialism, just as Kautsky's theory of ultra-imperialism does. Lenin pointed out that Hilferding, even before the war, in denying the parasitism and decay characteristic of imperialism, stood even lower than some of the bourgeois scientists who, on investigating imperialism, could not help noting these phenomena which stand out glaringly.

The theory of organized capitalism, promising a peaceful and painless transition to socialism, serves as a means of deceiving the more backward elements of the working class, of keeping them away from the revolutionary struggle.

This counter-revolutionary theory is *refuted* at every step by contemporary capitalist reality. This theory is completely shattered as soon as it is regarded in the light of the analysis of imperialism given by Lenin.

We have already seen that *imperialism* does not eliminate, but, on the contrary, strengthens and *sharpens* all the fundamental *contradictions* of the capitalist system. *Anarchy of production* not only does not disappear, but, on the contrary, assumes *gigantic proportions* and gives rise to particularly devastating consequences. *Competition* between the monopoly alliances is much fiercer than it formerly was between individual capitalists. Under imperialism crises become *severer* and more *devastating*, and their consequences affect the working class even more cruelly. The crisis of 1907 already bore witness to this fact, as it struck the country where monopoly had grown most—the U.S.A.—with particular force. The present *world crisis* of capitalism most thoroughly and completely exposes the futility of the legend about organized capitalism, disseminated by the lackeys of the bourgeoisie.

The legend of organized capitalism was caught up by the Right wing opportunists in the ranks of the C.P.S.U. and other Parties in the Communist International. Comrade Bukharin claimed that "the problems of markets, prices, competition and crises become ever more problems of world economy, being replaced within the country by problems of organization."

From this the Right opportunists drew the inference that the inner contradictions in capitalist countries are abating, that capitalism is getting stronger and that there could be talk about a rise in the revolutionary tide only after a new imperialist war.

The crude error with regard to the theory of organized capitalism is not accidental with Comrade Bukharin. This anti-Leninist position is closely connected with a whole series of errors in the field of the theory of imperialism, which he had committed beginning with the commencement of the war. Lenin fought Bukharin's mistakes over a number of years (1915-20). Against Lenin's theory, Bukharin counterposed his own theory of so-called "pure imperialism." Captured by "Left" phrases and masking themselves with them, the adherents of this theory, in practice, allied themselves to the opportunist social-democratic views on questions of imperialism.

The main fault in Bukharin's theory of "pure" imperialism lies in its extreme simplification and incorrect representation of imperialist reality. The adherents of this theory gloss over the deepest contradictions inherent in imperialism. They shut their eyes to the fact that imperialism grows out of and develops on the basis of the old capitalism, that because of this imperialism does not eliminate the fundamental contradictions of capitalism but, on the contrary, sharpens them to the extreme.

In his report on the Party program at the Eighth Congress of the Party in 1919, Lenin, touching on his disagreements with Bukharin, pointed out that

"... pure imperialism, without the fundamental base of capitalism, never existed, does not exist now and never will exist." *

In the same speech Lenin said further:

"Bukharin's concreteness is a bookish description of finance capitalism. Nowhere in the world does monopoly capitalism exist without free competition in a number of fields, nor will it exist in the future."

And Lenin continued:

"If we had to deal with an integral imperialism which had completely remade capitalism our problem would be a thousandfold easier. We should then have a system where everything was subject to finance capital only. Then we should only have to remove this control and leave the rest to the proletariat. This would be very agreeable, unfortunately it is not so in reality. In reality the development is such that we have to act entirely differently. Imperialism is a superstructure on capitalism. ... We have the old capitalism which, in a number of fields, has grown up into imperialism." **

The erroneous theory of "pure" imperialism, defended by Bukharin when he was one of the leaders of the group of so-called "Left Communists," served as the direct basis for the theory of organized capitalism.

The present crisis of capitalism clearly exposed the absolute untenability of this theory. It is quite evident that this opportunist fiction about organized capitalism, borrowed from the Social-Democrats, has nothing whatever to do with Marxism-Leninism. Lenin repeatedly emphasized that monopolies, growing out of competition, do not eliminate it but exist over and alongside it, giving rise thereby to a special sharpening of all contradictions and conflicts. Lenin has written:

* Lenin, *Collected Works*, Vol. XXIV, "Report on the Party Program," p. 131, Russian ed.
** *Ibid.*, pp. 133-34.

"Imperialism aggravates and sharpens the contradictions of capitalism, it intertwines monopoly with free competition, but it cannot *abolish* exchange, the market, competition, crises, etc.

"Imperialism is capitalism passing away, not capitalism gone . . . dying, not dead. Not pure monopolies, but monopolies alongside of exchange, markets, competition and crises—this, generally, is the most essential feature of imperialism." *

That is why Lenin emphasized that

"It is this very combination of contradictory principles, of competition and monopoly, that is the essence of imperialism, it is this that leads to the final crash, the socialist revolution." **

The parasitism and decay of capitalism

Imperialism is *parasitic* or *decaying capitalism.* Capitalist monopolies inevitably give rise to a tendency towards stagnation and decay. They tend to establish monopoly prices and maintain them at a high level. With free competition every capitalist tries to increase his profits by cutting down his outlay on production, and in order to cut down his outlay all kinds of technical improvements are introduced. Monopolies, inasmuch as they can maintain high monopoly prices, are not interested in the introduction of technical innovations. On the contrary, they frequently fear technical inventions more than anything else, since they threaten to undermine their monopolist hold on production or to make their tremendous capital investments valueless. Monopolies thus frequently *delay technical progress* artificially. The epoch of imperialism knows countless such instances.

In his work on imperialism Lenin cites the example of the Owens bottling machine which was invented before the war in the U.S.A. A German cartel bought the Owens patents and held up their utilization. The post-war period knows a number of such instances. Not so long ago an electric lamp that cannot burn out was invented, an "everlasting lamp." This invention has not been put on the market to this day because it would curtail the sale

* Lenin, *Collected Works,* Vol. XX, Book I, p, 331, International Publishers, New York, 1929.

** *Ibid.*

of lamps by the electrical equipment monopoly trusts. The Swedish Kreuger Match Trust that had its tentacles over practically the entire world and worked with the help of American banks was not a little disturbed by the invention of an "everlasting" match by a certain Viennese chemist. The method of obtaining oil from coal, discovered by Professor Bergius of Germany, has been bought out by the American oil trust which is holding up its application. The American railroads are not being electrified only because it would be disadavantageous to the monopolists.

Nevertheless, it must be borne in mind that the tendency to increase profits by means of technical improvements persists to a certain extent. That is why the biggest trusts establish excellent laboratories and scientific research institutes where thousands of engineers, chemists and physicists work. Because of monopolies, however, only a small part of the discoveries are applied. Under certain conditions now one, now the other tendency comes to the surface, now the tendency towards stagnation, now the tendency towards technical improvement.

Trotskyism distinguishes itself by a total lack of comprehension of the real character of the contradictions of imperialism as a parasitic and decaying system. Trotskyism does not perceive the *struggle* of two tendencies that is in effect under imperialism: the tendency to develop the productive forces on the one hand, and the tendency to retard technical progress on the other. It is this *struggle*, the continuous *conflict* of these tendencies, that gives rise to the *sharpening of contradictions* which is characteristic of imperialism. Trotskyism tries to make things appear as if there is absolute stagnation of technical development under imperialism, a complete "bottling up" of the development of productive forces. Such a viewpoint leads directly to the traitorous theory of the "automatic collapse of capitalism," with which we became acquainted above. This position is also inseparably connected with the Trotskyist denial of the Leninist law of uneven development under imperialism.

The parasitic character of the bourgeoisie is manifested with particular clarity in the epoch of imperialism. The overwhelming majority of the bourgeoisie has absolutely no connection with the process of production. The majority of the capitalists are people who live by "clipping coupons." The capitalists have become owners of shares, bonds, government loans and other securities which bring them an income. Enterprises are managed by hired technical forces. The bourgeoisie and its numerous toadies (politicians, the bourgeois intelligentsia, the clergy, etc.) consume the products of the arduous labour of millions of hired slaves of capital. Entire countries (like Switzerland) or whole regions (in the South of France, Italy, partly England) are turned into playgrounds for the international bourgeoisie where they come to spend their unearned incomes on mad luxury.

The epoch of imperialism brings with it a great *decline* of capitalist civilization. *Venality* grows and penetrates all spheres of politics, public life, art, etc. The biggest monopolies openly maintain in their pay definite groups of representatives in parliament, high government officials, etc. The heads of governments are most closely connected with the biggest banks, corporations and trusts. Millions in "presents" to the higher government officials make it possible for the banks and trusts to do anything they please in the country. The press is the hireling of big capital. The oldest and most "meritorious" bourgeois newspapers change their political physiognomy at once upon going over to a new owner. An enormous number of yellow journals prove to be owned by the same businessmen. Thus in Germany after the war the great majority of yellow journals and even a great many "serious" newspapers were owned by the big capitalist, Stinnes, who had grown rich during and particularly after the war, by the most unrestrained speculation. After the collapse of the Stinnes concern that had owned coal and ore mines, ocean steamship lines and cinemas, a large part of his fortune in newspapers fell to another big capitalist in heavy industry—Hugenberg (one of the leaders of the German bourgeoisie who did most towards the ascension to power of the bloody fascist dictatorship of Hitler).

Outright fraudulence, forgery, deceit and cheating become more and more the customary means of rising for the big capitalists and bourgeois politicians. These crimes are only rarely discovered—in cases of fiascos, when loud scandals result. Thus, in 1932 the scandal about Ivar Kreuger—the head of the Swedish match trust and one of the most violent instigators of anti-Soviet intervention—burst over the entire world. He committed suicide when on the verge of bankruptcy. After his suicide a whole chain of forgeries and misrepresentations were revealed, by means of which he wanted to save himself from the collapse that threatened him in the circumstances of the crisis. The same year, 1932, marked a tremendous scandal in France about the Oustric Stock Company, which proved to be the work of a few clever swindlers connected with the most prominent government politicians and bankers. With the help of all kinds of false promises this gang succeeded in drawing tens of millions of francs out of the pockets of credulous petty bourgeois. In 1933 in the U.S.A. much noise was occasioned by the discovery of a number of shady transactions by the biggest capitalist of that country—Morgan.

In America there are several well organized bands of gangsters which are particularly notorious and which even enjoy respect. They have their own trusts which maintain the best of relations with the police and the government.

In the foremost countries imperialism *bribes the upper circles* of the working class. From the enormous incomes obtained from the colonies, the super-profits squeezed out of the backward countries and at the expense of greater oppression and impoverishment of the great mass of the proletariat, trustified capital raises the wages and generally improves the conditions of a small, privileged section of the workers. This bribed section of the proletariat becomes a bulwark of the bourgeois order. Imperialism, however, can only bribe a very small minority of the working class. This bribery is at the expense of the continually greater exploitation of the basic mass of the working class. In the end, it leads to an even greater growth of class contradictions, to an even greater deepening of the chasm between the classes.

Imperialism—the epoch of the doom of capitalism

Imperialism is a distinct historical stage of capitalism. This *distinctiveness* is, as we have seen, *threefold*: imperialism is, first, *monopoly* capitalism; secondly, *parasitic* or decaying capitalism, and thirdly, *moribund* capitalism. This characterization of the epoch of imperialism, the epoch of monopolies, as an epoch of parasitic, decaying, moribund capitalism is the dividing line separating revolutionary Marxism-Leninism from all kinds of distortions and falsifications of Marxism. In the epoch of imperialism all the fundamental contradictions of capitalism reach their final limits, are sharpened to the utmost degree. The most important of these, as Stalin points out in his book on the foundations of Leninism, are three contradictions.

These are: first, *the antagonism between labour and capital.* Imperialism denotes the omnipotence of a handful of capitalists in the monopolies and banks. The oppression of the financial oligarchy is so great that the previous methods of struggle of the working class—labour unions of the old type, parliamentary parties—prove entirely inadequate. Imperialism, increasing the impoverishment of the working class to an unprecedented degree, increasing the exploitation of the workers by a small group of monopolist and banker sharks, puts the problem of new, revolutionary methods of struggle before the workers in its full force. Imperialism brings the worker face to face with revolution.

Secondly, *the antagonisms between the various cliques* of financial sharks and between *imperialist powers* in their constant struggle to seize new territories, sources of raw material and markets for sales and for the investment of capital. This frenzied struggle between the individual imperialist cliques inevitably leads to wars in which the biggest imperialist powers shed oceans of blood and pile up mountains of corpses in the struggle to redivide the already divided world, in the struggle to grab new sources of enrichment for a few billionaires. The struggle of the imperialists inevitably leads to their mutual weakening, to the weakening of the capitalist positions in general, and thus brings closer the day of the proletarian revolution, makes this absolutely necessary in order to save society from perishing altogether.

Thirdly, *the antagonism between the small number* of the so-called *"civilized" nations* and the enormous masses of the population of *the colonial and dependent countries.* Hundreds of millions of people waste away in the colonial and semi-colonial world under the domination of imperialist robbers.

> "Imperialism means the most shameless exploitation and the most inhuman oppression of hundreds of millions of the population of vast colonies and dependent countries." *

* Stalin, *Leninism*, Vol. I, p. 16, International Publishers, 1934.

Hunting super-profits, the imperialists build plants and factories in the colonies and semi-colonial countries, build railroads there, break up the old order of things, clear the way with fire and sword for new capitalist relations. The growth of imperialist exploitation leads to the strengthening of the liberation movement in the colonies and dependent countries, weakening the capitalist position throughout the world, undermining it at its roots, and leading to the transformation of these countries, as Stalin points out, "from reserves of imperialism into reserves of the proletarian revolution." The national liberation movement in the colonies becomes a threat to imperialism, a support for the revolutionary proletariat.

The extreme sharpening of all the contradictions brings about a situation in which imperialism becomes the *eve of the socialist revolution.* Capitalist contradictions sharpen to such a degree that the further maintenance of capitalist relations becomes an unbearable encumbrance to the further development of human society. Capitalist relations hinder the further progress of the productive forces; as a result of this, capitalism decays and begins to fall to pieces while still alive. This tendency to decay does not exclude the development of individual countries or individual branches of industry even in a period of a general capitalist crisis. Tremendous amounts of value are wasted unproductively under imperialism; the capitalist class with all its toadies finally becomes a most malignant parasitic cancer which presses more and more unbearably on the tremendous masses of disinherited toilers. Monopoly capitalism at the same time creates all the necessary premises for the realization of socialism.

> "The extremely high degree of development of world capitalism in general and the replacement of free competition by state monopoly capitalism, the fact that the banks and the capitalist corporations are creating an apparatus for the social regulation of the process of production and distribution of products, the rise in prices and increased oppression of the working class by the syndicates due to the growth of capitalist monopolies, the enslavement of the working class by the imperialist state, the gigantic handicaps imposed on the economic and political struggle of the proletariat, the horrors, calamities and ruin caused by the imperialist war—all make the collapse of capitalism and

the transition to a higher type of social economic system inevitable." *

Imperialism inevitably leads to devastating imperialist wars. The World War of 1914-18 plunged the entire capitalist system into a general crisis, characterized by the extreme acuteness and intensity of all the contradictions of imperialism. The principles laid down by the Comintern on the question of the general crisis of capitalism, which means a period of dissolution and collapse of capitalism, are based directly on the Leninist theory of imperialism and form an integral part of it, an inseparable link. The assertions of all kinds of Trotskyist contrabandists, who deny the principles laid down by the Comintern concerning the general crisis of capitalism, signify their complete renegacy from Marxism-Leninism, their complete break with the Leninist theory of imperialism.

Imperialism is the epoch of the downfall and destruction of capitalism, the period of the victorious proletarian revolution. Lenin more than once pointed out:

> "Imperialism is the highest stage of development of capitalism. Capital in the advanced countries has outgrown the boundaries of national states. It has established monopoly in place of competition, thus creating all the objective prerequisites for the achievement of socialism." **

Elsewhere Lenin says that the epoch of imperialism is the epoch of ripe and over-ripe capitalism which is on the eve of its collapse. matured to the extent that it must yield its place to socialism.

The epoch of imperialism is therefore the epoch of the collapse and destruction of capitalism, the era of proletarian revolutions.

Review Questions

1. How does competition lead to the formation of monopolies?
2. Do monopolies eliminate competition?
3. What is the source of the profits of the monopolists?
4. How does the role of the banks change in the epoch of imperialism?

* *The Program and Rules of the Communist Party of the Soviet Union (Bolsheviks)*, p. 6, Moscow, 1932.

** Lenin, *Selected Works*. Vol. V, "The Socialist Revolution and the Right of Nations to Self-Determination," p. 267.

5. What gives rise to the export of capital?
6. What is the function of tariffs?
7. What is the law of uneven development?
8. What is there essentially traitorous in the theory of organized capitalism?
9. How is the theory of organized capitalism connected with the theory of ultra-imperialism?
10. How does the decay of capitalism manifest itself under imperialism?
11. What are the five fundamental attributes of imperialism?

CHAPTER X

The War and the General Crisis of Capitalism

The fundamental contradictions of the capitalist order reach their *highest development* in the epoch of imperialism. On the one side—a handful of degenerate capitalist magnates; on the other—the tremendous majority of disinherited humanity. Such is the picture of capitalist society under the domination of imperialism.

Imperialism and the collapse of capitalism

In the epoch of imperialism the decay and decline of the capitalist order takes place. The existing order becomes an impediment to further development. Human thought, science and engineering record ever new victories over nature. Man subjects one after another of its most terrible forces to his will. The fruit of these victories, however, is gathered by a handful of the elect. More than that, capitalist relations narrow down the possibility of applying many of the most brilliant discoveries and inventions.

Mankind as a whole has become wealthy enough for everyone to be provided with a good existence. What prevents this is again capitalist relationships. Tremendous wealth is used not for the benefit of the broad masses, but to their detriment. Devastating wars, inevitable under imperialism, take many human victims, destroy the fruit of the hard labour of many generations.

Socialism or destruction, socialism or inevitable degeneration—that is how the question is put in the epoch of imperialism. The world proletariat must carry out a task of the utmost importance—they must tear mankind away from the clutches of imperialism. In the struggle for the overthrow of the reign of imperialism the proletariat finds many *allies* among the disinherited of the earth. The toiling masses of the colonial countries, who feel on their own backs the full "charm" of the imperialist regime, the ruined masses of the peasantry and the intermediate sections of toilers, are the source of assistance for the proletariat in its struggle for the overthrow of capitalism. Regardless of temporary defeats in one country or another, the final victory of the proletariat is inevitable.

Thus imperialism brings the class contradictions and the class struggle to an extreme acuteness. In this struggle the *fate* of the capitalist system is decided. Hence the struggle is a very stubborn one.

The unevenness of capitalist development, increased in the epoch of imperialism, creates different conditions for the victory of the proletariat in the different countries. Naturally the proletariat captures power and proceeds with the building of socialism first of all in those countries where and when conditions are the most favourable.

> "Enormous technical progress in general, and of the means of communication in particular, the colossal growth of capital and banks have resulted in a ripening and over-ripening of capitalism. It has outlived itself, has become a most reactionary hindrance to human development. It has reduced itself to the reign of an omnipotent handful of billionaires and millionaires, inciting nations to mutual slaughter in order to decide whether a German or an Anglo-French group of robbers are to get the imperialist plunder: power over the colonies, financial 'spheres of influence' or 'administrative mandates,' etc.
>
> "During the war of 1914-18, tens of millions of men were killed and maimed for this reason, and for this reason alone. An understanding of this truth is spreading with uncontrollable force and rapidity among the masses of toilers in all lands—and this so much the more since the war has wrought unprecedented ruin everywhere, and everyone, including the 'victorious' nations, has to pay for the war in interest on debts.
>
> "The collapse of capitalism is inevitable. The revolutionary consciousness of the masses is growing. Thousands of indications speak of this.
>
> "The capitalists, the bourgeoisie, may, under circumstances most favourable for themselves, delay the victory of socialism in one or another individual country at the cost of the destruc-

tion of additional hundreds of thousands of workers and peasants. But save capitalism they cannot."*

The imperialist World War

The struggle between the imperialists for a redivision of the world brought about the World War of 1914-18. This war shook the capitalist system to its very foundation and brought untold suffering to the masses of the people. In all the warring countries sixty-two million men were called to arms. More than ten million were killed and the number of wounded and maimed who remained cripples for life reached twenty-four million. Tremendous wealth of the most prosperous countries in the world was senselessly shot into the air. It has been estimated that the war cost three hundred billion dollars. In order to grasp this figure it should be noted that the entire wealth of all the warring countries on the eve of the war amounted to six hundred billion dollars. The war thus swallowed a sum amounting to half of what all the nations of Europe had been able to amass at the price of arduous, slave-like labour for many generations.

The war wrought havoc with capitalist world economy. It broke whatever connections had existed between certain states. Some of the countries became completely isolated (Germany). The supply of imported raw material and food was curtailed. Tremendous masses of the producing population, workers and peasants, were withdrawn from their occupations by the call to arms. In some countries almost one-third of all the workers in industry and agriculture was under arms. It must not be forgotten that the war took the best producing sections of the population—healthy young men. Only old men, adolescents and women, whose labour was of course much inferior, were left at home.

Tremendous regions were devastated and reduced to ashes in the process of military actions. The fronts in the World War were located not only in agricultural sections but often in most important industrial centres also. Ravaging artillery fire wiped plants and factories off the face of the earth. Mines were flooded. Entire

* Lenin, *Collected Works*, Vol. XXIV, "Answers to the Questions of American Journalists," p. 404, Russian ed.

cities, industrial regions, were wiped out as, for instance, Northern France where the most important front of the World War—the Western Front—was located.

Finally, the most important feature of the economic ruin wrought by the war was the transformation of the entire national economy, changing the character of production at the dictates of the needs of warfare.

With the advent of war the character of production changed radically. To the former three basic varieties of commodities—means of production, articles of consumption and articles of luxury—a fourth was now added, occupying an ever more prominent place: instruments of destruction and extermination—artillery, ammunition, war planes, submarines, rifles, tanks, poison gas, etc. The expenses of the World War amounted to $300,000,000,000 at a time when the entire wealth of the warring countries amounted to about $600,000,000,000. The annual national income of these countries amounted to $85,000,000,000. If we assume that the national income of each country during the war was reduced only one-third because of the tremendous withdrawal of workers and thus amounted to approximately $57,000,000,000, and if we further assume that the entire non-military expenditure absorbed 55 per cent, we reach the conclusion that the current national incomes could only cover war expenses to the amount of $25,000,000,000 a year. For the four years of the war this makes $100,000,000,000. Consequently, the other $200,000,000,000 had to come from the fixed capital of the warring nations. It therefore follows that the total wealth of these nations after the war no longer was $600,000,000,000 but only $400,000,000,000, *i.e.* one-third less.

The war wrought untold havoc in the field of human labour power.

In 1913 the population of Europe was 401,000,000 and with the normal growth of population, had there been no war, it should have been 424,500,000 in 1919. Actually it was only 389,000,000. In other words, Europe lost 35,500,000 people, or 9 per cent of its entire population. The influence of the war in the reduction of the European population was felt, first, in the direct loss of life—on the front in battles, and in the rear because of epidemics; secondly, in the reduction of the birth rate, since almost all the men were mobilized, and thirdly, in the increase in the death rate due to worse living conditions (hunger, privation, etc.).

If we take into consideration that this enormous loss of people was primarily the very best labour power of the warring nations, then the picture of the destruction of the human apparatus of production will become clear.

To this should be added the fact that during the war, wide sections of highly skilled workers were replaced by others of little skill. A decrease in the number of qualified workers employed thus took place, which brought great loss to the nations involved.

The war brought untold torture to the broad masses of toilers. The workers and peasants dressed in military uniforms were cannon fodder at the front where death or unendurable suffering awaited them. The workers who remained in the rear worked in the factories to the point of exhaustion for starvation wages. Under conditions of a military dictatorship, any sign of dissatisfaction on the part of the workers was suppressed in the most unmerciful and inhuman fashion. The workers at the rear lived under constant threat of being shipped to the front where death or injury awaited them. During the war the toiling masses were doomed to starvation.

The war *intensified* to the extreme all the contradictions of the capitalist system. The war widened the gulf between the workers and the capitalists. The war brought ruin to the broad masses of the peasantry. The war contributed towards the undermining of the position of the office employees and the petty bourgeoisie by bringing about their impoverishment.

> ". . . The war is imperialistic on both sides. . . . Both the German and the Anglo-French bourgeoisie are waging war for the grabbing of foreign territory, for the strangulation of small nations, for financial supremacy over the world, for the division and redistribution of colonies, for saving the tottering capitalist regime by means of deceiving and disuniting the workers in the various countries." *

* *Ibid.*, Vol. XX, Book I, p. 29.

The war was an inevitable result of the entire development of imperialism. The war showed that capitalism has finally become a hindrance to the further development of human society. The war disclosed what enormous danger and menace capitalism bears within itself for the further destiny of mankind.

Consequences of the World War and the general crisis of capitalism

The imperialist World War was the beginning of the general crisis of capitalism. A new page was turned in world history. The October Revolution broke through the imperialist front in Russia. In place of tsarist Russia—the bulwark of darkest reaction—the Soviet state arose. One-sixth of the globe was torn from the power of capital and became the country where socialism is being built. The October Revolution marked the beginning of the international socialist revolution of the proletariat. It divided the world into *two camps*—the camp of capitalism and the camp of socialism under construction. It made the first gaping breach in the capitalist structure. In place of the formerly universal capitalism, two systems, radically opposed to each other, are now struggling—the system of capitalism and the system of socialism.

Since the October Revolution capitalism has ceased to be the only existing social order, ruling the earth. Alongside it a new system has grown up, a new order—that of socialism. The Soviet Union is the fatherland of the world proletariat. The present epoch is the epoch of the *downfall and destruction* of capitalism, the epoch of the proletarian world revolution and the *victory of socialism.*

The World War remade the map of the world. It radically changed the relation of forces among the different capitalist countries. The proletarian revolution has triumphed on one-sixth of the world and has wrenched it from under the sway of capital. But in the rest of the world, which has remained in the power of capitalism, very important changes have also taken place.

The war thoroughly undermined the national economy of all the countries that participated in it. The victorious countries—the Allies—of course tried to transfer the whole burden of the war expenses onto the vanquished countries. Among the vanquished, however, it was possible to get something only from Germany since the allies of the latter (Austria-Hungary, Turkey, and Bulgaria) were in a very deplorable state. Germany was the principal enemy of the Allied countries. It had been competition with German imperialism that had brought the imperialist rulers of Great Britain and France to war. Hence the first business of the victors was to settle with Germany, to delete it from the list of possible competitors, to safeguard themselves against its competition by stopping or retarding its economic development for a long time to come. At the same time it was necessary to load the greater part of the war expenses upon Germany. The peace treaty signed in Versailles in 1919 provides a number of measures for pilfering Germany. A number of regions were taken away from Germany, France getting regions rich in coal and iron; Germany further had to turn over its merchant fleet to the Allies; she had to renounce her colonies and all the territories she owned beyond her own borders. Finally—and this is most important—tribute was imposed on Germany in the form of *payments* which were to reimburse the Allied countries for the destruction caused by the war (reparations). These payments were set in Versailles at 132,000,000,000 gold marks; according to the treaty the payments were extended over a number of years.

The pillage of Germany by the robber peace of Versailles resulted in Germany finding itself, of all the countries involved in the war, the most ravaged (with the exception of little Austria which American charity had to save from actual starvation).

The war radically changed the relation of forces in the camp of the victors. The U.S.A. gained most by the war, as it took a very insignificant part in the military action but profited tremendously on all kinds of war supplies. The sun of British capitalism set as a result of the war. Great Britain lost its primacy on the world market. It had to yield its place to its young competitor, the U.S.A. The contradictions between the U.S.A. and Great Britain are the pivot around which the imperialist contradictions of the entire post-war period revolve.

America proved sufficiently powerful to extract tremendous advantages from the war in which its old competitors (primarily, Great Britain and Germany) had cut one another's throats.

The warring countries could not themselves satisfy their growing war requirements of endless mountains of coal, iron, steel, bread, oil and cloth. This tremendous demand came to America.

At the same time the markets for manufactured goods in the agricultural countries of South America, Asia, etc., were freed. Before the war Great Britain, Germany and other European countries exported their goods to these markets. During the war there could be no thought of export from these countries. All this resulted in an unprecedented development of industry and agriculture in the U.S.A. America became the richest country in the world. The war shifted the centre of gravity of world capitalism from Europe to America.

Before the war, industry had not occupied a predominant place in the economy of the U.S.A. In 1905 the U.S.A. had exported agricultural products amounting to $1,000,000,000 and industrial products amounting to only $460,000,000. During the war industry developed with unparalleled rapidity. In 1914 the industries of the U.S.A. produced commodities to a total amount of $24,246,000,000, in 1918 the production already amounted to $62,580,000,000.

During the period of the war the production of textiles rose 40 per cent, of steel 40 per cent, of coal and copper 20 per cent, of zinc 80 per cent, of oil 45 per cent. From 1913 to 1918, the construction of ocean-going steamships increased more than tenfold, the production of automobiles doubled. For the period of the war the U.S.A. was transformed into an industrial country exporting manufactured goods. In 1919 the U.S.A. exported manufactured goods amounting to $2,072,000,000 and only $1,408,000,000 worth of means of consumption and raw material.

However, agriculture in the U.S.A. also made progress during the war. Between 1913 and 1918 the harvest increased 12 per cent and the number of cattle even more.

The war made the U.S.A. *the richest nation* in the world. Before that Great Britain had been the wealthiest: it had played a leading role in the capitalist world, it had owned capital in all lands including America—all were in debt to Great Britain. British currency—the pound sterling—was considered the most stable currency in the world; it was almost impossible to conceive of the depreciation of the British pound. The war changed all this: Great Britain lost a great part of its wealth in the war and receded to second place while the U.S.A. became monstrously wealthy.

From 1915 to 1920 U.S.A. export amounted to $18,000,000,000

more than its import, in other words, it gave the warring nations of Europe goods amounting to $18,000,000,000 more than the goods it received from them. How was this tremendous sum covered? What did the U.S.A. get for it?

First of all, enterprises in the U.S.A. which had previously belonged to European capitalists went over to American owners. The considerable sum of $3-5,000,000,000 went for this purpose. Further, more than half the world's gold reserve was concentrated in America; the warring countries had to give up their gold reserves to America for the great quantities of war supplies and means of consumption which the U.S.A. supplied for their troops and for their population. Finally the Allied debt to America amounted to the enormous sum of $10,000,000,000. Great Britain, in debt to the U.S.A. to the extent of £900,000,000 sterling, was supposed to receive £1,600,000,000 sterling from its debtors. As a result of the agreements reached between 1923 and 1927 on the regulation of the war debts, the indebtedness of the former Allies and other countries to the U.S.A. was set (with accumulated interest) at £2,400,000,000 sterling. The debts of Great Britain's old allies were reduced to such an extent that their payments only just balanced the British payments to the U.S.A.

As regards German reparations the sum originally set was 132,000,000,000 marks. The Dawes Plan adopted in 1924 left the total sum of reparations open but obliged Germany to make annual payments until 1929, amounting to 2,500,000,000 marks annually. The Young Plan, superseding the Dawes Plan in 1929, obliged Germany to pay an average annual sum of 1,900,000,000 marks for a period of 59 years. The Young Plan functioned for only a year and ten months. On July 1, 1931, the so-called Hoover Moratorium went into effect, holding up all payments on reparations and war debts for one year.

The amount of cash reparations payments by Germany for the entire period amounted to £645,000,000 sterling.

German reparations and the inter-Allied debts inherited from the World War constitute one of the sorest problems of the post-war capitalist system, one of the main points of contention and strife in the camps of the capitalist countries, one of the knots of sharpest contradictions. The U.S.A. occupies a position of non-interference in the matter of reparations: this is, as it says, an internal matter of the Europeans with which America has no concern. But so much the more insistently does it demand payment of the Allied debts to itself.

The development of the economic crisis brought about a virtual discontinuation of reparations payments as well as payments on other debts. It is self-evident that such a non-payment of debts sharpens the relations between the imperialists to an even greater degree.

The downfall of capitalism extends over an entire historical epoch. This is the period of the revolutionary struggle of the international proletariat for its dictatorship, for socialism.

Three periods of the general crisis of capitalism

The years since the imperialist war fall into three periods. The first post-war years 1918-21 were a period of the sharp disintegration of the entire capitalist system and of fierce struggle between the proletariat and the bourgeoisie, going over in a number of countries to open civil warfare. As a result of the destruction caused by the war, the tremendous losses in life and material values, the economic ruin reached unparalleled proportions. All the contradictions of capitalism were brought to a point. The dissatisfaction of the masses, who found themselves stranded in the same old misery, was tremendous. The Central European countries flared in the fires of civil war. A Soviet republic was set up in Hungary in 1919, lasting several months, and one in Bavaria held out several weeks. In 1920-21 a deep economic crisis gripped the capitalist countries causing the contradictions to become even more acute.

Soviet Russia during these years was repelling the attacks of the united forces of the Russian whiteguards and the international bourgeoisie. The Civil War ended in the victory and consolidation of the Soviet power, all attempts at intervention met with defeat at the hands of the iron force of the invincible proletarian revolution. The Communist International—the military staff of the world revolution—was established. For the first time in many capitalist countries, Communist Parties arose, which unfurled the flag of revolutionary socialism that had been stamped into the dust and steeped in blood by the traitors to socialism from the Second International.

With the help of the traitorous Social-Democratic leaders, the bourgeoisie succeeded in repelling the attacks of the revolutionary proletariat and breaking down its resistance in a number of countries. In 1923 the German bourgeoisie succeeded in again inflicting defeat on the revolutionary proletariat in that country. The first period thus ended, on the one hand, in the victory of Soviet power in the U.S.S.R. and, on the other, in the temporary defeat of the West European proletariat.

After inflicting defeat on the working class the West European bourgeoisie took the offensive. Thus, the *second period* began—the period of the gradual advent of partial stabilization in capitalist countries. A certain amount of "reconstruction," necessitated by the havoc left by the World War, took place in the capitalist camp. On the other hand, this period was a period of the rapid reconstruction of the national economy of the U.S.S.R., and of the most vital successes of socialist construction.

Having repelled the attacks of the masses of workers, the bourgeoisie proceeded to bind up the more gaping wounds left by the World War. Their method of curing these wounds was by transferring the entire burden of the heritage of the imperialist slaughter onto the shoulders of the working class. At the expense of an unbelievable reduction in the living standard of the workers, the bourgeoisie achieved a temporary and partial stabilization of capitalism. In a number of countries money circulation was re-stabilized after it had been completely upset by the war and post-war chaos. The bourgeoisie began to put capitalist rationalization methods into effect. Rationalization under capitalism means an enormous increase in the degree of exploitation of the workers. This is accomplished by the aid of technical innovations introduced by the rationalizers. Capitalist rationalization reduces the number of workers employed while increasing their productivity. Part of the workers are thrown out on the streets without the slightest hope of ever getting employment again. Those workers who remain are forced to work twice and three times as intensively, exhausting their entire strength for the benefit of capital.

Partial stabilization of capitalism could only be temporary, tottering, rotten. It could only succeed in deadening the effect of some of the contradictions of contemporary capitalism for a very short time indeed, as it is absolutely unable to solve these contradictions. On the contrary, these contradictions have made themselves felt more and more sharply from year to year.

The process of stabilization was characterized by an increase in the unevenness of development of the various countries. Some countries succeeded in getting on their feet after the ravages of war more or less rapidly, while others lagged behind in this respect. Currency was relatively stabilized in various countries at different times. The temporary revival of the production machinery also began at different times in the various countries. Unevenness of development in the years of stabilization was one of the sources of those contradictions which revealed themselves very soon afterwards.

Together with the temporary stabilization of capitalism, the reconstruction of the economy of the Soviet Union forged ahead with giant strides; the deep wounds inflicted on the economy of the country by the imperialist war and the civil war that followed were healed in a comparatively short time, independently and without recourse to any outside aid. The consolidation and growth of the power of the Soviet Union deepen the general crisis of capitalism and render it more acute.

The colonial countries, exploited by the imperialists, rise in a struggle against their exploiters. The revolution in China, regardless of temporary setbacks, does not let the imperialists rest. The revolutionary movement in India and other colonies of British and French capital continues to grow. The contradictions between the imperialist countries increase and become sharper. The transference of the world's economic centre to America, the transformation of the U.S.A. into a world exploiter, greatly sharpens the relations between the American and the European, primarily the British, bourgeoisie. The contradictions between America and Great Britain form the pivot around which the world imperialist struggles revolve. As capitalist industry reaches pre-war dimensions again in some countries (1927-28) the struggle for markets becomes more intensified.

The *third period* of the post-war general crisis of capitalism arrives. This period is characterized by the *sharpening* of the basic contradictions of contemporary capitalism. In 1927 as compared with 1913, world economy produced: oil—300 per cent, iron—102 per cent, steel—127 per cent, cotton—125 per cent, wheat—110 per cent, rye—95 per cent. The following year, 1928, resulted in a further increase in production for many commodities. *Capitalism*, about ten years after the war, *exceeded its pre-war limits*. Simultaneously, an exceptional *increase* in capitalist contradictions resulted both within individual countries and between them. The third period in the development of the general crisis of capitalism is the period of the shattering of the partial and temporary stabilization of capitalism; under the circumstances of the world economic crisis that began in 1929 and shook the entire economy of the capitalist countries to its very foundations, the end of capitalist stabilization finally arrives, as was pointed out in the resolution of the Twelfth Plenum of the E.C.C.I., held in the autumn of 1932.

Capitalist rationalization brings with it an unprecedented increase in the exploitation of the working class by the bourgeoisie. Rationalization sharpens the class contradictions to their extreme limits. Rationalization under conditions of capitalism results in the shutting down of a number of antiquated enterprises and a reduction in the number of workers employed at the remaining plants and factories. *Chronic unemployment* sets in. The condition of the working class becomes worse even in a number of the most highly developed capitalist countries.

Thus, for instance, in even the wealthiest capitalist country, which the reformists point to as being almost "heaven on earth" —the U.S.A.—the following changes took place between 1919 and 1925. The number of workers employed in industry, in agriculture and on the railroads decreased 7 per cent; production increased 20 per cent; the productivity of labour increased 29 per cent. During these years, the number of workers employed in these fields fell by almost 2,000,000 people. Part of these found employment in the sphere of trade and service, but the majority remained unemployed.

In Germany there were no less than three million unemployed at the beginning of 1929. During the later years of capitalist rationalization a constant reserve army grew, which even at times of industrial revival never fell below one to one and half million people in number. Of these, from half a million to a million people were permanently unemployed and their condition hopeless. These were real victims of capitalist rationalization, which had taken all their strength from them and then thrown them out onto the street.

The total number of unemployed, thrown out of employment by rationalization in the foremost capitalist countries, amounted to ten million people. Precisely the same number as that killed in the World War! Like the victims of the war, these also are doomed to death by capitalism; the only difference is that the capitalist victims of "peace" die slowly.

The impoverishment of the working class proceeds apace with the growth of technical improvement, throwing workers out of employment and at the same time enormously increasing the quantity of commodities produced. *Together with the tremendous increase in the quantity of commodities produced, the internal market contracts*, as it depends on the well-being of the broad masses. The increase in production conflicts with the decreased consumption of the masses. The difficulties of selling increase and compel the capitalists of the various countries to *conduct a savage struggle for external markets.*

In the third period the contradiction between the development of the productive forces and the contraction of the markets becomes particularly acute. The internal as well as the external contradictions grow, rending the capitalist countries asunder under the conditions of a general crisis of the capitalist system. The third period brings with it devastating crises and the ever growing danger of new imperialist wars.

At the same time, in the U.S.S.R. a transition takes place from the restoration to the reconstruction period. The great Five-Year Plan of reconstruction begins to be realized. The reconstruction of national economy, the colossal growth of socialist industry, the radical transformation of agriculture on the basis of collectivization—all this marks the victorious progress of socialism on the vast territory which covers one-sixth of the world. The third period intensifies the struggle between two systems—that of moribund capitalism and that of rapidly developing socialism. The absolute hopelessness of the capitalist system and all the advantages of socialism stand forth with particular clarity in this period when the enormous growth of socialism in the U.S.S.R. takes place against the background of a crisis of unprecedented depth which shook the capitalist countries to their very foundations.

During the years of partial stabilization the bourgeois scribblers and Social-Democrats made every effort to prove that the capitalist system had completely healed the wounds inflicted by the war and had definitely overcome the post-war crisis. They asserted that capitalism was full of strength and vitality, that it had a brilliant future before it. The Social-Democrats asserted that a period of capitalist prosperity and well-being had arrived, the millenium of organized capitalism which knows no shocks, wars or crises.

The opportunists within the Communist Parties repeated these ravings of the defenders of the bourgeoisie in a more concealed form. The *Right opportunists* repeated the Social-Democratic arguments about organized capitalism. During the transition from the second to the third period the Right opportunists tried to show that the third period is not the end of capitalist stabilization, but a period of its further entrenchment. The Right opportunists supported the fiction of American prosperity, creating the theory of American "exceptionalism," asserting that America was unaffected by the general crisis of capitalism. In the opinion of the Right opportunists, the stabilization of capitalism was permanent and unshakable. The Trotskyists, rather, at first tried to deny the significance of capitalist stabilization, disposing of it with a few "Left" phrases, but soon they joined the chorus of those who sang the praises of the permanence and steadfastness of capitalist stabilization. The Right opportunists and the Trotskyists did not want to admit the advent of the present world crisis even when the majority of the bourgeois politicians were compelled to admit its existence.

Even at the time of partial stabilization the C.P.S.U. and the Comintern foresaw the inevitability of the advent of a new crisis. They based themselves on the revolutionary, Marxist-Leninist analysis of those inner contradictions which inevitably develop in modern capitalism. In his report to the Fifteenth Congress of the C.P.S.U. in December 1927, Stalin emphasized that "from stabilization is born the growing crisis of capitalism." He said:

"As early as the Fourteenth Congress it was stated in the report that capitalism may return to pre-war level, may surpass the pre-war level, may rationalize its production, but that this does not yet mean—does not mean by far—that because of this the stabilization of capitalism can become durable, that capitalism can recover its pre-war stability. On the contrary, out of its very stabilization, out of the fact that production expands, that commerce develops, that technical progress and productive capacity increase, while the world market, the limits of this market and the spheres of influence of individual imperialist groups remain more or less stationary—out of this the deepest and most acute crisis of world capitalism is growing, pregnant with new wars and threatening the existence of any stabilization. Out of partial stabilization an intensification of the crisis of capitalism ensues, the growing crisis disrupts stabilization—this is the dialectics of the development of capitalism in the given historical period."

Later developments showed the absolute correctness of this estimate given by Stalin. Already at the end of 1929 the "deepest and most acute crisis of world capitalism" had set in. This crisis upset all the fairy tales of the bourgeois and Social-Democratic apologists of capitalism, all the opportunist theories. This crisis showed the full correctness of the estimate of the third period which was given by the C.P.S.U. and the Comintern. The present crisis, with its development, brought about the advent of the end of the relative stabilization of capitalism, as was pointed out in the resolution of the Twelfth Plenum of the E.C.C.I. of September 1932.

An unwonted sharpening of class contradictions takes place under the conditions of the general crisis of capitalism. In the new situation the bourgeoisie, feeling the approach of its downfall, makes use of the severest and cruellest methods of repression against the working class. In a number of countries the bourgeoisie, after repelling the first attacks of the working class in the very first years after the war, established fascist dictatorships (*e.g.*, Italy and Hungary). In Germany the bourgeoisie established a fascist dictatorship only after a number of intermediate steps, in February 1933, when the Hitler government came into power.

The bourgeoisie finds it continually more difficult to maintain itself in power by means of the more veiled forms of bourgeois dictatorship. It goes over to open fascist dictatorship. It represses the labour movement by the bloodiest methods. It passes over to open terror against the working class and its organizations. All this is clear evidence of the instability of capitalism, of the uncertainty of the bourgeoisie concerning what the morrow will bring.

The fascist form of open dictatorship of the bourgeoisie is extremely characteristic of capitalism in the epoch of its decay and downfall. Fascism tries to create a bulwark for the bourgeoisie against the working class. It appeals to the broad masses of the petty bourgeoisie, the peasantry, office employees and clerks, small businessmen, and the intelligentsia. It penetrates into the more backward elements of the working class. It widely mobilizes all the declassed elements. It conducts its frantic defence of capitalism, at least at first, under the mask of anti-capitalist agitation. The hazy demagogy against capitalism serves fascism as a decoy to catch adherents from among the disinherited but politically backward sections of the petty bourgeoisie.

"The principal aim of fascism is to destroy the revolutionary labour vanguard, *i.e.*, the Communist sections and leading units of the proletariat. The combination of social demagogy, corruption and active White terror, in conjunction with extreme imperialist aggression in the sphere of foreign politics, are the characteristic features of fascism. In periods of acute crisis for the bourgeoisie, fascism resorts to anti-capitalist phraseology, but, after it has established itself at the helm of state, it casts aside its anti-capitalist rattle and discloses itself as a terrorist dictatorship of big capital." *

Review Questions

1. What were the causes of the imperialist World War?
2. What destruction did the World War cause?
3. Which country profited most from the war?
4. How did the relation of forces among the Powers change as a result of the war?
5. What is the general crisis of capitalism?
6. What is the distinguishing feature of the first period of the general crisis of capitalism?
7. Why could the stabilization of capitalism only be temporary, partial and shaky?
8. What are the distinguishing features of the third period?

* *Program of the Communist International*, p. 25.

CHAPTER XI

The Contemporary World Crisis of Capitalism

The present crisis which has shaken the capitalist world for a number of years is distinguished by its unprecedented force.

The economic crisis amidst the general crisis of capitalism

The present crisis developed *amidst the general crisis of capitalism* that set in with the imperialist war. It broke out in the period of the decline and collapse of capitalism, in an era of wars and proletarian revolutions.

This crisis is distinguished from all previous capitalist crises by one extremely important circumstance. Side by side with the capitalist system there now exists a land where socialism is being built and is triumphing—the U.S.S.R. The world is now going through a period of *struggle and contest between two systems*—the system of moribund capitalism and the system of victorious socialism. A crisis of unwonted force is shaking the capitalist countries while a vast amount of construction work and an altogether extraordinary rise in socialist economy is taking place in the U.S.S.R. The struggle of the two systems renders the crisis of capitalism extremely acute. The existence of the U.S.S.R. is a constant reminder of the inevitable doom of the capitalist system. The victorious construction of socialism in the U.S.S.R. shows the disinherited and enslaved masses of toilers in the capitalist countries the only road of escape from the reign of slavery and oppression, poverty and ruin.

"It means first of all, that the imperialist war and its aftermath have intensified the decay of capitalism and destroyed its equilibrium, that we are now living in the epoch of wars and revolutions; that capitalism no longer represents the *sole* and *all-embracing* system of world economy; that side by side with the *capitalist* system of economy there exists the *socialist* system, which is growing, which is flourishing, which stands out against capitalist system and which, by the mere fact of its existence, is demonstrating the rottenness of capitalism and shaking its foundations." *

The world crisis began almost simultaneously in the autumn of 1929 in two opposite places: in the backward countries of Eastern and Southern Europe (Poland, Rumania) and in the foremost, most powerful country of contemporary capitalism—the U.S.A. From these centres the crisis spread over the entire capitalist world.

The crisis hit the most powerful and foremost country of modern capitalism—the United States of America—with the *greatest force*. For several years all the lackeys of the bourgeoisie, all its learned hirelings and toadies from the Social-Democratic camp glorified American "prosperity" and assured the world that there could be no end or limit to this prosperity. The crisis unmercifully exposed and refuted these traitorous arguments.

The present crisis came as the first post-war *world* economic crisis. It developed *unevenly* in the various countries: some countries experienced the crisis sooner, some later. The crisis hit various countries with various degrees of force. Nevertheless, it embraced the *entire* capitalist world and there is not a single capitalist country which it has spared. Thus, regardless of the unevenness with which it affected the various countries, the present crisis caught all the capitalist countries in its iron embrace.

In previous epochs, before capitalism had begun to decline, crises appeared after comparatively long periods of prosperity and a rise and growth of the national economy of capitalist countries. The present crisis, in this respect, differs radically from all previous, "usual" crises. The present crisis was preceeded by only temporary flares of revival in various countries.

These "booms" appeared in various countries at various times and were very short-lived. In Germany the year 1927 was one of revival. But 1928 already showed a decline. In Poland there was a certain revival in 1927-28; in Japan, in 1928 and the beginning of 1929. On the other hand in such countries as England, Australia, and Brazil there was no revival whatsoever before the

* Stalin, *Leninism,* Vol. II, "Poltical Report to the Sixteenth Congress," pp. 314-15.

crisis. In the economy of these countries the pre-crisis period was one of great stagnation.

Describing the condition of the capitalist world during recent years in his report to the Seventeenth Congress of the Communist Party of the U.S.S.R., Comrade Stalin said:

> "In the *economic* sphere these years have been years of continuing world economic crisis. The crisis has affected not only industry, but also agriculture as a whole. The crisis has not only raged in the sphere of production and trade, but has also swept into the sphere of credit and the circulation of money, and has overturned the established credit and currency relationships between countries.
>
> "Formerly, there were disputes here and there as to whether there was a world economic crisis or not, but now nobody argues about this because the existence of the crisis and its devastating effects are only too obvious. Now the controversy centres around another question, *viz.*, is there a way out of the crisis or not? And if there is a way out, where is it to be found?" *

Like all crises under the capitalist system, the contemporary crisis is one of overproduction. More commodities have been produced than the market can absorb.

A crisis of overproduction

> "It means that more textiles, fuel, manufactured articles, foodstuffs have been produced than can be bought for cash by the main consumer—the mass of the people—whose income remains at a low level. And as the purchasing capacity of the mass of the people in conditions of capitalism remains at the lowest possible level, the capitalists leave the 'surplus' commodities, textiles, grain, etc., in store, or even destroy them, in order to maintain high prices. They reduce production, dismiss their workers, and the mass of the people are forced to suffer privations because too many commodities have been produced." **

A crisis of overproduction means a lack of sales, the contrac-

* Stalin, *Report on the Work of the Central Committee of the C.P.S.U. (Seventeenth Party Congress)*, p. 7.

** Stalin, *Leninism*, Vol. II, "Political Report to the Sixteenth Congress," pp. 308-9.

tion of markets, the closing of factories and plants, a curtailment of production. Tremendous quantities of commodities *cannot be sold.* This leads to an *accumulation of reserves* of all kinds. Tremendous stores of raw material, industrial goods and agricultural products are accumulated. These stores exert pressure on the market. In order to maintain prices, a considerable part of these stores of goods is destroyed by the capitalists. For this purpose also, production is curtailed. By means of these measures the capitalists maintain the prices of some commodities at a comparatively high level for a short time, but the force of the crisis proves stronger than all the measures they adopt. The curtailment of sales, the contraction of markets, the accumulation of reserves of commodities inevitably lead to a *decline in prices.* Under contemporary monopoly capitalism the more powerful monopoly corporations do all in their power to maintain high prices on their commodities. Hence, there is a great lack of uniformity in the decline of prices. While the more powerful trusts and cartels maintain fairly high prices on their commodities, prices of all other commodities fall rapidly.

The lack of sales, the accumulation of reserves and the decline in prices lead to a *curtailment of production.* The decline in production has a number of serious consequences. The army of *unemployed* grows catastrophically. There is a progressive *under-employment of the working capacity* of enterprises. As a result the cost of production rises, while the sales prices of commodities sink. The weaker links of capitalist economy snap. Bankruptcies multiply. A *credit and financial* crisis breaks out.

The capitalists throw millions of workers out onto the streets. The unemployed are deprived of all means of subsistence or, at best, receive a beggarly dole. Those who remain at work receive greatly reduced wages. The earnings of the workers become continually smaller. But this only results in further lowering the purchasing power of the masses of workers. At the same time the agricultural crisis cuts down the incomes of the agricultural population. The peasant masses are ruined.

The contraction of the internal market compels the capitalists to conduct a frantic struggle for *foreign markets.* But foreign markets mean either other industrial capitalist countries, or colonial and semi-colonial agrarian countries. The bourgeoisie of every industrial country tries to fence in its own market from the encroachments of foreign competition. With this end in view, high tariffs, outright embargoes on the import of certain commodities, etc., are introduced, and the markets of the colonial and semi-colonial agrarian countries are ruined and drastically contracted because of the devastating effects of the agrarian crisis and the growth of colonial oppression and exploitation. All this leads to a catastrophic decline in foreign trade, to an extreme sharpening of the struggle for markets, to an *enormous growth of the contradictions* in the capitalist world.

There have been many crises in the history of capitalism, but never before has there been a crisis of such depth and acuteness.

The most profound and protracted of all crises

In scale, force and prolongation, in the extent to which it has affected all phases of capitalist economy, the present crisis far exceeds all previous crises.

> "The present economic crisis in capitalist countries differs from all analogous crises, among other things, by the fact that it is the longest and most protracted crisis. Formerly, crises lasted one or two years, the present crisis, however, is now in its fifth year and from year to year has devastated the economy of capitalist countries and has wasted the fat it accumulated in previous years. It is not surprising that this crisis is the severest of all crises." *

All the basic indices bear evidence of this and characterize the depth and acuteness of the crisis. According to the basic indices showing the decline of production, the extent of unemployment and wage reductions, the fall in prices of commodities, the decline in foreign trade, the drop in stock market quotations, etc., the present crisis far exceeds all the previous crises that have taken place in the history of capitalism.

The following table gives the index numbers of the present crisis in comparison with previous ones, in percentages of decline:

* Stalin, *Report on the Work of the Central Committee of the C.P.S.U., (Seventeenth Party Congress)*, p. 9.

Years of Crises	*World Production of Pig Iron*	*Building Industry of the U.S.A.*	*World Foreign Trade*	*Stock Prices U.S.A*	*Stock Prices France*	*Decline in World Prices of Commodities*
1873-74	8.9	—	5	30	—	20.2
1883-85	10.0	—	4	29	—	20.4
1890-92	6.5	—	1	—	21	—
1907-08	23.0	20.0	7	37	5	0.8
1920-21	43.5	11.0	—	41	25	21.0
1929-32	66.8	85.2	60	75	50	47.0

The decline in production during the present crisis reached proportions unequalled in the history of crises since the beginning of the existence of capitalism. During previous crises a decline in production amounting to 10-15 per cent was considered tremendous. In the present crisis the curtailment in the production of the capitalist world as a whole reached enormous proportions—a decline of from one-third to two-fifths; and in certain of the most important countries production declined to half.

Such an unprecedented decline in production sets the capitalist countries back considerably.

Exceedingly significant are the figures for individual branches of industry in capitalist countries. The following table shows the year in the past in which production was equivalent to that of 1932, when the lowest point of the crisis was reached.

Country	*Coal*	*Pig Iron*	*Steel*	*Consumption of cotton*
U.S.A.	1906	1898	1905	1893
England	1900	1860	1897	1872
Germany	1899	1891	1895	1889

Thus, the basic industries in capitalist countries have been thrown back twenty-five to forty years.

The unprecedented decline of production is intimately bound up with colossal unemployment. In extent of unemployment the present crisis has by far exceeded all previous crises. It is sufficient to point out that in the crisis of 1921, when unemployment reached what was then considered colossal proportions, the number of unemployed was about 10,000,000, whereas during the present crisis the number of unemployed in the most important capitalist countries was 40-50,000,000 people.

What are the causes for such a long and protracted character of the crisis, for its unusual extent and acuteness? In his report to the Seventeenth Congress of the Communist Party of the Soviet Union, Comrade Stalin thus analysed these causes:

> "It is to be explained, first of all, by the fact that the industrial crisis affected every capitalist country without exception and made it difficult for some countries to manoeuvre at the expense of others.
>
> "Secondly, it is to be explained by the fact that the industrial crisis became interwoven with the agrarian crisis which affected all the agrarian and semi-agrarian countries without exception, and this could not but make the industrial crisis more complicated and profound.
>
> "Thirdly, it is to be explained by the fact that the agrarian crisis became more acute in this period and affected all branches of agriculture including cattle raising, degrading it to the level of passing from machine labour to hand labour, to the substitution of the horse for the tractor, to the sharp decline, diminution in the use of and sometimes to the complete abandonment of artificial fertilizers, which caused the industrial crisis to become still more protracted.
>
> "Fourthly, it is to be explained by the fact that the monopolist cartels which dominate industry strive to maintain the high prices of goods, and this circumstance makes the crisis particularly painful and hinders the absorption of stocks of commodities.
>
> "Lastly, and what is most important, it is to be explained by the fact that the industrial crisis broke out amidst the conditions of the *general* crisis of capitalism, when capitalism no longer has, nor can have, either in the home states or in the colonial and dependent countries the strength and stability it had before the war and the October Revolution, when industry in the capitalist countries is suffering from the heritage it received from the imperialist war in the shape of the chronic working of enterprises under capacity, and an army of unemployed numbering millions from which it is no longer able to release itself.

"Such are the circumstances which determine the extremely protracted character of the present industrial crisis." *

The crisis of overproduction leads to a colossal decline in production in all fields of economy. Beginning with the autumn of 1929 a *stoppage* and a *curtailment of production,* hitherto unprecedented, has been taking place in capitalist countries.

The decline in production

While there is a considerable increase of production in the U.S.S.R. every year, the capitalist world, caught in the iron vice of the crisis, curtails production to an unprecedented degree.

Here is a table, compiled on the basis of official data, showing the trend of the volume of production in the U.S.S.R. and in capitalist countries (given by Comrade Stalin in his report to the Seventeenth Party Congress of the C.P.S.U.**):

VOLUME OF INDUSTRIAL PRODUCTION
(Percentage of 1929)

	1929	*1930*	*1931*	*1932*	*1933*
U.S.S.R.	100	129.7	161.9	184.7	201.6
U.S.A.	100	80.7	68.1	53.8	64.9
England	100	92.4	83.8	83.8	86.1
Germany	100	88.3	71.7	59.8	66.8
France	100	100.7	89.2	69.1	77.4

This table is very significant.

It shows, first of all, that industrial production in the biggest capitalist countries suffered an extraordinary reduction, while industrial production in the Soviet Union more than doubled.

It shows, in the second place, that the lowest point of the decline in industrial production in capitalist countries was reached in 1932, when the volume of production diminished by fully one-third. Only in 1933 did the industries of the capitalist countries begin to pick up; production, however, even in 1933 was almost one-fourth lower than in the pre-crisis year of 1929.

It shows, thirdly, that the crisis did not affect all countries with equal force and that its effects in various countries differ greatly.

* *Ibid.*, pp. 9-10.
** *Ibid.*, p. 12.

It should be borne in mind, however, that the situations of the various countries at the beginning of the crisis were also different. From the table it might appear that England is in the most favourable position. But this is really not so. If we compare the present level of these countries with their pre-war level, this becomes quite evident. Here is a table showing this:

VOLUME OF INDUSTRIAL PRODUCTION
(Percentage of pre-war level)

	1913	*1929*	*1930*	*1931*	*1932*	*1933*
U.S.S.R.	100	194.3	252.1	314.7	359.0	391.9
U.S.A.	100	170.2	137.3	115.9	91.4	110.2
England	100	99.1	91.5	83.0	82.5	85.2
Germany	100	113.0	99.8	81.0	67.6	75.4
France	100	139.0	140.0	124.0	96.1	107.6

From this table it is plain that the industries of England and Germany are below their pre-war level. The industries of the U.S.A., which in 1929 had reached 170 per cent of the pre-war volume of production, now exceed the pre-war level by only 10 per cent. At the same time the industries of the Soviet Union have increased practically fourfold compared with the pre-war output of the industries of tsarist Russia.

The catastrophic decline of production in capitalist countries signifies an unprecedented waste of productive forces.

The production apparatus created by the sweat and blood of the toiling masses is utilized to an extremely small degree. A considerable portion of the blast furnaces, open hearths, mines, machine-building plants and textile mills is not utilized. Enterprises equipped according to the last word in engineering stand idle. Tremendous means invested in these enterprises are wasted; the plants themselves go to pieces as they are not used or attended to. The overwhelming majority of enterprises work at only part capacity. The considerable under-employment of the working capacity of enterprises is one of the clearest expressions of the general crisis of the capitalist system.

Thus, for instance, in the United States, the chronic utilization of plants below capacity expressed itself in the fact that even up to the beginning of the crisis in 1929 coal mines were worked only to 68 per cent of their capacity, oil wells to 67 per cent, oil refineries to 76 per cent, iron smelters to 60-80 per cent, automobile plants to not more than 50 per cent, machine-building plants to 55 per cent, textile mills to 72 per cent, and in some branches even less—as in the polygraphic industry to 50 per cent, in the flour-milling industry to 40 per cent and in the woollen mills to 36 per cent. Thus the basic industries, even before the crisis, could not utilize their enormous production capacity in full. The under-employment of the working capacity of the enterprises increased enormously as a result of the crisis and the decline in production.

Only 13 per cent of the equipment of steel mills and only 11 per cent of the machinery used in the manufacture of automobiles were still in operation in the U.S.A. in October 1932. In Germany the entire industry worked at 36 per cent of capacity in December 1932, in heavy industry the percentage was even smaller.

In the United States 60 blast furnaces were reduced to scrap in 4 years. In 1931, 12 open-hearth steel furnaces, with a total capacity of 710,000 tons of steel, and 13 rolling mills were torn down. In Germany 23 blast furnaces and 38 open-hearth furnaces were destroyed.

In bourgeois newspapers one can find dozens of descriptions of tremendous machinery "cemeteries" that have sprung up in all capitalist countries. Plants and warehouses with boarded up doors, powerful cranes standing in dusty neglect, abandoned railroad branch lines overgrown with grass, whole fleets of freight and passenger steamships, forests of dead factory chimneys extend for miles in the industrial regions of the richest capitalist countries.

The decline in the national income and reduction in the national wealth

The curtailment of production in industry and agriculture and the reduction in transportation involve a reduction in the total values produced annually in the capitalist countries. This means that the *national income declines* in capitalist countries.

But it is not only the national income which declines in the capitalist countries under the influence of the crisis. Factories that are standing idle go to wrack and ruin. Houses that are not repaired become uninhabitable. Fields that lie fallow become over-run with weeds. For lack of use and care machinery rusts and becomes useless. Tremendous quantities of goods that cannot be sold are destroyed in various ways.

A wanton *waste* and *destruction* of wealth, accumulated by scores of years of persistent toil, take place in most diverse forms. An extraordinary *squandering of productive forces*, accumulated by the toil of many generations, ensues.

The sum total of values in any country—plants, factories, buildings, machinery, equipment, manufactured goods and raw material—is usually called the *national wealth* of that country. It is self-evident that in capitalist countries this wealth is not at all in the hands of the nation. On the contrary, under capitalism it is concentrated in the hands of a small group of exploiters and parasites, just as the preponderating part of the national income in capitalist countries does not at all go to the nation's masses but to the minority of drones.

Here is a table showing the decline in the national wealth and national income of the most important capitalist countries for the first two years of the crisis (in billions of dollars):

Country	*National Wealth*		*National Income*	
	1929	*1931*	*1929*	*1931*
U.S.A.	400	240	90.0	54.0
England	115	69	19.0	11.4
Germany	80	48	15.5	9.3
France	68	51	9.0	6.7
Italy	30	18	5.0	3.0

These figures show that for two years of the crisis five of the most important capitalist countries lost almost 40 per cent of their national wealth ($267,000,000,000 out of $693,000,000,000 at the beginning of the crisis). Their national income also fell from $137,500,000,000 a year to $84,400,000,000 a year, that is, also about 40 per cent.

These figures give a universal picture of the unprecedented devastation wrought by the crisis in the capitalist world. These figures clearly illustrate the senselessness, the criminality of the capitalist system which blindly destroys untold wealth while condemning tens and hundreds of millions of people to hunger and death.

The present crisis has far exceeded previous crises in the extent of the decline of the national income and the destruction of national wealth. For comparison it is sufficient to point out that in the 1901 crisis the national income of Germany fell 6 per cent; the 1907 crisis reduced the national income of Germany 4 per cent, and the national income of England 5 per cent.

Unemployment and the conditions of the working class

The entire weight of the world crisis of capitalism fell on the working class. The crisis brought about an unprecedented aggravation of the conditions of the working class, an extraordinary increase in the unemployment and exploitation of the proletariat.

The general crisis of capitalism which started with the World War called forth a considerable increase in unemployment. After the war, unemployment in the principal capitalist countries reached enormous proportions. The industrial reserve army, which formerly disappeared in times of prosperity, has become a permanent army of unemployed since the war. The size of this army of permanently unemployed was quite large even before the beginning of the present crisis. Thus in England the number of unemployed since 1920 has never been below a million. Unemployment increased with the wave of capitalist rationalization that spread in the years from 1925 to 1927. Because of the increase in the intensity of labour the capitalists achieve "economies" in labour power. Hundreds of thousands of workers prove "superfluous" for this reason.

In June 1927 the percentage of unemployed in England amounted to 8.8 per cent and in February 1929 it was already 12.2 per cent; in Germany for the same period 6.3 per cent and 22.3 per cent or 2,622,000 were unemployed; in the U.S.A. in 1927 there were 2,100,000 unemployed, and at the end of 1928 and beginning of 1929 there were 3,400,000 unemployed.

The crisis which began in 1929 brought about a colossal increase in unemployment. The curtailment of production threw millions of workers out of employment. Under pressure of the crisis a further intensification of labour was inaugurated and the exploitation of those workers who remained at work was increased.

In the period of the present crisis unemployment reached proportions never before experienced in the entire history of capitalism. According to the most conservative estimates the number of unemployed in the major capitalist countries was 45,000,000 people. If we take the families into consideration this constitutes the entire population of a country like the U.S.A. To this number must be added the tremendous number of workers who are employed only part time, that is, who work one to two days a week. Finally, these figures do not include the vast masses of toilers in the colonial countries whom the crisis deprived of their last piece of bread. For the period of the crisis world unemployment increased four to five times, and in a number of countries even more.

It must be kept in mind that the most important capitalist countries have no really adequate or reliable statistics on unemployment. Usually the statistical data *greatly underestimate.*

In a country like the U.S.A. there are no official data on unemployment. But even bourgeois newspapers cannot hide the fact that at the very lowest point of the crisis there were approximately 17,000,000 unemployed in the U.S.A. This amounts to about half the working class in this richest of industrial countries. In England there are some data on the number of unemployed from the social insurance lists. These lists show about 3,000,000 unemployed. But during the years of the crisis several hundred thousand workers were removed from the social insurance list. Hundreds of thousands received no social insurance. In Germany the official data on unemployment very much underestimate the actual situation, particularly since the Hitler fascist regime came into power; nevertheless, the number of unemployed there, even according to official data, is not less than 5,000,000.

At the present time it is rare to find a worker's family in a capitalist country in which the head of the family or at least the children or some member of the family is not unemployed. This means that the meagre wage of the one who is working must feed a greater number of mouths. It means that the one who is working cannot be sure of the morrow, cannot be at ease as to his fate, since the threat of losing his job is always over him.

Capital conducts a desperate onslaught on the miserable dole that is handed out to the unemployed in capitalist countries. On the pretext of "economy" in government expenses the aid rendered the unemployed is greatly reduced. In such countries as France and the U.S.A there is no social insurance against unemployment and the unemployed must die of starvation or apply to private charity. But even in those countries where unemployment insurance does exist there is a desperate attack on the unemployment dole. In

Germany and England the dole has been cut down considerably. In addition, part of the unemployed have been deprived of the dole altogether.

Under the conditions of the crisis the bourgeoisie conducts an attack against the standard of living of the working class. In all countries the *degree of exploitation* of those workers who were still employed *increased* enormously. In a number of cases the working day was lengthened. The intensity of labour grew. Those who were partially employed were paid exceedingly low wages. Working conditions were aggravated in every way.

The bourgeoisie makes use of the crisis conditions for an organized attack on the wages of the workers. During the crisis a reduction in wages was effected in all capitalist countries, in every branch of the national economy.

During the years of the crisis the amount of money paid out in wages to the working class as a whole decreased considerably. In the U.S.A. the amount paid out in wages in 1932 was only 33 per cent of what it formerly was. The wages of the working class in Germany fell off 26,000,000,000 marks for three years of the crisis. During this same period the wages fund in the U.S.S.R., the land of socialism, increased from 8,000,000,000 to 30,000,000,000 rubles.

A certain German economist has investigated how the level of the real wages of workers in the principal capitalist countries has changed in the past ten years. On the basis of his investigation he came to the following conclusion:

> "If we compare the level of real wages at present with that of previous decades we find the following: in Germany and the U.S.A. the level of real wages is lower than it has ever been for the last half century; in England real wages are at the same level as they were at the end of the nineteenth and the beginning of the twentieth centuries."

Data from various countries prove this.

Germany. The level of real wages for the latest period has been continually reduced. Thus, taking 1913-14 as 100, we get the following index numbers (in 1928 the level of real wages as a result of slow increases was 100, but the years following show a continuous decline):

1925	98
1928	100
1930	89
1931	79
1932	64

In 1933 there was a further reduction in the standard of living of the German working class.

The conditions of the unemployed are even worse. Not to speak of the great number of unemployed who were altogether deprived of government aid mainly for political reasons, the fascist administration has reduced the dole of all others.

England. The average wages of English workers were (taking 1895-1903 as 100) 98 in 1927, 97 in 1929, 94 in 1932.

In the *U.S.A.* the wages of the working class as a whole, rising from 1922, reached their highest point in 1929. Taking 1898-1908 as 100, in 1929 they were 125. But at this point a sharp decline began to pull the standard of living down to the level of years ago. In 1930 the index number fell to 105, in 1931 to 91, in 1932 to 71.

Unemployed raking about in garbage cans for something to eat, forming endless queues at the doors of charity soup kitchens—this is a common picture in any capitalist city now. Tramping the highways has become common in the U.S.A. Hordes of people, in entire families, including their children and their whole miserable household, can often be met on the highways roaming about in a vain search for work. An investigation conducted by some charity organization pointed out that in the U.S.A. over a million and a half unemployed thus wander over the highways.

Hunger drives people to desperation. The number of suicides all over the capitalist world is continually increasing. In Berlin alone an average of sixty people daily commit suicide because of starvation.

The so-called help for the unemployed becomes a means of compulsion to slavery, of forced hard labour. Forced labour for the unemployed is very much in vogue now in many capitalist countries. At the threat of being deprived of all assistance, the unemployed are driven to so-called "public works" (these are mostly either unskilled labour requirements of some big landlords or some kind of military construction), concentrated in various camps and settlements where prison discipline prevails. The pay for this work, taken away from industrial or agricultural workers, is also prison pay. The fascist government of Germany is hurriedly building such forced labour camps for the unemployed youth. This example is most tempting to the other capitalist countries which a few years ago raised such a self-righteous hue and cry about "forced labour" in the Soviet Union where labour has really became "a matter of honour, a matter of glory, a matter of valour and heroism."

The attacks of capital against the vital interests of the workers call forth *resistance* on the part of broad sections of the proletariat. A wave of strikes sweeps over the capitalist countries. Under conditions of the present crisis these strike struggles are distinguished by a special pertinacity. They help the workers to understand the real situation. They show up clearly who is their friend and who their enemy. Under the conditions of the crisis, strikes soon assume the character of a challenge to the bourgeois order which criminally condemns millions of people to hopeless misery.

Interweaving of the industrial and agricultural crises

The special acuteness and depth of this crisis are the result of the fact that both industrial and agrarian countries, both industry and agriculture in capitalist countries have been affected by it. The present crisis has sharpened and exposed all the fundamental contradictions of the capitalist system, including the contradiction between industry and agriculture.

> "In the course of development of the economic crisis, the industrial crisis in the chief capitalist countries has not simply coincided, but has become *interwoven* with the agricultural crisis in the agrarian countries, aggravating the difficulties and predetermining the inevitability of a general decline in economic activity." *

The industrial crisis leads to an unprecedented growth in un employment, to the extreme impoverishment of the toiling masses. The poverty of the masses means a *curtailment in the sales* of agricultural products. In addition to this the curtailment in produc-

* Stalin, *Leninism,* Vol. II, "Political Report to the Sixteenth Congress," p. 314.

tion also means a curtailment in the demand for agricultural raw material: cotton, wool, etc. In its turn, the agricultural crisis, in ruining the masses of the peasantry, deprives them of the ability to purchase industrial commodities, thus contracting the sales market for industry.

The agricultural crisis is a glaring instance of the inability of capitalism to manage the modern development of productive forces. Modern engineering makes it possible to use entirely new methods of labour, opens up opportunities for mechanization which means a colossal increase in productivity. The limits of capitalism are, however, too narrow for modern technical achievements. Sharpening the contrast between city and village, capitalism dooms the village to stagnation and decline. Capitalist relationships are a stumbling block to the further development of agriculture.

The decline and stagnation of agriculture in capitalist countries is revealed particularly glaringly when compared with the U.S.S.R. While the area under cultivation in the Soviet Union increased in only the one year of 1931 by about ten million hectares, the area under cultivation for grain in all capitalist countries has increased in the past twenty years by only thirty million hectares. The World War evoked a profound crisis in the agriculture of capitalist countries. The pauperization of the masses of the peasantry and the curtailment of production in a number of countries were results of this crisis. The present crisis, in which the industrial and agricultural crises are interwoven, is fatal to the existence of tens of millions of farmers.

Giving rise to an unprecedented impoverishment of the proletariat and the toiling masses in general, the crisis drastically cuts down the demand for agricultural products and contracts the sales market for these products to its smallest possible limits. This extreme contraction of the market results in the accumulation of tremendous *reserves* of agricultural products and a *catastrophic decline in prices.* The accumulation of reserves, the decrease in sales and the decline in prices in their turn bring about a *restriction of production* in agriculture.

Warehouses and grain elevators in capitalist countries are filled with reserves of agricultural products. The leaders of the bourgeoisie see only one way of getting rid of this abundance—to burn, allow to rot, throw into the sea and destroy these reserves, but mainly to reduce the area under cultivation in order to compel agriculture to produce less. Mountains of wheat and maize were allowed to rot or were burned, rivers of milk were poured out, in Germany grain was treated with a special chemical which made it unfit for human consumption, so that it could be fed only to cattle.

Prices of agricultural commodities have fallen sharply during the crisis. For instance, the wholesale price of wheat on the world market declined 70 per cent, cotton, sugar, coffee and wool became half price. It would seem that the city consumers, the masses of the population, should gain by this. In practice, however, this is not so. Before the commodity reaches the ultimate consumer it passes through the hands of dozens of middlemen, wholesalers, who are united into big monopolies that do not let the retail prices drop. Retail prices in most capitalist countries did not decline much during the years of the crisis and in some countries they even rose (Germany, for instance). But the farmer, the mass of the toiling peasantry, has to deal with the wholesaler and sell his products at extremely low prices which often do not cover his expenses on seed and equipment, not to speak of the labour he has expended.

The farmer has to pay taxes to the government, rent to the landlord, interest on bank loans, just as before and even in greater amounts. The payments in interest on loans and taxes take the lion's share of what the poor and middle farmer realize on the market. The farm and all the farmer's household goods are sold at auction for debts and taxes. Hundreds and thousands of farms have thus been lost by the poor and middle farmers not only in Europe but also in the U.S.A., the land to which the capitalists have always pointed as the paragon of the well-doing and thriving of agriculture under capitalism. Such unprecedented ruin gives rise to a growing resistance on the part of the toiling farmers against the pressure of capital, landlord and bank. The farmers strive to unite, organize against the sale of their goods at auction, refusing to buy the property. There have been cases in America where the farmers of a district have gathered in an organized fashion at auction sales of ruined farmers and kept the bid down to one dollar for the entire property. In this way, the representatives of the banks were compelled to call off the auction and prolong the term of debt payments.

Abandoning their farms the ruined peasants swell the armies of beggars that crowd the highways. The conditions of the hired farm hands in capitalist countries are even worse. In both Europe and America it has become a common thing for landlords and rich exploiting farmers who hire farm hands to refuse to pay in money for the labour power. For a handful of grain, a peck of half-rotten potatoes they can get an unemployed worker from the city to do the same work. The bourgeois scribblers shout about returning to the land. Special societies are formed for the organization of so-called "settlements" for the unemployed. But this only means that there is an increase in the number of petty farms which without equipment can hardly raise enough to feed the workers who spend their hopeless days and nights in working on them. The crisis of capitalist agriculture clearly shows the hopelessness of the situation of small-scale production under capitalism.

The *poor* and *middle* farmers suffer most from the blows of the agrarian crisis. The crisis leads to the impoverishment of the broad masses of farmers. The crisis *speeds up the differentiation* among the farmers, the transition of many of them into the ranks of the proletariat. The burdens which the peasantry has to bear in capitalist countries under the influence of the crisis are especially unbearable. Taxes, rent, interest on debts and all other charges—all this presses most heavily on the great masses of the peasantry under conditions of the crisis.

The agrarian crisis causes a curtailment in the production of agricultural products. Bourgeois governments in a number of countries frankly advise curtailment of production declaring that this, in their opinion, is the only way to alleviate the agrarian crisis. The curtailment of production in agriculture, as in industry, involves a tremendous destruction of productive forces. Wheat and maize fields stand bare and unsown, cotton, rubber and coffee plantations remain unattended or are altogether cleared. And this at a time when millions of people are starving, have no roofs over their heads and lack even the most necessary clothing.

The agrarian crisis and the ruin of the masses of the peasants brought about a decline in agriculture. The sale of agricultural machinery and artificial fertilizers has fallen off catastrophically. In the foremost capitalist countries the use of tractors, sowers and harvesters has been curtailed. The crisis brought about the degradation and ruin of agriculture in the capitalist world.

One of the most important distinguishing characteristics of the contemporary crisis is its development on the basis of monopoly capitalism.

The crisis and monopolies

"Present-day capitalism, as distinguished from older capitalism, is monopolistic capitalism, and this inevitably gives rise to the struggle between the capitalist combines to maintain high monopolist prices of commodities in spite of overproduction. Obviously, this circumstance, which makes the crisis particularly painful and ruinous for the mass of the people, who are the basic consumers of commodities, cannot but lead to the dragging out of the crisis, cannot but retard its dissipation." *

For many years the lackeys of the bourgeoisie claimed that the growth of monopolies indicates a transition to organized capitalism. The apologists of capital told fairy tales about crises being things of the past for monopoly capitalism. The present crisis revealed the absolute falsity of these inventions. Actually, the monopolistic nature of modern capitalism has led to an extreme *sharpening* of the crisis, to its deepening and protraction.

The lords of monopoly tried, first of all, to shift the entire burden of the crisis onto the shoulders of the broad masses of consumers, attempting to maintain inflated prices even under conditions of overproduction. And actually, irrespective of overproduction, prices on a host of products of monopolized branches of industry fell much more slowly than prices of commodities produced by other branches.

Years	*Germany (1926 = 100)*		*Austria (1923-31 = 100)*		*Poland (1928 = 100)*	
	Cartel Prices	*Free Prices*	*Cartel Prices*	*Free Prices*	*Cartel Prices*	*Free Prices*
1928	102.1	106.8	—	—	—	—
1929	105.0	97.4	99	100	107.7	93.6
1930	103.1	79.7	96	87	108.9	80.9
1931	93.6	60.8	91	76	107.8	63.8
1932	83.9	47.5	93	73	106.1	52.5
1933	83.9	48.3	94	73	94.8	48.8

* *Ibid.*, p. 314.

In a number of cases the pressure of the crisis nevertheless proves stronger than monopolistic ties and then prices drop precipitately and the monopoly itself goes to pieces. This is particularly true for the branches engaged in the production of raw material. The sharp decline in the demand for raw material and the accumulation of tremendous reserves compel the producers ultimately to reduce prices considerably. In these fields the monopolists proved unable to maintain prices at a high level.

All the contradictions inherent in the nature of monopoly capitalism greatly increase under the circumstances of the crisis. It is perfectly clear that the trend of monopolies towards maintaining high price levels leads to the sharpest kind of conflict between a few monopolies, on the one hand, and the entire mass of the consumers of their products, on the other. This conflict becomes more acute between the monopolized branches of industry and those branches where monopoly is negligible. Further, the conflict between the monopolies themselves is sharpened tremendously. The contradictions that rend individual monopolies increase sharply, the struggle within separate monopoly organizations grows severer. A number of monopolies cannot stand the blows of the crisis and fall to pieces.

The following big monopoly combinations, for example, were dissolved during the crisis: the International Zinc Cartel, the European Pig Iron Cartel, the International Tin Cartel. The European Steel Cartel, under continual powerful pressure, was practically compelled to sanction a return to free competition among its members. In Germany the organization of the artificial silk producers fell apart and the zinc cartel failed; in France the pig iron syndicate was dissolved, etc.

The governments of capitalist countries give the monopoly associations powerful support. Monopolies which get into difficulties receive all kinds of subsidies and other help from the government treasury. Many hundreds of millions of marks, dollars and francs have thus been transferred from the lean pockets of the taxpayers to the coffers of private capitalists.

The monopolistic nature of modern capitalism leads to a protraction of the crisis. In the epoch of free competition, the general reduction of prices, the failure of the weaker business organizations and the curtailment of production led to a gradual dissipation of the crisis and to a renewal of the cyclical movement of industry. With the prevalence of monopolies this method of the natural dissipation of the crisis becomes very much more difficult. The reign of monopolies leads to a sharpening of the crisis and to its further deepening.

The crisis of overproduction and the contraction of markets lead to a decline in foreign trade. The present crisis exceeded all previous crises in the history of capitalism with respect to the decline in foreign trade.

The decline in foreign trade

The following table, showing the decline in foreign trade for 1929-31 as compared with that of previous crises, bears eloquent witness to this.

DECLINE IN FOREIGN TURNOVER

Crises	*Percentage*
1873-1874	5
1883-1884	4
1900-1901	1
1907-1908	7
1929-1932	65

The decline in world trade weakened the economic ties without which capitalist economy cannot exist. Industrial countries greatly reduced the amount of imports of raw material. Agrarian countries reduced the import of manufactured articles. This led to a still greater curtailment of both production and consumption by the broad masses of the workers.

The decline in world trade most forcibly affected the biggest capitalist countries, which occupy a dominant position in the world market. Here are the index numbers showing the reduction in export and import of the most important capitalist countries. (The figures for 1929 are taken as 100.)

DECLINE IN FOREIGN TRADE OF THE MOST IMPORTANT IMPERIALIST COUNTRIES

	1930		*1931*		*1932*	
	Import	*Export*	*Import*	*Export*	*Import*	*Export*
U.S.A.	70	73	48	50	30.1	30.8
Germany	77	90	50	73	34.7	42.6
England	86	78	72	53	57.6	50.1
France	90	85	72	61	51.2	39.3
Italy	80	79	51	66	38.7	45.6

Such a decline in foreign trade leads to an unprecedented *sharpening of the struggle for markets.* The competitive struggle between various countries assumes extraordinarily acute forms. In every country the capitalists try, first of all, to ensure the internal market for themselves, not to admit any foreign competition. Unusually high tariffs are introduced. This unheard-of rise of protectionism in all capitalist countries results in a great *increase in dumping.*

The monopolistic nature of modern capitalism has put its stamp on the whole process of development. One of the consequences of the monopolistic character of modern capitalism is a certain peculiarity in the development of the credit crisis. In previous crises the *sphere of credit* was one of the first in which the crisis openly and stormily manifested itself. Sales difficulties soon resulted in the crash of enterprises which did not find it possible to sell their products; having no money to meet their obligations they were compelled to declare themselves bankrupt, *i.e.*, unable to pay their debts. In pre-monopoly times the failures of enterprises were quickly followed by the failure of the banks with which they were connected. At the same time, the bankruptcy of these enterprises led to a curtailment of production, eliminating the weaker enterprises from the market, which was thus left to the stronger and more adaptable ones. In this way, the crisis strengthened the position of some groups of big capital even more, by destroying the small and part of the medium-sized enterprises.

The credit crisis, inflation and the struggle for markets

The monopolistic character of modern capitalism led to a situation where the credit crisis openly broke out only in 1931, after the crisis had already deeply affected the entire economic life of capitalist countries.

From the very beginning of the crisis, the monopolies reigning in modern capitalism began to shift the losses caused by the crisis onto the shoulders of the non-monopolized fields where enterprises of medium magnitude predominated. At the same time the monopolies had to restrict production drastically in order to maintain a high level of prices on a rapidly falling market. The restriction of production inevitably led to a *fall in profits*, to losses and tremendous changes in the *distribution of profits* among the various groups of capitalists.

The crisis led to an unprecedented number of *bankruptcies* of all kinds of enterprises.

NUMBER OF BANKRUPTCIES

	1929	*1930*	*1931*	*1932*	*1933*
U.S.A.	22,909	29,355	29,288	31,882	17,732
England	5,900	6,287	6,818	7,321	4,927
Germany	9,846	15,486	19,254	13,966	3,718
France	6,092	6,249	7,220	9,014	8,362
Poland	516	815	738	545	259

The credit crisis has been maturing for a long time. The failures of enterprises connected with banks, government budget difficulties, the decline in profits and the increase in losses, the fall in the prices of stock—all this prepared the way for an explosion of the credit crisis, which burst forth with extraordinary force in 1931. Industrial failures caused by the decline in production and prices, the impossibility of realizing products, the depreciation of the stock in hand, etc., inevitably brought about the failure of credit institutions. Bank failures, in their turn, created difficulties for industry and resulted in new industrial bankruptcies.

The credit crisis first developed in *Germany* and *Austria.* As early as in the spring of 1931 the biggest bank in Austria, which had control of 75-80 per cent of all the industries of the country, crashed. This was followed by a number of bankruptcies of the largest industrial enterprises in Germany. In June 1931 the third biggest bank in Germany (the Darmstadt and National Bank) and another big bank—the Dresden Bank—failed. From Central Europe the wave of the credit crisis engulfed *England*, resulting in a credit crisis in *France, America* and other capitalist countries.

Under the blows of the crisis a number of the biggest enterprises, constituting the "pride and glory" of world monopoly capital, failed during the second half of 1931 and in 1932. The Swedish Kreuger Match Trust crashed. Working on American capital, Kreuger wanted to seize the match monopoly of all countries. He led a frantic campaign against the Soviet Union: the export of matches from the Soviet Union was an unwelcome obstacle to him. Kreuger shot himself on the eve of his bankruptcy. After his death it appeared that in the last years he had held himself afloat by a number of frauds and swindles by means of which he delayed the moment of his failure. It was also revealed that very high state officials of a number of countries had been in his pay. Many Social-Democratic leaders were supported by him.

One of the biggest American business men—Insull—also proved to be an outright swindler. In the spring of 1932 the corporation which he headed and which owns electric power stations, gas plants and water supplies in sixty cities, having a capital of half a billion dollars, crashed.

> ". . . the crisis has not been restricted to the sphere of production and trade, but has also affected the credit system, currency, the sphere of debt obligations, etc., and this has broken down the traditionally established relations both between separate countries and between social groups in the separate countries.
>
> "An important role in this was played by the drop in the prices of commodities. Notwithstanding the resistance of the monopolist cartels, the drop in prices increased with elemental force, and the drop in prices occurred primarily and mostly in regard to the commodities of the unorganized commodity owners, *viz.*, peasants, artisans, small capitalists; the drop was gradual and smaller in degree in regard to the prices of commodities offered by the organized commodity owners, *viz.*, the capitalists united in cartels. The drop in prices made the posi-

tion of debtors (manufacturers, artisans, peasants, etc.) intolerable while on the other hand it placed the creditors in an unprecedently privileged position. Such a situation had to lead and really did lead to the colossal bankruptcy of firms and separate entrepreneurs. During the past three years tens of thousands of joint-stock companies were ruined in this way in the United States, in Germany, in England and in France. The bankruptcy of joint-stock companies was followed by the depreciation of the currency, which to some extent eased the position of the debtors. Depreciation of currency was followed by the legalized non-payment of debts, both foreign and internal." *

The development of the crisis led to the broadest *inflation*, that is, depreciation of currency. The drop in prices results in great difficulties for the debtor: a debt of the same amount payable when prices have declined costs him a considerably greater quantity of commodities than when he contracted the debt. The drop in prices places additional burdens on the shoulders of debtor entrepreneurs and makes the positions of entire countries that are considerably in debt much worse. What is the way out of this difficulty? The capitalists and their governments seek a way out in two directions: by moratoriums, a stoppage of payment on debts, and by inflation. With the development of the crisis capitalist countries one after another stopped their debt payments. But that was not sufficient. They also adopted the course of inflation. At first the weaker countries introduced this measure. Then in the autumn of 1931, England took up the course of inflating its currency; the British government stopped changing its paper money into gold, and the pound sterling began to fall in value. The depreciation of currency eases the position of the debtor—he can now repay his debt with depreciated, that is, cheaper, money. But inflation is also of tremendous importance in the *struggle for foreign markets*.

Depreciation of its money gives the capitalist country an advantage over other countries on the world market. The reason for this is that its commodities cost less on a gold basis. The price in paper money may even rise, but if this money is exchanged

* Stalin, *Report on the Work of the Central Committee of the C.P.S.U. (Seventeenth Party Congress)*, pp. 10-11.

for gold the commodities of the country with an inflated currency will prove to be cheaper than the commodities of the countries which have remained on the gold standard. And with a low price it is easier to overcome competition on the world market. Those countries whose commodities are still priced in the old money, which is based on the gold standard, are at a disadvantage. Thus we see that another of the biggest capitalist countries in the world, the U.S.A., the richest country of all, also inflated its currency, in March 1933. The American dollar and the English pound sterling were considered the most stable currencies in the entire capitalist world. They were looked up to, the business men of all capitalist countries firmly believed in their stability, they were valued on a par with gold, the accumulations of other, less wealthy countries were converted into these currencies. And these two strongholds gave way, pulling down with themselves the currencies of other countries dependent on them. The third big country that was enriched by the war, Japan, depreciated its money to almost one-third of its former value in gold. With this wave of currency inflation on the part of the more powerful capitalist countries a new wrangle arose, a new scramble among the capitalists. The country with an inflated currency, since it can sell its commodities cheaper on the world market, can beat its rivals. Thus in the fight for markets, a new weapon came into use—inflation. And with this weapon a *currency war* is being waged.

Towards the end of 1933 only four countries in the entire capitalist world had currencies based on the gold standard: France, Belgium, Switzerland and Holland. All other countries had had recourse to inflation.

> "It goes without saying that these phenomena which shook the foundations of the credit system had to bring in their train, and did bring in their train the cessation of payments on credits and foreign loans, the cessation of payments on inter-Allied debts, the cessation of the export of capital, the further diminution of foreign trade, the further diminution of the export of commodities, the intensification of the struggle for foreign markets, trade wars between countries and—dumping. Yes, comrades, dumping. I do not mean the alleged Soviet dumping, about which only very recently certain noble deputies in noble parliaments of Europe and America were shouting until they

were hoarse. I mean the real dumping that is now being practised by nearly all the 'civilized' states, and about which the gallant and noble deputies maintain a prudent silence." *

The present depression and its peculiarities

The data on the movement of industrial production in capitalist countries show that the point of greatest decline was reached in 1932. The following year, 1933, industry in the capitalist countries began to show a slight upward trend. During the course of 1933 there were frequent fluctuations up and down, nevertheless, industry did not drop to the low point it had reached in the summer of 1932.

It would be incorrect to explain this phenomenon exclusively by the policy of inflation and the feverish war preparations which a number of governments of capitalist countries have adopted. In some countries, Japan for instance, colossal orders for the war industries have actually played a great role. Improvement in the condition of industry is, however, to be observed in all countries, including those which have a stable currency. It is consequently evident that "side by side with the war-inflation boom the operation of internal economic forces of capitalism also has effect here." **

By means of the fierce intensification of the degree of exploitation of the working class, by means of the ruin of the masses of the farmers, by means of the robbery of the toiling masses of colonial countries, capitalism has succeeded in obtaining a slight improvement in the condition of industry. The increased exploitation, the heightened intensity of labour, the reduction in wages—all this makes it possible for a number of capitalists to continue production even with a small demand and low prices of commodities. Prices of raw materials and foodstuffs have declined at the expense of the peasants and toilers in the colonies; this also means lower costs of production for the capitalists. The crisis has destroyed a tremendous part of the productive forces. The destruction of large quantities of goods has at last so reduced the reserves that the ratio between supply and demand has in a number of cases become more favourable. The wiping out of weaker

* *Ibid.*, p. 11.
** *Ibid.*, p. 14.

enterprises has here and there cleared the market for the surviving stronger ones.

Thus industry in the principal capitalist countries has passed its lowest point. From this low point industry has entered the phase of depression,

> ". . . not an ordinary depression, but a depression of a special kind which does not lead to a new boom and flourishing in industry but which, on the other hand, does not force it back to the lowest point of decline." *

In ordinary times when capitalism had not yet reached its period of decline and fall, crises were replaced by depressions, which were in turn replaced by periods of prosperity. But at the present time, capitalism is moribund capitalism. It is undergoing its general crisis, rent by the most profound contradictions, which propel it to its doom. The present economic crisis broke out amidst the general crisis of capitalism; that is why it is distinguished by such depth and protractedness, such power of devastation and acuteness. The new phase of depression has also been entered upon amidst this general crisis; that is why this depression differs radically from the usual type of depression and is not the forerunner of a new boom, a new period of prosperity,

> ". . . because all these unfavourable conditions which prevent industry in the capitalist countries from rising to any serious extent still continue to operate. I have in mind the continuing *general* crisis of capitalism in the midst of which the *economic* crisis is proceeding, the chronic working of the enterprises under capacity, the chronic mass unemployment, the interweaving of the industrial crisis with the agricultural crisis, the absence of tendencies towards any serious renewal of fixed capital which usually heralds the approach of a boom, etc., etc." **

The crisis raging in the whole capitalist world since 1929 has sharpened to the utmost all the internal and external contradic-

* *Ibid.*, p. 15.
** *Ibid.*, pp. 14-15.

tions of the capitalist system. The protracted crisis has brought about an unparalleled aggravation of the conditions of the toiling masses. Colossal unemployment, ruthless reduction in wages, the intensification of exploitation—this is the fate of the working class under the conditions of the present crisis. The crisis has also subjected the broad masses of farmers to unprecedented ruin. Together with their impoverishment there is a tremendous upsurge of the resentment of the toiling masses against the capitalist system.

The eve of a new round of revolutions and wars

In the face of the indignation of the masses, the bourgeoisie is more and more abandoning the old methods by means of which it formerly held the working class in subjection and is passing over to open terrorist, fascist dictatorship. In Germany the bourgeoisie set up the bloody dictatorship of Hitler in February 1933. Fascist tendencies are growing among the bourgeoisie in other countries as well. The establishment of fascism in Germany bears evidence not only of the disruptive role of the Social-Democratic leaders who split the ranks of the working class and thus weakened its resistance to the bourgeois dictatorship, it also bears witness to the weakness of the bourgeoisie which can no longer maintain power in its hands by the old methods of administration. The bourgeoisie is throwing off its democratic tinsel and is going over to open, bloody terror against the working class. But this only results in a further sharpening of the class struggle, threatening to explode the entire structure of capitalism.

The protracted crisis has extremely sharpened all the existing antagonisms between the capitalist powers. Under conditions of the crisis every country tries to shift its burden onto other countries. The struggle for markets has grown exceedingly acute. Having recourse to dumping on foreign markets every country, at the same time, raises barriers around its own markets against the encroachments of foreign competition. The non-payment of debts sharpens the antagonisms between creditor and debtor nations. The crisis has intensified the action of the law of uneven development under imperialism. It affected various countries with varying force and thus produced a shifting in the relation of forces among the imperialist nations. All this has sharpened the relations between countries to the extreme. The preparations for a new im perialist war are already proceeding in the most open fashion. Capitalist countries are arming to the teeth in preparation for a new battle for the redivision of the world. While all branches of industry restricted production as a result of the crisis, one branch of industry—the war industries—did not contract, but on the contrary, expands from year to year. A number of years have already passed since Japan first occupied Manchuria with armed forces and began pushing deeper into Northern China. The Sino-Japanese war renders the struggle for the Pacific Ocean, where the imperialist interests of Japan, the United States and Great Britain clash, extremely acute.

In the secret chambers of imperialist staffs the plans for future wars are already being worked out. Prominent among these plans are projects for armed intervention against the Soviet Union.

> "The tremendous strain of the internal class antagonisms in the capitalist countries, as well as of the international antagonisms testify to the fact that the objective prerequisites for a revolutionary crisis have matured to such an extent that at the present time the world is *closely* approaching a new round of revolutions and wars." *

The correctness of this estimate of the situation has been confirmed by a tremendous number of facts. The countries where fascism was "victorious" are in turmoil. In Germany the Communist Party is conducting an heroic struggle against fascism and in the exceedingly difficult circumstances of a deeply "underground" existence is preparing the forces for the overthrow of the fascist dictatorship. In France fascist provocations called forth such powerful resistance on the part of the masses of the workers that bourgeois politicians were thoroughly terrified by the indignation of the proletariat. In Austria in February 1934 tens of thousands of workers conducted an armed struggle for many days against the greater forces of the enemy and under the extremely difficult circumstances of the treachery of their leaders. Soviet China, embracing a number of regions with a population of over sixty million people, has now become a powerful factor. It has successfully resisted a number of crusades launched against it by the counter-

* *Theses and Decisions of the Thirteenth Plenum of the E.C.C.I.*, p. 5, Modern Books, Ltd., London, 1934.

revolutionary generals, and has created its own powerful Red Army.

> "The masses of the people have not yet reached the stage when they are ready to storm the citadel of capitalism, but the idea of storming it is maturing in the minds of the masses—there can hardly be any doubt about that." *

We already know that capitalism will not go off the stage on its own initiative, that it will not collapse automatically. We know that all the theories of the automatic collapse of capitalism only bring untold harm to the cause of the working class, lulling its will to the long persistent struggle which is necessary in order to triumph over the exploiters. No sharpening of the contradictions of capitalism creates a situation where the bourgeoisie can find absolutely no way out. Only a persistent struggle will decide the collapse of the capitalist system.

> "The victory of the revolution never comes by itself. It has to be prepared for and won. And only a strong proletarian revolutionary party can prepare for and win victory." **

Review Questions

1. How is the protracted character of the present crisis to be explained?
2. In what is the exceptional acuteness and depth of this crisis expressed?
3. In what is the character of the present crisis as a crisis of overproduction expressed?
4. How did the crisis affect the position of the proletariat?
5. How did the crisis affect the position of the peasantry?
6. What are the characteristics of the present depression?
7. What indications are there of the approach of a new round of revolutions and wars?

* Stalin, *Report on the Work of the Central Committee of the C.P.S.U. (Seventeenth Party Congress)*, p. 17.

** *Ibid.*, p. 22.